D1049823

WOMAN OF THE DAWN

✳

Other books by the author

Walk in Balance: The Path to Healthy, Happy, Harmonious Living
by Sun Bear with Crysalis Mulligan, Peter Nufer, and Wabun

Lightseeds: A Compendium of Ancient and Contemporary Crystal Knowledge
by Wabun Wind and Anderson Reed

Sun Bear: The Path of Power
by Sun Bear, Wabun, and Barry Weinstock

The Bear Tribe's Self-Reliance Book
by Sun Bear, Wabun, and Nimimosha

The Medicine Wheel: Earth Astrology
by Sun Bear and Wabun

The People's Lawyers
by Marlise James, aka Wabun

WOMAN OF THE DAWN

A Spiritual Odyssey

WABUN WIND

Prentice Hall Press

New York London Toronto Sydney Tokyo

This is a true story, but names and places
have been changed to protect the privacy
of the individuals involved

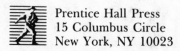 Prentice Hall Press
15 Columbus Circle
New York, NY 10023

Copyright © 1989 by Wabun Wind

All rights reserved,
including the right of reproduction
in whole or in part in any form.

PRENTICE HALL PRESS and colophon are registered
trademarks of Simon & Schuster, Inc.

Library of Congress Cataloging-in-Publication Data

Wind, Wabun, 1945–
    Woman of the dawn: a spiritual odyssey/Wabun Wind.
        p.   cm.
    Includes bibliographical references.
    ISBN 0-13-961699-3:
    1. Wind, Wabun, 1945–   . 2. Shamans—United States—Biography.
3. New Age movement.
BP605.N48W563   1989
299′.7′092—dc20
[B]   89–37659
                                                          CIP

Manufactured in the United States of America

10   9   8   7   6   5   4   3   2   1

First Edition

To Sun Bear
With thanks for everything you teach me
and
Special thanks for teaching me life is beautiful
and sacred

Acknowledgments

Woman of the Dawn has been a long project. First I lived the experiences, then I had to synthesize them before I could even conceive of putting them on paper. What this means is that many people have contributed to this book, in many ways. When trying to acknowledge people who span a twenty-year period of life, it's inevitable that, if you try to list everyone, you'll leave someone out.

So I'd like first to thank all of the people who have been part of my life these past twenty years. Each of you gave me some gift, some insight that has helped to form me, and this book. Particular thanks go to those who have been part of the Bear Tribe in the past, those who are part of the Tribe now, and those yet to come.

Special thanks go to my teachers over those years. Some of you prefer privacy, so the thanks will be silent, but heartfelt. To those who allow me to use your names—Sun Bear, Morning Star, Nimimosha, Yarrow, Shawnodese, Richard and Joyce Rainbow, Twylah Nitsch, the late Evelyn Eaton (Mahad'yuni), and all those who have spoken at the Medicine Wheel gatherings—more heartfelt thanks.

I'd like to offer my gratitude to those people who were of special help in the writing of this book. More thanks than words can express go to my husband Shawnodese for the encouragement, love, emotional support, and honest feedback. Thanks to my friend Anderson Reed for the writing advice and for reminding me that what I was doing was more important than the fact that I was doing it. Thanks to both Shawnodese and Reed for steadfastly assuring me I could do this book at times when

ACKNOWLEDGMENTS

cleaning the toilet seemed a more enjoyable task. Particular thanks to all those who read parts of the book and commented upon them: Shawnodese, Reed, Morning Star, Nimimosha, Jerry Chasen, Oscar Collier, Steven Foster, Meredith Little, Verna Sanchez, Raven, Susan James, JoDee Rottler, and Sun Bear. There were many other people who gave me emotional support in this project. I'd like to thank all of them, including, but not limited to: my brother Robert James, Michelle Buchanan, Beth Davis, Regina Kerr, Sheila Mulligan, Peter Nufer, Chris Morgan, Jean Wanner, Nancy Zega, Kohlyne Morgan, Amie Carter, Jan Tew, Elisabeth Robinson, Dawn Songfeather, Diane Duggan, Yarrow Goding, Donna DuPree, Ruth Moon Deer Traut, Omifunke, Jude Davis, Maureen Dion, Mary Lynn Niederhauser, Rosemary Gladstar, and Jaya Houston—all whom I'm proud to call friend.

I send prayers and grateful memories to three recently departed friends—Cougar, Terry Towle, and Michael Galinis. May you go shining.

Thanks to the people who helped with the concept for or editing and production of this book. They include Bill Thompson, Pam Thomas, Josh Baskin, Andy deSalvo, Michael Moore, Marilyn Abraham, Philip Metcalf, Carol Mayhew, and John Morgan. Special thanks to David James for helping find the cover photo location, and to Douglas Kirkland, the excellent photographer who took the cover picture.

People have not been my only helpers with *Woman of the Dawn*. My thanks to the special crystal that stood behind me to represent the elemental kingdom; to the fern and the oak to my sides, representing the plant kingdom; to the squirrels, crows, cardinals, sparrows, and songbirds that sang to me through the window throughout the time I was writing. Special thanks to the owl who came the night I finished writing Chapter 11, to the thunder beings for visiting the night before I completed the book, and to Akeem and Maize, feline friends who frequently remind me that giving and getting affection is just as important as writing.

To sum up, I use the words I have been taught, "Thank you, all my relations."

—Wabun Wind
April, 1989

Contents

Prologue

NORTHERN CALIFORNIA, 1982

Our egalitarianism had gotten us into trouble once again. I knew it the instant I handed over my microphone to the stranger. The man had appeared an hour before at the gate of Camp Cazadero near Guerneville, the site of our second Northern California Medicine Wheel Gathering. These are gatherings to honor the earth and are held to fulfill a vision that had come to Sun Bear four years earlier. The man said he had a gift for Sun Bear. The person at the gate, put off by the man's aura of wrath, sent someone to get either Sun Bear or me. We both came, talked with the man, then invited him into the gathering hoping the atmosphere of respectfulness and peace would diffuse his anger. It didn't. He had a gift all right: disruption. For some reason we needed to accept it.

He was a self-styled radical political Native who felt non-Native people didn't have the right to participate in ceremonies for earth healing or anything else related to the indigenous people of the planet. I've met this kind of person, in several shades of skin, both before and since this incident. Under their radical rhetoric is as much racism and fascism as you would find at a meeting of any white supremacy group. While they claim to want freedom, they want it only for themselves and those whom they deem fit.

We had agreed to let this man speak to the 800 or so people gathered because, although we did not agree with his views, we respected his right to have them. He spoke after the final words from the teachers who had spent the weekend instructing participants how to connect with and respect the earth and each other and how to help with the healing of the Earth Mother. After these words we were to have the closing ceremonies. The people in the crowd were in ebullient spirits. Many of them had succeeded in opening themselves to the earth's energy this weekend, and they wore the glow only she can give. Both the people and the land felt good and peaceful to me. Consequently, it was as if a bucket of ice water hit me when the politico's words shattered that peace.

"You white people are trying to steal our ceremonies just like you stole our land and everything else we had," he shouted, his voice loud with anger.

Some of the participants began shouting back at him.

Taking another microphone, I loudly and firmly asked people to show this man respect even if they didn't agree with what he was saying. Things quieted down for a minute. The man began his diatribe again, and people let him talk.

Without someone to fight, he ran out of steam pretty quickly. Angry after he couldn't have his fight, he left the stage and tried to involve Sun Bear in a screaming match near the back of the crowd. Sun Bear wouldn't yell back, so the man constantly increased his own volume.

Sensing the depression his talk had engendered in the audience, I began to speak to them. To the best of my ability I spoke straight from my heart. I told them I knew why I was there, and that it had nothing to do with "stealing ceremonies." I was there to do what I could to help heal our beautiful Earth Mother, the planet that gives us life and nourishment from the moment we are born. I was there to honor and learn from those Native people willing to teach me.

I spoke quietly, but with the conviction I felt in my heart about the earth and all her children. I told them some of my own story about coming to this path. I noticed some people were crying as I spoke. I continued until I felt their depression lifting, then I said, "I am here to help the earth. I am not going to let someone else's negativity stop me. If you feel the same way, join me at the Medicine Wheel and we'll prepare for the closing ceremonies there."

As we walked to the Wheel, many people came up to embrace

me and to tell me that the way I had handled the situation had
been a powerful emotional healing for them. When we got to the
Wheel, I took a mental inventory of the teachers who were
nearby. There was Bear Heart, Wallace Black Elk, Brooke
Medicine Eagle, Rosemary Gladstar, Steven Foster, Meredith
Little, Grandpa Roberts, Adele Getty, Sunwater, Norma
Cordell, Hyemyhosts Storm, Harley Swift Deer, and my dear
spiritual grandmother Evelyn Eaton. I was sorry Dr. Elizabeth
Kubler-Ross and a couple of other teachers had had to leave
early. I saw that Sun Bear was still talking to the politico, and
steering him off the grounds.

I asked Brooke to use her lovely voice to draw people together
again and raise the energy, and then I asked the elders to make
prayers. By the time the prayers were completed, Sun Bear had
joined us and the closing ceremonies began. They were powerful
and, by their end, people once again were glowing.

A woman touched my arm and said she had a gift for me.
Because of the experience with the man I was a little anxious
about any gifts. However, the anxiety quickly lifted when she
presented me with a very large and beautiful clear quartz crystal
that had come from Washington State. She told me that the
crystal wanted to be used in the center of the circle when next I
did the Rainbow Crystal Healing Ceremony. That crystal has
been with me at more than two dozen Medicine Wheels since
then, and was partly responsible for bringing Anderson Reed and
me together to write *Lightseeds*. I sincerely thanked the woman for
her gift, then made my way over to Grandmother Evelyn.

"You were wonderful Wabun," she told me. "You really trans-
formed the energy. I am so glad I know you."

I hugged her with tears in my eyes.

"Wabun," Sun Bear said as he put an arm around my shoulder.
"I'm really proud of you. You're such a good woman. It's been
a long trail but you really have found your power."

I hugged him, a little embarrassed by all this praise. But I had
done a good job, and I felt happy about it. Finally, I understood
it was okay to be proud of a job well done.

It had been a dozen years since I had first met Sun Bear; eleven
since I had begun living with the Tribe and been given the name
Wabun. Those dozen years sometimes have seemed like 100; at

other times like the blink of an eye. They have been magical, frightening, painful, ecstatic, intense, and never boring. It's good I had so little idea of what would happen when Sun Bear first walked into my life. Otherwise I might still be locking myself into an apartment in New York every night, and thinking Manhattan is the center of the universe.

1

THE PREPARATION

Who could refuse an invitation to a *Rolling Stone* magazine party in New York? There was sure to be a copious amount of booze as well as gourmet snacks and an interesting conglomeration of people attending, many of whom would probably be happy to share the drugs they smoked, drank, sniffed, or swallowed. This, after all, was the early seventies extension of the good old psychedelic sixties. Saying "yes" was as fashionable then as saying "no" is now. Being a freelance writer, with more ambition than financial resources, I certainly was not about to turn down such an invitation.

I carefully chose my most flamboyantly hip dress, one that reminded me of the ladies in the court of King Arthur (I fancied myself Guinevere then, not yet knowing that Morgaine was more my style), went against my moral fabric by ironing it, applied full makeup, and took a cab to the restaurant in the east sixties where the party was being staged. I sought out Alan, the speed-freak advertising man who had worked for me on a magazine I was editing that had just folded. He was even thinner than I remembered, and it saddened me to see this promising man throwing his life away. The story went that he had become hooked because he went to a doctor who mixed amphetamines with vitamins for his largely celebrity clientele. Alan now worked for a company somehow connected with the Stone. He had invited me to this party. We spent a few minutes talking, but his amphetamine-propelled chatter began to annoy me, so I looked to see if I knew anyone else there.

Seeing no familiar faces, I got a scotch on the rocks, some

hors d'oeuvres, and began to play one of my favorite party games. I'd stand toward the side of the room, looking happily self-contained, and see what number I could count to before someone came up to talk with me. I'd learned that appearing happy being by yourself drives many people nuts. They can't understand how anyone could be alone and happy in a public place. I'd gotten to ninety-two (an average of forty to 300 being the usual range) when an academic-looking man in his late thirties wearing a conservative suit came over to talk. I wasn't surprised by his looks. Intellectuals, particularly conservative ones, were often both angered and intrigued by a woman alone looking happy. In the first few minutes of conversation, I learned that Steve was not only an editor at Random House but was, in fact, the editor who had recently turned down my book proposal on the subject of radical lawyers. He was flustered at this discovery and quickly began to rationalize his decision. I assured him that I wasn't offended since Holt, Rinehart & Winston had taken the book. He told me if he had known how charming I was he would have considered the book even more seriously than he had. It became obvious he liked me, and he looked as good as anyone else in the visible vicinity, so I encouraged him to begin the thrust and parry that indicated he hoped we would greet the dawn together. I did not share this hope. I was more interested in a good dinner and the prospect of having some intelligent male company.

As is the way at such parties, we drifted to talk to others after he ascertained that I would have dinner with him. There was a group of interesting UN diplomatic types there who invited me to a party that would be going on all night. I tucked the address in my purse. They were Spanish men and, my own feminist dogma be damned, I've always been a sucker for those limpid brown eyes and charming manners. I also like to kick up my heels in a flamenco every now and again.

Suddenly, the room began to shake. Holding on to a nearby chair, I looked around. The shaking intensified, but no one else was paying any attention to it.

"Dear God," I prayed, "I know I promised never to drink again after I lived, hungover, through the February earthquake in Los Angeles this year. I know I'll break that promise again if I make it now. But I don't want to die in an earthquake in the middle of a roomful of people who are too stoned even to know that it is happening."

The shaking stopped for a moment. I tried to walk casually to the doorway, remembering from my L.A. experience that this is the safest place to be when the earth is rumbling. I got to the doorway just as the shaking began again. I looked back into the room, astonished that nobody else was concerned. From my vantage point, I looked out and saw parts of buildings coming loose and falling to the ground. They barely missed hitting some of the people walking in the street. Yet, the people just kept walking, oblivious to the danger all around them. I saw the top floors of several skyscrapers begin to crumble and come down. I was terrified. My stomach was quaking as strongly as the earth. It took all of my rather considerable self-control to keep from shouting or screaming. I would have yelled warnings to the people in the street but none of them were being hurt, and I did not want to precipitate a panic.

Steve came over behind me and said, "Hey, you're not going to get away that easy."

I looked at him with raw fear in my eyes.

"What's wrong?" he asked.

"Don't you feel anything strange?"

"Could it be, dear lady, that you have been mixing too many of the fine consciousness-altering substances available here?"

I saw no fear in his face, and I began to wonder whether I had been having some sort of drug-induced experience. Then I remembered that the only drug I'd had was one glass of scotch. Still, knowing that unusual behavior was rigidly circumscribed in such circles, and discussing an earthquake no one else noticed was far outside the acceptable framework, I decided to go along with his evaluation. Anyway, the shaking had ceased.

Smiling into his eyes I took his arm and said, "I better take it easy on that stuff tonight. After all, I want you to know just how charming a writer I can be."

We stayed, circulating at the party for another hour or so. The earthquake experience had upset me more than I thought. I drank scotch fast enough that my hollow leg, which usually allowed me to drink almost anyone under the table, filled up, the extra alcohol seeping into my brain. I could not allow myself to be mentally impaired with Steve, so I went to the ladies room and rid myself of whatever scotch was still in my stomach. If the term "bulemic" was in use then, I certainly hadn't heard it. I probably wouldn't have paid anymore attention to it than I would have to the term "social alcoholic." Drinking was almost a prerequisite for budding writers in 1971. My Columbia Journalism classmates and I spent enough afternoons in the West End Tavern to label the sessions "Drinking 201." Drinking, dancing, smoking, doing drugs, having sex, staying up (in all the meanings of the word) for days on end were the fitness events of hip, humanitarian, liberal to radical, concerned young citizens in the sixties. I'm amazed so many of us made it to the seventies in a relatively healthy state.

Steve and I dined that night at a fine Chinese restaurant. Later, we went to the diplomat's party, where I did a little flamenco with some of my new-found Spanish acquaintances, while Steve watched with a mixture of envy at my slightly soused uninhibited- ness and admiration for my courage at doing what I wanted. There was no way he could have known that my expansive nature only became fully apparent when I altered my consciousness in some way. The rest of the time I was quiet at best, repressed at my worst. Being a closet part-time conservative, I did not alter my conscious- ness very often. I liked to take full advantage of the times I did.

When I became bored with dancing and flirting, Steve and I adjourned to the White Horse Tavern in the village, one of my favorite places to drink in my expansive moments. The White Horse had been frequented by Dylan Thomas when he visited the City. My heritage is Welsh, and I could loosely trace family ties to the spirituous latter-day poet. I harbored a secret wish to find his ghost sitting in a corner, ready to recognize me as his worthy descendant and to lay the mantle of bard upon me.

The earthquake experience was still bothering me. Fear made it hard for me to stay expanded, so I kept drinking until I went beyond slightly soused. I didn't care. I had been afraid and was still afraid. The more I drank, the less I remembered the nauseat- ing, dizzying feeling of the earth—the earth, which is supposed to be solid and dependable—shaking. Steve faded from impor- tance in my consciousness. I just wanted to be rid of the fear that had left me feeling insecure about the things I had always taken for granted.

Ignoring whatever train our conversation had been taking,

I turned to Steve and said, "It's scary to feel the earth move."

Looking at me with a puzzled expression, he said, "I beg your pardon?"

I realized I had just gone beyond the commonly accepted framework, so I tried to cover by mumbling something about always liking the Hemingway description of the earth moving in one of the love scenes in *The Sun Also Rises*. In an attempt to further cover my lapse, I launched into a soliloquy about Hemingway being my favorite writer. When Steve finally managed to get a word in, he said that he'd like to make the earth move for me. I realized then that the train of the conversation must have been about seduction. I really didn't feel like being seduced, but I was afraid of going home alone. The fear won. If I were going to die in an earthquake, I decided I'd rather have company. I went to his apartment, just a few blocks away.

Unfortunately for Steve, when I lay down the memory of the earth shaking, mixed with the unreasonable amount of alcohol I had consumed, produced a reaction that reminded me of the seasicknesses I had once experienced for a few hours on a ship going from Barcelona to Naples. I faced that dawn at Steve's on my knees, worshipping the virgin of the porcelain. Steve has not yet been the editor of one of my books.

The next morning I managed miraculously to make myself functional. I had an interview with a magazine editor. Steve and I took a cab uptown together, parting, and making insincere but polite promises to be in touch.

I had no time to get home and change, so I decided to use all my panache and act as if I often dressed in a floor-length low-cut gown with gold trim on Wednesday mornings. My panache was tested sorely when, on my way from the cab to the office building, I met two people I knew walking up Fifth Avenue. As everyone who has ever lived in Manhattan knows, it is very unusual to meet a non-coworker acquaintance on the streets of New York. The odds of meeting two acquaintances on the same morning must be about the same as those of winning the lottery. I smiled and carried on brief conversations, excusing myself to get to my appointment. Luckily, I could still shield myself behind the sixties mentality and the rather bohemian reputation I had. Both acquaintances smiled indulgently at my outlandish outfit. Thankfully, so did the editor.

I did get an assignment from her to write an article eventually entitled, "Dare You Give Birth If You Are Fat?" I thought it was appropriate for me to be writing that article since I always believed I was battling the bulge, with the bulge most often winning. That mission completed, I decided to splurge on a cab ride home, telling myself I did not want to risk meeting anyone else I knew. If I had been willing to tell myself the truth I would have admitted I was afraid of being in the subway when the earth started to shake again. It wasn't until I found myself ready to put out cab fare (a luxury at the time) that I realized just how sure I was that the earth was going to shake some more.

I didn't have to wait long. Two days later I was walking by the East River near the Upper East Side rent-controlled apartment I had fortunately been bequeathed by a former boyfriend who had gotten married. I'd just left the apartment building in a huff because Terry, my friend and neighbor, had insisted I should see a psychologist about the earthquake incident.

She contended I was really shook up by what happened the other night, which was true. She continued by making me admit there could not have been an earthquake no one else had felt.

I conceded her point.

Pressing her advantage she continued by pointing out that I had been very up-tight about earthquakes ever since I had been in the Big One in Los Angeles.

I admitted I had found it disconcerting to see palm trees almost bent into a 'C' shape, especially when I was looking out the window of some unfamiliar apartment. I contended any sane person would be frightened by that, but that I had dealt with that fear. I hadn't been having dreams about earthquakes or fears about them in the four months separating the two incidents. I had just been left with a dislike of going to Los Angeles. I suspected that might be a very sane prejudice.

Terry pointed out the discussion wasn't about my prejudices. It was about my thinking there had been an earthquake no one else noticed.

I told her I'm not the hysterical sort of person who regularly imagines things or has fainting spells. She said I certainly was sounding hysterical about this. She felt I had a problem, and she had no idea what it was so she wanted me to see someone who might. She didn't understand my sudden fear of psychology when

I was always the one going to encounter groups and conscious-ness events.

I conceded that point but said I did not want to be pushed into something that felt wrong. I left the apartment to cool off. I really didn't understand my own hesitation to talk to a psychologist. I believed in personal growth, in therapy, in honesty, in letting it all hang out (to a point). But, prior to this time, I had just been dealing with the usual fears, angers, frustrations, and tears of an American upbringing. This incident was different. Now I was perceiving things dissimilarly from everyone else. But I could not accept the logical next step, which was that I was having some sort of psychological problem. It didn't feel like a problem. It felt as if I were seeing something other people were not. That didn't make it less real.

As I was walking, I turned to look at the river. Suddenly, the water began to rise. With increasing speed the water rose higher and higher. Although I could not see it, I knew the rising was becoming a tidal wave, a tidal wave that would cover the city and wash all the filth out to the cleansing sea. I almost panicked. Tsunami, tidal wave, is an old dream-fear of mine. Ever since I was a child I have had a recurring dream of being by the ocean and turning to see a tidal wave rushing toward me and the shore. The scenery and characters in the dream changed, but the plot always remained the same. I would watch as a wall of water rose from the sea and came toward me. I would be terrified. I would awaken before the wave hit.

This time I wasn't sure I would awaken in time. Seeing the level of the East River rise did have a dream-like quality to it, but it felt very real and it terrified me. I knew I was going to be swept into the Atlantic. I knew there was no point in running. I could never outrun a tidal wave. I grasped the closest nearby bench so tightly that both hands turned white. I watched the level of the river continue to rise. I heard the noise of the approaching wave. Abruptly, it stopped and the river receded. Relief flooded through me. But I didn't know what to do. I couldn't stand many more of these experiences without having someone with whom to talk about them.

I knew what Terry's response would be if I told her, and I was fairly certain most of my other friends would share her opinion. I suspected my women's consciousness-raising group would read some sort of sexual meaning into the experiences and, once again, tell me that I put too much emphasis on the men and romance in my life despite my feminist leanings. I doubted I'd get much understanding or support from that quarter. Finally I decided to wait to discuss these incidents with the spiritual group I attended. I figured that if anyone could explain what was happening, they could.

Before that meeting took place on the following Wednesday, I had more experiences. They were not as dramatic as the previous two. I'd leave my apartment or another building and, when I walked into the street, I would feel the earth quaking. Every time it happened I got dizzy and disoriented. A couple of times I got nauseous.

Gavin, the Australian-born, Sufi-trained leader of the spiritual group listened to me recount the experiences, then asked the other members of the group what they felt was occurring.

Their answers ranged from true mystical experiences, to schizophrenic breakdown, to major paranoia, to messages from flying saucer people. Gavin said, "My dear, while these experiences are certainly real on a finer, spiritual level of reality, obviously they did not happen. You are, it appears, being given messages of some sort for some reason. I would not worry about the experiences. Just keep a record of what occurs and the circumstances surrounding it. And keep your mouth shut. Most people don't understand these finer levels of reality."

They certainly don't. As June pushed toward sultry July I had one other extraordinary experience. Since I started coming into the City as a teen I have enjoyed walking from Port Authority to Grand Central Station, viewing all the manifestations of humanity represented on 42nd Street. While parts of the street were seedy even then, it vibrated with life—raw, real life. I vacillated between envy for the nonintellectual vitality of the people there, disgust for the seamy scenes, and compassion for the people who obviously were in real need. Walking there always left me feeling excited, and both grateful for and guilty about my fortunate lot in life—a winning combination of turmoil for a woman weaned on the concept of original sin. I remember having a recurring daydream of bringing some of the people there home for Thanksgiving dinner. I've always been a secular humanist, even when I became intellectually sophisticated enough to realize the harm one-night-stands do, whether in matters of charity or matters of the heart.

On a Sunday in June I was making that walk when, suddenly, the earth began to quake again. Now, other than the subway, 42nd Street would have to be one of the worst places you could be in an earthquake. Its enormous electrical billboards and marquees could easily come crashing down on the crowds below— crowds not known for decency and compassion. I walked down the street while destruction reigned all around me. One man, crouching in a doorway with his bottle in a brown paper bag, was hit by a sign that came hurtling from the other side of the street. A woman fell into a crack in the earth, screaming, with terror clearly written on her face as the john with whom she had been negotiating jumped away from her hands as they tried to clasp his ankles. Gasoline tanks exploded as cars violently crashed into one another, sending balls of fire ripping through the air. People were engulfed in the flames. Few people stopped to help those falling into cracks, or injured, or burned, although some people stopped to relieve them of their purses, wallets, or jewelry. It was every man for himself, and it didn't take long for looting to begin.

Terror prevailed on 42nd Street, and I knew I had to just keep walking. I did not know if everything was real on this physical level, or whether I was again perceiving "the finer levels of reality." I just knew if I stopped I was in imminent danger either way. If it was "real" I could be hit by falling debris, or a fireball, or I could fall through a crack into whatever lay beneath. If it wasn't real, I knew that if I stopped and started to cry or scream or vomit, the police would take me to Bellevue and I would have to explain everything to some probably unsympathetic resident doctor.

As I continued walking, the strangest experience of all began. Time ran outside of its normal track. It seemed as if I were walking through a time tunnel. Behind me was the earthquake as it was happening. Ahead of me was the aftermath of the quake, and that was full of new terrors. The looting intensified as people took everything of value from all the businesses in the area. Then the people set some buildings on fire just to watch them burn. By the light of the flames I could see people beginning to assault each other for no apparent reason. No one on the streets was safe. People or groups who came in to try to restore order were either beaten or chased out of the area. People did unspeakably cruel things to each other. I kept walking, my stomach in knots and sobs threatening to rip themselves out of my eyes and throat.

Time passed. People were hungry. No food was left. If someone found a crust of bread, other hands would try to rip a crumb from it. People began to hunt the pigeons and the rats. I did not want to see anymore. I knew what would happen next, and I did not want to see it. I shut my eyes and continued walking. I prayed that when I opened them again, I would be on 42nd Street in late June, 1971, and the streets would have stopped shaking.

I opened my eyes and my prayer had been answered. Then, and only then, I wept . . . with relief.

2

THE MEETING

I first heard about an Indian named Sun Bear when I was out in California researching my book about radical lawyers. I got most of my information from my friend Gene, a poet who had deserted the Big Apple for sunny mellow California about a year earlier. From Gene's reports, this Sun Bear sounded like quite a character.

I was looking for a spiritual teacher with a little more flair, vitality, and grasp of this physical level of reality than Gavin, the man who led my spiritual discussion group in the City. This Sun Bear certainly sounded like he had flair. I knew nothing about American Indians, having received my public education at the time when school districts only grudgingly admitted that minorities existed in this country. Radical Indian politicians had not yet become popular with the people in the New York liberal circles with whom I associated. Indians were a whole new area for me, and one that sounded fascinating.

Gene filled my imagination with stories about this man who was leading a group of city dwellers—both Indian and non-Indian— into the country where they could learn to live in harmony with the land, whatever that meant. Sun Bear apparently believed that changes were coming on the earth pretty soon, and that people needed to learn about the earth again in order to survive these changes. He taught about old Indian prophecies, earth spirituality and earth ceremonies. Gene also thought Sun Bear taught that there were many reincarnated spirits of American Indian people reborn now, waiting for these changes that would make the earth new again. To cap it all off, it sounded like this Sun Bear fellow

11

was pretty old, yet fairly robust. It was rumored he had an eye for the ladies; and they, for him.

I wanted to go right out to Medicine Rock, the place where this community was starting. I really did not have time. I had a tight and preplanned schedule, limited finances, and a lot of lawyers and law commune people to interview. Sun Bear would have to wait.

When I returned to New York, Gene kept me up-to-date on the flamboyant activities of Sun Bear and his Bear Tribe. Gene or his friends attended a couple of fundraisers the Bear Tribe gave, and Gene enjoyed telling me all about them. One was in San Francisco at that famous rock palace, the Fillmore Auditorium. Headlining the performers were the New Riders of the Purple Sage, a Grateful Dead offshoot band featuring several of the Dead musicians. Sun Bear apparently got up and told the people about his philosophy between sets. It was a great San Francisco hippie event, and Gene was impressed. The other was in Sacramento. It was something called a potlatch and featured American Indian food and music, dancing and crafts. Approximately 3,000 people came to it—a very impressive crowd, especially for Sacramento.

I decided Sun Bear would at the least make a good story. I found out from Gene that Sun Bear was planning a cross-country trip to tell people about his Tribe. I got an address, wrote there and asked if I could interview him while he was in New York. In an action quite unlike me at that time in life (being a New Yorker and careful with the extent of my hospitality), I also suggested he could stay in my apartment if he needed a place in New York.

To my mild surprise I received an answer from someone whose name I didn't know from Gene's stories of the important people in the Tribe. Sun Bear would be happy to do both, and I would get a call when he neared New York, which was supposed to be in late July or early August.

I prepared my proposal for a story on Sun Bear and submitted it to *Life* magazine. They saw me to discuss the proposal further but decided, ultimately, it wasn't for them. They did, however, give me an assignment to write a story about a commune for the elderly in Florida. The *Life* rejection didn't bother me because I was sure one of the music or politically/humanistically oriented magazines for which I wrote would take the story about Sun Bear. If someone had told me then that I'd never write that article, but would instead, collaborate with this man on a new way of living, I would have told them they were crazy—and I might have retracted my offer of a place for Sun Bear to stay. Like most people with a fairly successful and comfortable life, I talked about liking change and variety, but I certainly didn't want it to come to me too quickly or radically. And of course I wanted a vibrant spiritual teacher—but one who wouldn't make many demands upon my life. However, on the day in July, 1971 when Sun Bear came to my door, spirituality was not my paramount mental topic. What I was thinking about was finding my true love, and/or doing something to make those damn earthquake experiences stop. I had suffered through a minor one just that morning.

Although the incidents had continued following the 42nd Street debacle, they had come with decreasing frequency and severity. Consequently, I had almost become used to them; almost, but not totally. They still scared me and my taxi bill was getting way too high.

In fact, I had taken a taxi home the previous night after a date with a lawyer. That dreary date, and the fact that my well-thought-out plan for finding the perfect mate was fizzling, had put love and the lack of it foremost in my thoughts. I had expected that an unwritten benefit of my lawyer book would be meeting this perfect man. I had met and dated a number of lawyers that year, but none of them seemed perfect, or anywhere close to it. I was getting worried. I was twenty-six years old and, despite all my efforts at raising my consciousness away from convention, I nevertheless thought I should be considering marriage, that disdained but desired institution. In recent years, I'd had several beaus who were definitely serious about me, but I did not return the feeling. I had even developed a sixth sense about when someone was going to propose, and would do something outrageous to stop them. Sometimes I would become a scandalous flirt, or I'd say how much I hated children and dogs, or I'd give an impromptu soliloquy about why I thought marriage was both antiquated and insane. My prospective partners were all nice guys, but I had not met my true love. I was certain I would know that perfect man when he appeared.

When Sun Bear rang the buzzer to my apartment and identified himself, I remember expecting him to be a wizened old man with a blanket around his shoulders supported on the arm of the person traveling with him. His companion, Morning Star, would be a tall, solid Indian man who greeted you with grunts rather than speech.

So much for my assumptions.

When I opened my door I saw a handsome, virile Indian man accompanied by a slender blond woman. Both were wearing jeans, Western shirts and wide, open-faced grins. Sun Bear wore what I would come to know as his trademark black hat. His face had a lot of character, and yet a certain innocence. He radiated charisma and vitality.

"Hi, welcome, I'm Marlise," I managed. "Come in."

They introduced themselves, smiling broadly, then entered, carrying suitcases.

"Sit down. Can I get you something to drink? Or eat? I made up some sangría, and I've been working since the spring perfecting a three-bean salad, There's some in the refrigerator. You must be tired. How was your trip? Did you have trouble finding a place to park?" I gabbed away anxiously.

They sat down.

"Sister," Sun Bear spoke to me, "Come sit down for a minute and let's talk." He patted the cushion next to his.

I sat. He took both my hands in his and said, "Thanks for asking us to be here. I've been looking forward to meeting you since I saw your letter. But tell me, what is troubling you?"

"Well," I replied, "I'm nervous about meeting you, of course, and hoping the interview will go well, and that you'll both enjoy being here."

"No," he said, "that's not what I mean. Something more is troubling you, and I think I can help."

Did this man read minds?

I sincerely hoped not because I couldn't stop wondering what the relationship was between him and Morning Star. I wanted to dislike her just for being there, but the beams of warmth directed at me by her spectacular blue eyes prevented that. This was definitely not a situation for which the normal rules of cosmopolitan society had prepared me.

"Sister, what is troubling you?", he asked again.

These two people could beam acceptance at me all they liked, but my guard was up. I was afraid any talking might reveal my attraction to this man. That would be inappropriate until I knew where he stood with Morning Star. Besides, just because I was attracted to him didn't mean that I trusted him.

"I'm just nervous about meeting you, as I said. Now, can I get you some sangría?"

"We don't drink alcohol."

"Okay, can I get you some iced tea then?"

"Good. That would be good."

I poured them each a glass of tea and myself a tall sangría. At that point I felt as if I'd be needing it.

Sun Bear noted that need of mine. He didn't say anything but I could feel him noting it.

I tried again to take control of the situation with some more polite questions about their trip. They answered in some detail, telling me a couple of amusing travel anecdotes. After about a half an hour Morning Star said she felt like taking a walk. I offered to accompany her but she said she wanted some space to herself.

When she left, Sun Bear took both my hands and told me that he liked me. I asked what his relationship was with Morning Star.

"She is a good sister, and a real good traveling companion."

Here the problem began. Sun Bear was telling me the truth as he saw it, given his cultural understanding and his very obvious maleness. But I was hearing a different truth, the only one possible for me with my conditioning and my understanding. Here we began speaking different languages, and first encountered the translation problems that would hinder our relationship for almost a decade. Over the years I've wondered whether, to some degree, all relationships between men and women involve difficulties with language. I have since learned that in some Native cultures there were separate languages for women and for men, with a third language spoken by all.

At that moment, however, I wouldn't have been interested in these linguistic concepts even if I had known about them. I just wanted to ascertain that this man was free to be *the one*. From the moment I'd first seen him I suspected he was. I'd been immediately overwhelmed with the feeling he was the true love, the perfect mate for whom I had been waiting. What else could account for the strong feelings I already had about him? It seemed as though I'd known him before and had just been waiting to again lay eyes upon him.

"Then she's not your woman?" I asked, just to be sure.

"She's her own woman," he laughingly replied. "I don't believe that people can or should own each other."

"Oh, I totally agree," replied my mouth, responding only to the neural impulses coming from my left brain, not from those originating in my right brain or in that deep, mysterious, misunderstood region we call the heart.

"Good," he responded as he drew me closer and sealed our agreement with a kiss. Since he was so adept at mind reading, I took this kiss to mean he was in agreement with all the thoughts that had just danced through my brain.

. . .

After Star returned and in my best Jewish mother mode, I managed to cook and serve a huge meal, Sun Bear returned to the question of what was troubling me. Trusting him more now that he had accepted my cooking and hospitality, I told him, still somewhat reluctantly, about the first earthquake incident at the party in June.

"A, ho!" he exclaimed when I finished that story. "I knew you were special since that first look at your letter. Sister, you have been having visions of the earth changes. You have seen this great city crumbling as it will in your lifetime. You are not crazy. You just have a gift for seeing far greater than most people do."

When he said that, I felt a huge sigh of relief go through my being. Finally there was someone I could talk to about the strange and frightening experiences that had been plaguing my life— someone who would not tell me to go find a shrink. With gusto, I launched into a full account of the other incidents. It was obvious he was impressed, although I had no idea why he would be.

When I finished my personal story, I told him I had never heard of the "earth changes" nor of "vision." In short, I had no idea what he was talking about.

Star, knowing Sun Bear's drive to share his visions, and knowing that I had just spoken the magic words, took out some beading and comfortably settled herself. Despite my desire not to, I had grown to like this woman more and more as the afternoon turned into evening. She was intelligent, lively, curious, outspoken, and definitely had opinions of her own. She was just the sort of woman I would choose for a close friend. As I was thinking this, she looked at me and smiled. Was this mind reading ability contagious?

Sun Bear asked me for some more coffee and also made himself comfortable.

Beginning, "Well, sister, I surely have a lot to teach you," he launched into a discourse that tilted the world I knew, but certainly brought the strange incidents I'd been experiencing into balance.

Sun Bear, it seemed, was a medicine man and a man of vision. After questioning him for several hours about what both those terms meant, I came to a basic intellectual understanding of the words. It took several more years for me to *know* what medicine meant, and a few years beyond that to have the visions that brought me a full understanding of that concept. What I could grasp then was that a medicine man was a combination minister/priest, doctor, psychologist, and prophet. Some medicine people also work with earth ceremonies, and with the elementals—the earth, air, fire, and water. This meant that some of them could bring rain or other changes in the atmosphere. Later I learned Sun Bear has this medicine.

A person of vision is one who has had some strange experiences—such as mine with the earthquakes—and, rather than being frightened by them, bases her life and work upon them. I had real trouble grasping that concept. Sun Bear explained that it was a vision that made him stop working for Office of Economic Opportunity programs for Indian reservations, and begin working to form the Bear Tribe.

Every few minutes I had to interrupt Sun Bear to ask for an explanation of some new concept: medicine men, medicine women, medicine societies, dog soldiers, earth changes, back-to-the-land communities, prophecies, the pipe, sweatlodges, herbalists, sand-painters, suck doctors, rain dances, chicken pulls, corn dances, dream medicine, moon ceremonies. I felt as confused as I had when first I worked for congressmen or the state department while at George Washington University and had had to learn the alphabet soup of acronyms that hold the federal government together. Sun Bear was speaking about a culture so foreign from the one I knew that he could have been speaking an altogether different language.

It all sounded very strange to me, bordering on spooky. The earth was supposed to just be there, the way I had been taught. It was a resource for man to harness: better living through chemistry and all that. You were not supposed to be able to talk to the earth and expect that talking to make changes; or to call the thunder clouds and have them come; or to pray to a plant before you picked it; or to ask the deer people to sacrifice one of their relations so humans could eat. That was all in the category of supernatural. But then, I had to admit, so was experiencing an earthquake or tidal wave that didn't really happen.

"Now do you understand, sister?", asked Sun Bear after his lengthy discourse.

"I think I have some sense of what you are talking about," I replied, "But I can't wait to get out my tape recorder and officially interview you tomorrow. All this is really fascinating material. I know I'll write a good story about it."

"I'm sure you will sister. But now it's time for resting and renewing," he replied.

It was time. What followed certainly renewed me. By the next day I knew with absolute certainty Sun Bear was the one for whom I had been waiting. Now that I had met him I could be patient until he saw this truth.

Miraculously, to my way of thinking, Morning Star and I got along increasingly well. She became my translator and guide over this strange new terrain. It had not, after all, been so long since it had been new to her too. She and her husband John, a high school teacher in an alternative school in Sacramento, had heard about Sun Bear in 1969 when he was teaching Native American philosophy in the experimental college at the University of California at Davis. Sun Bear also inspired and helped with a large experimental garden there.

At that point Sun Bear had been told by the Great Spirit, the Creator, that now it was time for him to begin the Bear Tribe— the medicine society he had been shown in various visions throughout his life. It certainly was a prime time in contemporary history to begin work with such a radical new idea.

A medicine society is a group of people who share a common vision. Historically, the Cheyenne dog soldiers are examples of one medicine society. The Bear Tribe was to be a multiracial medicine society composed of people who wanted to understand, then teach others about, the coming earth changes and how to prepare for them. Bear Tribe members were also to try and build a true love relationship with their brothers and sisters in the group, and to avoid being negative, violent, or possessive—a large order for people who had grown up in the same society I had! In the beginning they were also to abstain from alcohol and all drugs except "medicine weed," or marijuana. Not being a person who had ever smoked anything recreationally, Sun Bear certainly wasn't enamored of medicine weed himself, but it would have been nearly impossible then to find a group of alternatively minded people who were willing to give up that herb—their common denominator of rebellion against the rest of the culture.

Star and John volunteered their home as the meeting place for the group originally interested in Sun Bear's vision, and in bringing it to fulfillment. They were among the first people to move to Medicine Rock, and were responsible for much of the coordination of the beginnings of the Bear Tribe. In the spring of 1971, tragedy struck their family. Their eldest son, by then seven years old, accidentally drank some water contaminated with kerosene. Unable to face the death together, they drifted apart. John, then known as Eagle Wing, began relating to another woman. Star began traveling with Sun Bear. Their younger son, Little Eagle, stayed with Eagle Wing and the community while Star made long journeys.

It was the death of a child—the most grievous of misfortunes—that turned Star into this beacon of unconditional love. In her heart she felt she had nothing left to lose. Only those with this feeling seem to have everything to give. Give she did—to me, to Sun Bear, and to the stream of people who heard Sun Bear was in town and wanted to talk to or visit with him. I don't think I had ever before met such a variety of people in New York.

In between these activities, I launched a full-scale public relations campaign for Sun Bear and the Bear Tribe. I had had (unfortunately, in my mind) to take a public relations job after graduating from the Columbia University Graduate School of Journalism. It paid more than any of the magazine jobs I was offered, and had the possibility of advancement. Having learned how to generate publicity for something I did not believe in, I decided to use these skills for something I did believe in. I prepared releases on Sun Bear's vision, community, and philosophy.

I hand-delivered them, then followed through by phone. I leaned on some of my Columbia classmates. I got publicity: a few articles, a couple of radio interviews.

I was determined to show Sun Bear and Star *my* New York. At that time, every Manhattanite had her own New York. Mine was a mixture of liberals—lawyers, literary people, rock writers, folks from the human potential movement, some off-off-Broadway theatre types, feminists, political radicals, poets, and people interested in spiritual advancement. I wanted to show these folks to Sun Bear, and show Sun Bear off to them. Between his stream of people, my mixture of folks, and the groups to which he had already promised a visit or talk, we had quite a schedule.

Two days after they had arrived, I accompanied Sun Bear and Star to a commune in upstate New York. This was quite a cultural revelation to me—almost as big as the time that I, as a student producer at Columbia, took a student television crew into an apartment in Harlem and had to give the supposedly methadone-cured addict money for a fix if I and said crew and equipment wanted to get out in the same state in which we entered. The Harlem episode almost made me quit Columbia because I feared journalism was irrelevant to the real-life problems of poverty and hopelessness. The commune incident made me question just how different from mainstream society alternative living really was.

The commune was a big house in the country filled with people, most of whom seemed to be children. The decor was decidedly below the tasteful early thrift store and gift mix in which I had decorated my own apartments up until then. The women wore long hair, long skirts, and long faces. I soon understood why. The men were doing most of the talking. My feminist dander rose quickly. Seeing me about to boil over, and wanting to keep the peace for Sun Bear's talk, Star firmly suggested I accompany her on a walk.

"How can you stand it?", I hissed.

She explained that Sun Bear himself was as egalitarian as most men she knew, and that young guys had the same big egos whether they were in alternative or regular society. She assured me she had seen some changes in the men who stayed with the Tribe for a while. In any case, she was more concerned that Sun Bear have a chance to see if this was a community with which the Tribe could connect than she was with trying to liberate the women in the group. She told me that if I had more connection with the earth I would have more balance and less anger. I wasn't sure I agreed with any of this, but I felt I should keep quiet. I was the stranger to these ways, and I was the interloper. I shut my mouth and felt sorry for myself, being stuck in this unpleasant situation for the rest of the day. I also felt I was flunking my first test with Sun Bear. After all, if I couldn't stand being around the sort of people with whom he associated, how could I convince him—or myself—that he was my perfect mate.

Sun Bear made the connection he wanted to. The group leaders assured him they would be happy to trade goods or services with the Bear Tribe whenever the need arose. I believe I heard that that commune ceased to exist before any trades were made. I wasn't sad to hear it, and I certainly wasn't sad when we left that day.

I liked returning to the City and being back on my own turf.

The next day we were taking the subway to midtown to meet a *Newsweek* reporter for lunch at a fancy French restaurant, my favorite kind. Sun Bear and Star were playing their favorite subway game: grinning at the person across from each of them. They used those same friendly, open-faced grins I had seen when I met them. Nobody smiled on New York subways, even then, unless they also talked and sang to themselves a lot and perhaps had their shoes on the wrong feet. Most people would return their look, skeptically at first, checking to see if these were crazies, then, noting their Western appearance and deciding they were just two friendly country hicks, would capitulate within a minute or two and begin smiling back, shyly at first, but then with increasing boldness. Within a couple of stops these two would have half the people in the car smiling. That was a significant accomplishment. I was in a good mood, knowing I had the day to show them my New York, so I began smiling too. We almost got the whole car smiling that time—proof, I thought, that one person could make a difference.

When we met Dan in the lobby of the restaurant, he helped us to get past the maitre'd who insisted that Sun Bear wear a tie. Sun Bear pulled a piece of jewelry he called a bolo tie out of the pocket of his Western jacket and asked if that would do. This confused the maitre d', an unusual state for someone in that position in New York, who instead insisted that Sun Bear wear the loaner tie

kept in the cloak room for the rare occasions when a man tried
to pass the portals without the proper uniform. Sun Bear graciously accepted the tie, Dan gave the maitre d' a nice tip, and the
rest of the lunch was quite pleasant. Dan was interested in Sun
Bear and his work. He promised to try to get some mention of
it in the magazine, which ultimately did not happen. But I felt that
even the possibility of a *Newsweek* article was quite a coup for me.
I hoped it would make up for my failure to appreciate country
communal living.

Following some sightseeing in midtown we met with Oscar
Collier, my literary agent. Sun Bear had already authored two
books, *At Home in the Wilderness* and *Buffalo Hearts,* both then
published by Naturegraph Publishers. I thought Oscar could help
with any future book projects (which was a good intuition on my
part, although Oscar worked with us first as an editor, not as an
agent) or with some magazine articles. The meeting went well
and I was feeling good about myself as I took Sun Bear and Star
to a rock party at a restaurant on the end of the South Street pier.
Sun Bear wasn't real fond of loud music, so he spent more time
looking at the river than he did talking with the other guests. But,
he assured me, he enjoyed it all. He urged me to try to relax and
enjoy myself too. Eventually he found some people interested in
his visions, and he was off and talking. I mingled then, speaking
with some of my acquaintances.

When I drifted back to where Sun Bear was now speaking to
a larger group, I heard him saying "What happens between a man
and a woman is their private business. No one should force anyone else to do anything, including being with just one person if
they feel energy toward others. People can't possess each other."

My mind jumped in in total agreement. After all, I had long
been an intellectual advocate of free love, open marriage, and all
the other tenets of the sexual revolution we were all supposed to
be promoting and practicing in the sixties.

The problem was with my feelings. While Sun Bear was speaking and my mind and mouth were agreeing, my heart was translating his statements to be, "What happens between a man and a
woman is their private business, except, my darling, with you, to
whom I will tell everything and always be faithful. No one should
force anyone else to do anything, but force will never be an issue
between us. I will always want to do whatever you ask me to do.

With you by my side, I won't feel energy toward anyone else. I don't want to possess you, but already you possess my heart. I've been waiting my whole life to meet you."

Honestly, I was not a reader of, nor writer for, romance books or magazines. I steadfastly believe that family and society started feeding me "one true love, knight in shining armor" messages along with my mother's milk. Unknown to my very refined and developed mind, my feelings did not know nor care about, let alone accept, any tenet of that much-touted but little understood revolution of the sixties. I was an intellectual futurist and an emotional neanderthal, like so many of my generation.

Even my dearly beloved feminism had not changed my feelings. I talked a lot about not being dependent upon any man in any way. I advocated having my own life, my own career, my own friends, and my own goals. But my archconservative emotions would lay it all down in an instant for Mr. Right. And the moment they saw Sun Bear, my feelings bellowed that this strange Indian was Mr. Right.

The stage was ever-so-ripely set. Sun Bear said and lived all the things my mind wanted to believe. My mouth enthusiastically agreed with all of his forward-looking wisdom. But my feelings lurked like a cat behind a doorway, waiting to pounce upon any sign of atavistic thought in this man that they felt should be mine.

While I was plotting my relationship with Sun Bear, I found out later he was doing some plotting of his own. According to what he has told me since then, he had recognized me as an important part of his vision from the time he first read my letter When we met he "knew" me, and what my tribal name would be. It didn't matter to Sun Bear that all these new concepts confused me. His vision showed him where I would fit. He could afford to dance with my mind until I saw my own path clearly

• • •

After a week of having lived in the cocoon of unconditional love and acceptance Sun Bear and Star had spun around me, I was a little depressed on the day they left to go to Washington, D.C. for some lectures. They were to return in a couple of days. I waved goodbye as they pulled off from the curb, and returned to my apartment intent upon shaking the depression through intense work on the lawyer book.

I did work, but calls for Sun Bear kept coming in. I felt like an answering service, and became quite annoyed at this interruption to my privacy. I began by trying to be helpful to each caller, but my humanitarian resolve began to falter when callers got angry at me because I didn't know where to reach Sun Bear, or expected me to know how to heal their bodies, minds, souls, or lives. I had never aspired to social work. I considered myself a writer, and one who needed peace and privacy.

I wondered if this was how it was at his base camps in California. Then I realized few of them had phones. But, from the sound of the people calling me, they would have dropped by if they couldn't phone. Each person seemed to feel that Sun Bear had something special just for them—healing or a message or advice. They seemed to communicate that he owed them, and they had no responsibility for giving him anything back for his gift. Frankly, it seemed quite rude to me. I didn't think these people would phone a doctor, psychologist, or priest and make the same kinds of entreaties. If they thought this Indian medicine man could do so much for them, why didn't they treat him with more respect?

When Sun Bear phoned later that day I asked him about this. "People in America have always had a lot of conflicting opinions about Indians," he said. "That's a long story, and one you'll understand better as time goes on. I'm going to put Star on now and you can quickly tell her if it sounded like any of the people who called were in really bad shape."

It had seemed to me that most of the callers were in bad shape. However after discussing the first few with Star I realized none were really critical, and they could wait until Sun Bear returned.

After the call I fantasized about what it would be like working with Sun Bear. I admitted to myself that talking to the people who had called made me feel useful. Since Sun Bear had walked into my life I felt for the first time I could remember that my vast reserves of energy were being put to good use. Usually people were put off by or were afraid of my intensity and energy. Sun Bear and Star were not. In fact, Sun Bear even stretched me at times. I liked that.

Then I thought about "living off the land." Other than the weekend I spent at the Woodstock Festival in 1969, I had never slept out in the open. Even the summer camp I attended had cabins. I had been really high after Woodstock (without leftover additives), but who wasn't? Could I stand roughing it, especially for an indefinite period of time? Did I want to? And what would it really be like? Would I be living in a tent, foraging for greens, roots, and berries? Would I actually have to hunt animals for meat as Star told me they had done at some of the bases? That, I decided, would definitely be more than I could stand. When I was a little girl my Aunt Ruth used to take me to a park where there were fenced deer. There was a little doe Aunt Ruth helped me name Bubanu. Bubanu used to come over to see me whenever we went there, probably because I always carried a treat in my pocket. I knew I could not go deer hunting and risk hurting Bubanu's relatives. Besides, the thought of blood or gore was just more than my delicate stomach could stand.

It was then that I realized I was actually considering living with the Bear Tribe. While I had known before that I wanted to be with Sun Bear, I had somehow managed to separate that from the fact that it would mean living with his group. I was the sort of person who considered dinner with eight to be group living, and almost intolerable. Other than crowds at concerts and things of that nature, I preferred people in twos and threes. The idea of being part of a group of 200, with frequent guests, would require a lot of thought.

I was very happy when Sun Bear and Star returned a few days later. After being around their warmth, my life had begun to seem cold by comparison. They had come back to New York to spend more time with me and to accompany me to a meeting of my spiritual group. When I had told Gavin about Sun Bear's visit, he wanted to meet him. It seemed Gavin knew something about Indian prophecies and wanted to compare notes.

It had begun raining just as Sun Bear drove into the city. When we went to the car to drive to the meeting, we were greeted by a clap of thunder followed by a bolt of lightning.

"Ho, brothers," Sun Bear said, looking toward the the sky. "It's good. It's good. Thank you. I always like it when the thunderbeings are around. They are bringing me a sign for this meeting."

When we went into the room where the meetings were held I was surprised by the number of people who were there. Sun Bear was cordial and quite willing to answer questions. As I watched him talking with Gavin, I was struck by the difference between the two men. Not only did Sun Bear have more vitality, charisma, and warmth, but also he had more humility and a less rigid view of the world. While I was grateful for the help this spiritual group had given me, it seemed they approached the metaphysical in a much more intellectual way than I'd realized before. And intellect, I was beginning to think, had its limits.

Toward the end of the meeting Gavin began to be quite cutting with his questions. It almost seemed he wanted to discredit Sun Bear in the eyes of the people there. Sun Bear retained his equanimity, which seemed to make Gavin even more intent in his efforts. A few minutes more of this strange behavior and Sun Bear thanked Gavin for having him there and said he needed to leave.

Although I felt somewhat torn, I decided to leave with Sun Bear. I said my good nights to Gavin and the group. As we were walking out the door, a big clap of thunder seemed to shake the building. We returned to my place.

Sensing my distress Sun Bear said, "You don't realize what was going on there do you?"

I shook my head no.

"It's too soon for you to know the whole story," he said, almost talking to himself. "Let's just say that Gavin saw you were thinking of leaving his group and he didn't want you to. He tried to engage me in a power struggle to make me look bad in your eyes."

"I don't understand," I said. "Why wouldn't he want me to leave?"

"You have a special energy my sister, and a particular path to walk in this life. Don't worry about it now."

He sat quietly lost in thought for a few minutes.

"I'm concerned you're going to have some difficulties after we leave," he said. "I want to give you some methods of dealing with them, although I'm not sure you'll be ready to use these ways. What do you do when you get upset, besides cry or drink?"

I was going to be self-righteously indignant about what he said, but realized it would be useless. He had noted every drink.

"Sometimes I go down and stand, watching the water flow in the East River."

"Good, remember to do that. Water is very healing, and it is the element to which you feel closest. Let's go down there now and see if anything else is available."

As I closed my door and used the key to lock the two dead-bolts I had besides the regular door locks, Sun Bear chuckled and said, "In zoos they have to lock up the animals. In the big cities, the people lock themselves up. Come on, let's see if there is anything natural left in that park."

We found a couple of small trees, and a few plants bravely pushing their way up between the sidewalk cracks.

"Here's what I want you to do if it gets to be too much. Come here, or find another place with bigger trees, and hug them. Put your body up against the trees like I'm doing, and stand there until you feel better. Then turn around and lean your back against them, staying that way until you feel calm."

"But people will think I'm crazy."

"What's more important, what people think or how you feel within yourself?"

3

THE AFTERMATH

A day after Sun Bear and Morning Star left to resume their cross-country travels, I felt devastated. I lay curled up in my bed, unwilling to get up and face the day. What was the point? Nothing I had known in the past seemed to have any real meaning. The future was so murky it was anybody's guess what would happen. I didn't care. I had glimpsed paradise, snuggled in that cocoon of love and acceptance. Now I had lost it. Why didn't I just pack a suitcase and take off with them? I cursed my overblown sense of responsibility and commitment that kept me here to finish a book and live out the last months of my lease. Were these more important than true love?

None of my ponderings really mattered. The fact was that Sun Bear had not asked me to go along, and I had not had the courage to ask if he wanted me to. True, he had said he hoped I would think about joining the Tribe. But he hadn't said when. Nor had he made the declarations of undying love I had so wanted to hear. After the night when he took me out to hug trees, there was a decided coolness between us. I thought it came from him, perhaps because I had implied he was nuts for hugging trees. It would be a long time before he told me he was purposely being cool because he didn't want me to make a spiritual decision based largely upon my feelings for him as a man.

But, I wondered now, grinding my head into the pillow as I twisted and turned some more, whether the coolness had come from me. The meeting with Gavin had upset me. For all my unvoiced complaints about how Gavin had treated Sun Bear, I had to admit that his group had given me some foundation during

29

the time when I was just opening up to the fact that there is more to life than what meets the eye. I felt grateful for that help, and torn because there was obviously some sort of animosity between Gavin and Sun Bear.

It was late in the preceeding year that I had resolved to turn some of my energy toward the spiritual. I had decided that I could not change the world for the better—the only goal I thought worthy of having—if I could not make some changes in myself. Neither politics nor psychology seemed to be helping me to change as quickly as I thought I should. Spirituality was all that I knew was left.

I'm not sure how I would have defined spirituality then: probably as anything but the organized religions I knew from my childhood. I was not antireligion; in fact I've often thought the Presbyterian church lost out on a great minister when I found out in the early sixties that women were encouraged to be ministers' wives, but not ministers. I had had a multidenominational childhood. I had almost been confirmed in the Lutheran church until I lost respect for the minister. I had called a peer "asinine" because of a statement she had made about a story I wrote in seventh grade. The minister came to my house and told my parents I had cursed at another young lady. Since my mother had encouraged me to have a vocabulary that set me apart from my schoolmates, she had to agree that the man did not have a very open mind, or an adequate grasp of language.

When we moved to the suburbs I joined a Presbyterian church, but my dad and I would occasionally go to revival meetings. I loved the emotions at those meetings—the loudness, the rowdiness, the singing, and the confessions of conversion. Sometimes they made me cry with happiness. But, much as it appealed to my repressed emotions, I couldn't bring my body and mouth to open up and join in. I never could take the step from evangelical voyeur to participant. Besides, I really liked the minister at the Presbyterian church. He was a good listener, even to teenagers, and had a lot of common sense. He helped me through a couple of the crises of adolescence. Because of our friendship I ended up at the College of Wooster, a Presbyterian college in the Midwest my freshman year.

The problem I encountered at this college was the homogeneity of the people. I was used to being around folks who were not all white Anglo-Saxon Protestants (Wasps). In fact, in the high school I attended we Wasps, along with anyone who wasn't Italian and Catholic, were in a distinct minority. We formed our own adolescent United Nations clique. I became used to hanging around with people of various nationalities and religious backgrounds, and I liked the diversity.

When I transferred to George Washington University in D.C. I found that diversity again. I was also in the small group of women who wanted to either go into politics or the foreign service, so I was a happy member of a minority again. I discovered the Episcopal church. I loved the services. They had more ritual than the Catholic masses I had attended with friends. The singing, the chanting, the frankincensing, the vestments of the priests all seemed wonderful. They evoked the emotions of the revivalist meetings without the rowdiness.

As college liberated me from my conditioned ideas, I began to question why I went to some church or other every week. I discovered fear and guilt lying beneath my other motivations. I missed a couple of Sundays. To my wonderment, no lightning bolts struck me, nor did I sense that I was destined to burn in hell. Following this revelation I missed quite a few Sundays. I fancied myself an agnostic for a while, then I just turned away from religion altogether—until the year when I decided spirituality might help me make the somewhat vague changes I desired in my life.

There was a theory popular with some of my friends at the time that when you decide to pursue spirituality you become a magnet that draws different spiritual experiences and teachers to you. Having seen it happen for so many people over the course of time, I have concluded that it is more than a theory; it is one of those elusive but discoverable universal laws. Because of it I easily found people who helped me explore Buddhism, Sufism, Zen, yoga, meditation, and a strange conglomeration of new practices that seemed to originate on the hippie turf of the Lower East Side.

It was these strange practices that upset my friend, boss, and mentor, Evan. When I first met Evan he was editing a small, humanistically oriented magazine entitled *Homo Sapien.* I met him in the bar that was under the apartment I was renting at that time. When he learned I was a writer he asked me to do a story. I did, and he tore it apart, telling me I should have begun with the last paragraph. Having written for a variety of magazines since I was eighteen (many of which were, objectively, of higher quality and better known than *Homo Sapien*), and, rarely having more than a word changed in my articles, I was challenged by this arrogant bastard who thought he knew so much. I loved challenges.

I became his contributing editor within a few months, and half a year later he hired me as his managing editor for the expanded version of *Homo Sapien,* which had financial backing and was hopefully going national. This turned out to be the first of several magazine jobs that gave me a unique specialty—expert dummy issue editor. The dummy issue of a new magazine doesn't have real stories. It has titles, real ideas for the first issue, and spectacular artwork. All copy reads the same: "Xxxxxxxxxxxx xxxxxxx xxxx xxxxxxx xx xx xxxxxx xxx xxxxx xx xxxxx xxxx xx," etc. This shows the importance of actual writing to the advertising world.

The dummy issue is designed to sell advertisers on the need for and potential success of the new publication. Unfortunately, after a couple of months of two professional ad men pounding the pavement it became obvious *Homo Sapien* would not attract enough advertisers to keep the backing of the money men. We got different backers and tried again with a magazine called *New Human*—a new dummy, a new staff, the same story. Later, on my own, I got the opportunity to try once more with a magazine called *Motion,* which was financed by a major shoe company. It was after this magazine folded that I decided to try writing books, at least until I could get a job with a well-financed magazine.

When Evan saw *New Human* fold, he went to work for a more specialized publishing company and eventually edited one of the airline magazines. With that job and a formal engagement to Elaine, his patient girlfriend of many years, Evan became a born again straight, and he worried about me. It didn't matter that he had introduced me to some of the most unusual people from all quarters that I, or anyone, could ever hope to meet. It didn't matter that he had encouraged me to date some of them "just for the experience," which he vicariously shared through our intimate conversations. Evan had become respectable and, as my mentor, he felt it was his duty to make me follow suit, particularly in the important area of spirituality. It was Evan who had become involved with Gavin. He convinced Elaine to study with them. Then he turned his attention to my soul and its possible evolution.

Evan almost lost on this one because I had heard about Sun Bear and his Tribe just before I committed to study with Gavin's group. I was going to wait before making a commitment; but then, with Evan's urging, I decided I needed to begin progressing spiritually as soon as possible. I voraciously read all the material written by the mystic who founded the group (no mean feat since he wrote big books) and by many of his followers. I felt these folks did have a larger understanding of the universe and of human nature than anything I had explored up to that point. Their literature seemed to have answers to all the questions facing humanity. I liked that. Seeing things in black and white was so much easier than having to deal with shades of grey. But I also felt something was missing for me on this path.

Whatever it was, and "heart" seemed the best word I could find to describe the lack, Sun Bear had it. As I twisted the pillow once more I wondered whether I could possibly conceive of going to join him not because he was *the one* but because he was the spiritual teacher I had been seeking? "Oh, yes," my brain answered, as I turned to cry some more into my already soggy pillow.

When my neighbor Terry got home from her vacation that afternoon, she knocked on my door to get the mail I'd been collecting for her. Reluctantly, I answered the knock. All I had managed to do that day was get myself up, dressed in a robe, and planted in front of the afternoon soaps.

"Hi," Terry said with a worried expression on her face, "are you sick?"

Responding to the sympathy in her voice I began to cry all over again.

Terry was, by nature and conditioning, a very kind, calm, and compassionate person. She made a wonderful friend for me. Her imperturbable nature was a good counter-point to my intensity, which sometimes bordered on hysteria. In return, I suspected my tempestuous nature helped to draw her out.

I was sorry she had been away and missed the Sun Bear stream of humanity. She would have enjoyed it.

She sat down and put her arm around my shoulder.

"Come on, tell me what's going on."

An hour later we were both laughing as I told her about hugging trees by the East River.

"But I don't know what to do," I entreated.

"I can see that," she replied. "Do you have to decide today?"

"No."

"Then why don't you get dressed and we'll go to that little French restaurant on 86th and I can tell you about my vacation."

That was only the first of many times Terry saved my sanity over the next few months. As we were walking to the restaurant, I felt the earth begin to rumble again—much to my great surprise, since the "incidents" had always occurred when I was either totally alone or alone in a crowd. I didn't see anything this time. I just felt the viscousness of the earth's mantle and heard the strange, high-pitched noise that precedes the more visible parts of an earthquake. It was enough to make me head for a doorway.

Terry followed me.

"Is it happening right now?" she asked.

I nodded yes.

"Tell me exactly what is happening."

I began to do so. I found as I described the sensations, they began to recede. In a very short time the earth felt still, and my nausea disappeared. I was ecstatic at this discovery, hoping it meant I could always talk away these incidents or visions when they occurred.

"But what if someone else besides you is with me, or I'm alone?" I asked Terry.

"Then you'll either have to let your companion or the people in the street think you're nuts, or you'll have to go on feeling the incident."

Another tough choice, like hugging the trees. Appearing to do the proper or correct thing was quite important to me then. I had been inculcated with the Wasp's concern for the neighbors' opinion—a rather foolish interest given the lack of intimacy and community feeling in contemporary society, yet one that seemed to me a foundation for civilized society. It was concern for the neighbors' opinion, and punishments for turning it against me, that had changed me from an ebullient, energetic, and mischievous child into a "proper little lady"—a quiet, dull, and stodgy goody two-shoes. It was this concern that taught me later to appear to do the proper thing, while doing what I really wanted. Such hypocrisy does indeed seem to form the basis for most of "civilized" society.

Terry and I did have a nice dinner that night. I enjoyed hearing all about her vacation, and we laughed a lot over the anecdotes about Sun Bear and the stream of people I'd encountered. She was truly supportive of my doing whatever I felt would make me happy.

"When you were a kid did you count buttons to see who you'd marry?" I asked.

She said no.

"You'd say, 'Rich man, poor man, beggar man, thief, doctor, lawyer, Indian chief' and whatever you said when you ran out of buttons told you who you were going to marry. I wonder if I got the Indian chief a lot?"

I counted the buttons on the blouse I was wearing and, sure enough, got Indian chief that night, which cracked us up. I didn't realize it then but it was to be one of the few pleasant meals I'd have with someone else over the next few months.

Terry, it turned out, was one of the few of my many friends who thought I should do whatever would make me happy. Evan's reaction was more representative. He truly believed I was losing my chance for a good life and true spiritual salvation. He was adamant in his opinion that Sun Bear and his Tribe were a vast mistake for me. He contended they were a cult. Suspecting I'd hear that from more than one source I had turned to the dictionary. Cult was defined as: "1. worship; reverential honor; religious devotion 2. the system of outward forms and ceremonies used in worship; religious rites and formalities 3. devoted attachment to, or extravagant admiration for, a person, principle, etc., especially when regarded as a fad; as, the cult of nudism 4. a group of followers; sect." Given those definitions I had to agree the Bear Tribe was a cult. So was Gavin's group, Protestantism, Catholicism, Judaism, Buddhism, and every other spiritual system existing on the face of the earth.

"Come on, Marlise," he said when I gave him the dictionary definition, "you know what I mean."

"No I don't."

"This group is trying to brainwash you and force you to go out and join them."

"*Au contraire,* Evan, I'm here now, aren't I? If what you are saying were true I'd be somewhere out West. Sun Bear didn't even ask me to join him when he left, damn it. I wish he had. And I didn't see him brainwashing anybody else who came by to see him. He's been doing this for a couple of years now and he has only 200 or so people spread over a dozen or so places. He doesn't believe more than twenty or twenty-five people should be in any community because most pieces of land that are affordable can't support more people than that, and it's hard for more people than that to become a real community. He does dishes and drives a beat-up Ford that used to be a police car before he bought it in a city auction. When I called him 'Rimpoche,' then explained it was a Tibetan Buddhist term for a special teacher and meant 'precious one,' he laughed and told me he wasn't more precious than anyone else. Does that sound like guru behavior? *You* come on, Evan.

"Gavin has more than 200 people in his groups, and that body of knowledge he teaches certainly changed my attitudes and beliefs," I continued. "Can't you call any radical shift in thought brainwashing?"

"I guess so. But I don't like this guy. He's using your attraction for him to get you to do what he wants you to."

"Like you used my attraction to you to get me to quit my job and work for you? Or like you used it to get me into Gavin's group? Shall I go on?"

He didn't want me to. What he really wanted was for me to sit quietly while he explained to me yet again why I was doing the wrong thing.

I received a call the next day from Josh, my direct guide in Gavin's organization. He wanted to meet me for coffee and talk about this Sun Bear. We met, we drank coffee, he talked, and I listened. When he was done he asked me if I still intended to go out to join Sun Bear.

"I think so Josh," I replied, "but I'm not sure yet."

That answer won me a private consultation with both Josh and Gavin.

After stating their reasons for thinking I was doing the wrong thing, they asked for my response.

"I'm not intending to do anything now," I said truthfully. "I still have my book to finish, and I was just assigned an article for

Life. But I've had no luck finding a full-time job I like here, and I've had those earthquake experiences, so I'm thinking I might make the move West toward the end of the year, but definitely not to Los Angeles."

They were relieved to know they had me to reason with for four more months. They suggested we talk again as the time came closer. Gavin also recommended I consider going out to see Sun Bear and his Tribe for a limited visit the first time—something like two weeks to a month. I agreed to consider what he said.

Over the next month I also agreed to consider the opinions of many other acquaintances I had and groups with which I was associated. Generally, my radical political friends were glad I was finally committing myself to something, rather than continuing with the "gad-fly journalistic tendencies that took me from cause to cause and concept to concept." My psychologically oriented acquaintances were interested, but wary. They held the picture of the stoic Indian in mind and felt I would become emotionally atrophied being around such people. My journalism buddies thought I was taking the concept of participatory journalism to a ridiculous degree. My feminist friends felt I should keep trying to raise my consciousness. They'd heard about commune women in long hair and long skirts baking bread when they had a minute break from caring for their numerous children. My family didn't like the idea of my moving West but had become resigned to my "strange ideas about life" and knew the less said, the less stubborn I became on any topic.

The funny thing was that I still hadn't made a decision when I began talking to people about the possibility of my move. But they assumed I had, and many of them tried to talk me out of it. The more they talked, the more the scale tipped toward the West. However, just because I was contemplating going West did not, in my mind, necessarily mean I would join the Bear Tribe. I had enjoyed Northern California, and had Gene and a couple of other friends there. And I kept getting calls from Benjamin Wahyu, an Indonesian lawyer I had interviewed when we were both in Los Angeles. Benjamin was also a political activist and writer. He proclaimed himself to be the last of the world's great hedonists in his spare time. He wanted me to come to Denver, his home base, and check out that claim myself.

That was tempting. I figured if we did stand on the brink of the earth changes Sun Bear talked about, there were two alternatives. You could prepare for them as the Bear Tribe was doing, or you could have such a good hedonistic time that you went out with a smile on your face. I vacillated about which was the best alternative for me, as I did about almost everything in those months. Besides having problems deciding my future, I was also having problems with my present. For one, the earth changes incidents continued happening. I had a couple of experiences as dramatic as those that occurred before I met Sun Bear, but most of the time I just heard the earthquake noise and felt the earth moving. However, these experiences must have had some kind of cumulative effect because each one was making me feel more vertigo and nausea.

One of these events became even more dramatic and frightening to me because during it Sun Bear seemed to appear out of thin air.

I was walking out of the 72nd Street subway station on the West Side when I heard the then-familiar noise. I began to run but it was rush hour and I couldn't get through the crowds quickly enough. This, of course, was my worst nightmare—to be caught in a subway station with an earthquake happening. The urge to scream was becoming stronger by the minute. At this point Sun Bear appeared. He took my arm and told me to be calm and not scream. He reminded me that many people would not understand the visions I was having. He lead me to the street. Since I was still shaking, he continued walking with me to my destination.

"Why do you continue to fight your destiny sister?" he asked. While I was forming my answer, Sun Bear disappeared, again into thin air. I think my mouth must have dropped with amazement.

I was as shaken by his appearance and disappearance as I was by the earthquake incident. I was even more upset when he called me a few days later and asked if I was okay now.

When I asked what he was talking about, he replied, "My helping you the other day when you had the earthquake incident in the subway."

"How did you know it was happening?", I demanded.

"I was out walking and a little bird told me. Aren't you glad I helped?"

"Yes," I replied without much conviction. In fact, I wasn't sure I was glad. I didn't know much about this mind reading business, but I did not like the idea that someone else 3,000 miles away could know what I was thinking. I felt that Sun Bear's reply about the bird was flip, and did not show proper respect for the seriousness of the incident. Beyond that, his ability to appear and disappear had to go in the category of "unsolved spooky stuff" that had been growing steadily since first I heard about the Bear Tribe. I did not like unexplained mysteries.

Again, we were experiencing a translation problem. It would be several years before I would understand that Sun Bear was being totally honest when he said a little bird told him.

In addition to these experiences, I was also experiencing a build up of emotional pressure from my indecisiveness and the opinions other people had been giving me. The effect of this pressure was a paralyzing confusion. I didn't know what I believed in anymore, or what I wanted. That was the hardest of all for someone who had been as goal-oriented as I had been.

I spent many hours crying because of this confusion and the despair it evoked. One time I actually cried for twenty-four hours. Terry finally convinced me to go to an emergency room where they gave me some kind of sedative that turned off the fountain and brought sleep. Sometimes even sleep brought little respite, because I would have dreams that rehashed all my waking concerns, or it would bring strange dreams as frightening in their own way as the earthquake incidents.

Despite all the people I knew, I felt totally alone. No one really understood my feelings—not even Terry, although she really tried. No one could help me. Frankly I felt as though I were coming unglued, and it was only a matter of time until I was a pile of mush on the floor of life.

The occasional letters and phone calls from Sun Bear or Star gave me some sense of sustenance, but it wasn't enough. Even though I had showed it to them, they did not really understand or appreciate *my Manhattan.* They had tried, but they couldn't comprehend why I was staying in the City even when it was making me physically ill. They kept assuring me I could write anywhere, even out West. But I didn't feel I could leave until my book was completed. My perceived lack of human support left me alone with my mind, the tyrant that ruled me with its incessant arguments, facts, disclaimers, and questions.

My emotional turmoil was also taking its toll on my work. It was hard to write or to talk to magazine editors when I felt I was constantly teetering on the brink of tears or phantasms. I constantly had to force myself to plunge ahead.

Everything began to rush toward the final unhinging on an early December day when I was supposed to attend a friend's wedding. I began the day by tripping on a loose step outside of a shop. I fell, hit my head, and sprained an ankle. An ambulance took me to a hospital where I was x-rayed for brain, head, or neck damage, treated for cuts and the sprain, and released.

Now a reasonable person would have gone home to bed. I went home, got dressed, hid the cuts as best I could and went to the wedding. At the reception I proceeded to consume enough booze to make me forget all my pains—physical, mental, emotional, and spiritual. I couldn't dance up a storm as I wanted to, so I talked the ears off of a couple of friends. Hearing about my problems they, of course, offered their solutions. While the solutions were of no more value than any of the others people had made, these friends were kind enough to see that I got home safely. Otherwise I doubt I would have.

When I went to lie down that night, I couldn't. I had such a severe pain in my right side that I could not straighten up, either standing or lying. I sat up and watched old movies until I could call my doctor in the morning. He saw me immediately and sent me on to a surgeon.

The surgeon said, "We'll take your gallbladder out this afternoon."

"Like hell you will," I replied. "I want to keep all my parts as long as possible. Have you ever heard of testing before cutting, or do you need just one more gallbladder operation to get that vacation in the Bahamas?"

I did not have a high opinion of the medical profession. Seeing that I meant what I said, we compromised. I agreed to be hospitalized and have all my internal organs tested, and he agreed not to cut unless there was a real need to. He also agreed that I could fast rather than have intravenous feedings, which were only sugar water. It's too bad I hadn't worried about the sugar content in the drinks I'd had the night before. I considered consistency the hobgoblin of little minds and politicians. I still do.

After four days of being pushed, punctured, dyed, x-rayed, and otherwise manhandled, the doctor concluded I was suffering from muscle spasms, probably brought on by stress. He prescribed a muscle relaxant and sent me home. My first experience of being a patient advocate had been successful.

Awaiting me at home were all the things that had caused the stress: the almost-finished book, the article that needed one more rewrite, and the messages from friends hoping to influence my future.

I decided I needed to make some decisions, and quickly. I returned the calls from friends and listened once more as they advised me to stay in New York. I made a list of reasons to stay and reasons to go. Although there were more reasons to stay, my last reason to go was, "I really want to!"

Sun Bear and Star now were living in Reno. I made reservations to go there, then I called everyone back and told them my decision. I did not indicate it was open to discussion. Most people did assure me that I could turn around and come back home if I found I had done the wrong thing. Gavin even called to assure me I would be accepted back in the group, as long as I returned within a reasonable amount of time.

Finally freed of my agonizing, incapacitating indecision, I set to work and finished the book. I rewrote the *Life* article. I gave away most of my possessions, and packed what I wanted to go with me. I prepared for Christmas. I kept myself very busy.

One time-consuming Christmas project was finding the proper dog to give my parents for Christmas. They hadn't asked for this gift but our family dog had died of old age a few months before. After researching and writing an article about pets for *New York* magazine, I had concluded that a soft-coated wheaten terrier would be ideal for them. A family in a brownstone was giving one away because, they said, he needed more room to run. What they didn't tell me was that Zachary had almost every bad habit a dog could have. He never learned the meaning of "heel," "stop," "sit," or "lie down." And he was strong. *He* walked *you.* He was a barker, a fighter, a whiner, a shredder, and a humper. Despite all this, he was affectionate, adorable, loving, and, in his own way, loyal. In short, Zachary was the perfect substitute for an errant, eccentric, grown child. I think my parents eventually forgave me this gift.

All my activity made things all right during the day but, when I went to bed at night, I was plagued by all the doubts work kept

at bay. Since Sun Bear's "appearance" I'd been having thoughts
come into my mind that claimed he was an evil medicine man.
These were strange thoughts, foreign to me. They appeared in
my mind of their own volition, rather than originating in any
thought that preceded them. And they were strong messages.
Partly because of them, at the last moment I decided to see
Benjamin in Denver before I went to Sun Bear. Maybe Benjamin
could help me understand what was going on in my mind.

On my last day in New York, I felt only relief that—finally—I
was going. I, a successful New York writer, was preparing to go
West and find my spiritual destiny with the Indians! It seemed
almost as romantic to me as Hemingway and the other expatriates
who had wandered the streets and byways of Europe when I was
just a toddler. I would find love and spiritual fulfillment in the
place where the sun sets. As I looked around the apartment one
last time, the phone rang.

"Sister," Sun Bear's voice said. "Remember how I showed you
to connect with the earth?"

When I said yes he continued, "Good. This is your first test
coming up. I will be praying for you."

He hung up.

That was a strange way of saying "Bon Voyage." I hugged
Terry goodbye, picked up my suitcase, and headed out.

4

THE FIRST TEST

Benjamin met me at the airport in Denver. Something about him seemed different. What was it? It wasn't the way he looked. He still was an attractive man, dressed stylishly, with his black hair cascading over his forehead and collar. He smiled at me. There was an appreciative glimmer in his warm brown eyes. But something definitely was different.

He insisted we have a drink. One drink turned into two, and two was about to become three when I said I was going to claim my luggage. Reluctantly he accompanied me.

When we had the luggage he told me to wait with it while he fetched his borrowed car.

It was an old Ford. I didn't understand what was going on. We had been talking on the phone for months about the fabulous New Year's eve celebration we could have during these last few days of the year and the beginning of the new one. We had planned to stay in a suite at the top of the finest downtown Denver hotel. We were to have meals at the best restaurants, flowing champagne, and any consciousness-altering substances we desired. Our bacchanal was to begin with his meeting me at the airport with a limousine. This beat-up Ford definitely wasn't in our plan.

I was beginning to get worried. I didn't like the change I sensed in Benjamin, or the changes he was making in our plans. Maybe the money he had expected to get before this holiday had not come through. Was that it? I had made it clear from the beginning that, while I would enjoy a luxurious time, I did not have the money to pay for half of it. He had assured me he'd have the money and would be honored to treat me.

"I have the money," he answered my unspoken question when I was settled in the car, "but before we start in on our good time, we have to do something more important. I have the first couple of chapters done on my autobiography, and I want you to read them and tell me what you think of them."

Red flags popped up in my mind. I had, of course, known about his book and known he wanted my opinion, but we had agreed we would not discuss writing or other work until after New Year's Day. This was a real change in plans, and one dangerous to our having fun. Like me, Benjamin now thought of himself first and foremost as a writer. He had stopped taking cases or participating in politics until he had finished his book. Also like me, he was an Aries. I didn't know much about astrology then, but I knew that an Aries man and woman had vast potential for tumultuous times. Once I had had an Aries beau who was also a writer. I met him when I was on the barricades during the Columbia demonstrations and he was a reporter covering the event. We had one of those relationships in which one feels an almost hypnotic attraction to another person, while never being quite sure one actually likes him.

I was thinking that my stop in Denver had been a mistake.

"You should be happy I'm letting you read my book," Benjamin said, feeling my hesitation. "I haven't let anybody else see it yet."

We drove to a nice older home in what appeared to be a good section of the city. During our phone conversations Benjamin had vaguely mentioned that, between the legal and political activities, he traveled so much, he felt that renting an apartment was a waste of money. He told me he lived in the basement apartment of some friends when he was in Denver, but I hadn't paid much attention thinking we'd only see the hotel suite. We went in. It was dark, dank, foul-smelling, and a mess. He had clothes, bottles, and the remainders of take-out meals strewn all over. From the carton-to-bottle ratio, and from the smell, it appeared he had been taking most of his nourishment in liquid form.

"What are you looking at?" he asked irritably. "Haven't you ever messed up a place when your creative juices were flowing?"

"Not this much," I replied honestly.

"Well, maybe you aren't as creative as I am. I don't think women can be. All the great writers are men, as it should be. I don't even know why I'm letting you look at my work," Benjamin said.

"I'm not asking to see it," I replied. "It was our agreement not to get into work until later."

"My writing and what I have to say is the most important thing happening right now for both of us."

I was worried. This man certainly wasn't acting like the humorous, easy-going Benjamin I had liked. There was a hardness to him I had not seen before if, in fact, it had been there. Also, he was acting like a megalomaniac and a dominating asshole. If I had sensed either of these tendencies before, I certainly wouldn't have come to Denver. Hoping to retrieve our fling, I decided that Benjamin was either experiencing writer's frenzy or had partaken of some substance that was making him irritable.

I cleared a place to sit and said, "Let's see what you have."

He brought a sheaf of papers to me, sat down, picked up a bottle, and watched me read. Now for those of you who are not writers, let me state that this is very dirty pool. No one should have to read infant writings while the author watches, measuring every nuance of facial expression. Luckily, I had a great poker face in those days. When I got to the end of the first chapter I asked if I could have a drink. Benjamin wanted to know what I thought but I refused to talk until I had read it all. I hoped to buy myself time to think of some diplomatic way to tell him I did not like what I was reading.

There was a dark quality to the writing, a negativity that seemed unnecessary to his story line. It was as though he wanted his readers to go away feeling guilt and shame. I knew this was a popular school of radical writing then, particularly among men, but I didn't like it. Benjamin's life, I knew from both my interview with him and our conversations, had a very inspirational quality. He was the oldest child of an Indonesian family that had moved to San Francisco when Benjamin was six. He had seven younger brothers and sisters. He had been involved with gangs in his adolescense, but had turned himself around and managed to work his way through college and law school. He hadn't chosen to emphasize any of that in his story.

I knew he wasn't going to like my comments. I considered

giving him some pap about the parts I did like and omitting criticism. That would have been smart, but it wasn't what he'd asked for. If someone requested my honest opinion, he was going to get it.

I was not prepared, however, for the intensity of his reaction to my comments.

"How can you presume to judge me!" he cried. "You have not lived the life of poverty and deprivation I have. You don't know how terrible it is to be an Asian-American in this great, hypocritical nation. You don't know what it is to starve. You don't know what it is like to have your father come home drunk because he can't find a job, and beat you. You come from the charmed life of the white capitalist pig bosses."

I did not think it would be wise to cut in to tell him he had asked me to criticize his writing, or to explain I had spent most of the first thirteen years of life in a two-room apartment in Newark, New Jersey. Like anyone in the middle of a tirade, particularly one with racist or sexist subject matter, he didn't want his hysteria cut with facts. I was, because of my skin color, tossed in with the bad guys, regardless of what my situation had actually been. I had been politicized enough to carry a good, constant dose of "white man's guilt," which disposed me to listen quietly to harangues such as this one.

While I had been reflecting, Benjamin had worked himself more and more into a rage. He began moving toward me.

"What do you know, you honky woman?" he screamed as he lifted his arm to strike me. He caught me off-guard because I had been paying more attention to my thoughts than to his actions. It was all I could do to lift my arm to shield my head.

The strangest thing happened. Benjamin's arm fell to his side like a puppet cut from a string.

"My dear," he said, "I'm so sorry. I would never strike you or any woman. I hate men who do that. I appreciate your honesty about the book, and I think you've made some valuable comments. I don't like everything you've said, or agree with it, but I've certainly overreacted. I don't know what is the matter. It feels like something has gotten into me today."

Whatever had gotten into him made me want to get out of there. I told Benjamin I was leaving and wanted to use his friends' phone to call some people I knew in town to see if I could stay with them.

"Please give me another chance," he asked contritely. "I know I have acted like a bastard, but that's over. Let us go have one of those wonderful meals we talked about. I know a restaurant downtown I think you'll really like. And to make sure neither of us gets angry again, I have some wonderful little pills to cool us right out."

I was wary, particularly of downers, but I agreed. I anticipated a spartan existence with the Bear Tribe and, already, I was missing the lavish dinners and expensive wines to which, sometimes, I had been treated in New York. I felt I really needed this celebration we had planned, and I hoped the little pills would calm Benjamin so we could finally have a good time.

We went to an elegant restaurant and Benjamin encouraged me to have anything I wanted to eat and drink. It didn't take much urging. I splurged. I felt he owed me after his horrible conduct. I ordered another bottle of champagne figuring my strong mind could manage the effects of any consciousness-altering substance. I knew I would become more loquacious when I was drinking. In fact, having an "excuse" to act uninhibited was the main reason I drank. But I always knew what I was saying and doing. The downers I had taken were, however, an unattractive and consequently unfamiliar area for me. I liked having energy, not surpressing it. I had little idea how those pills would affect me when they met the cocktails and champagne.

As the evening went on, I began to find out. First I became sleepy. Benjamin ordered some coffee and kept me talking until that feeling passed. Then I felt as if I were in a warm and safe place where I could talk about anything. I did. I told this man I barely liked and did not trust all sorts of things about my life. Eventually I began to talk with him about my experiences with Sun Bear and the reasons I was going to Reno to see about working with his Tribe. I even mentioned the earthquake experiences and Sun Bear's telling me they had been some sort of vision.

Benjamin, who had been paying rapt attention to everything I had said, laughed at those statements. "My grandfather was a sort of shaman in Indonesia," he told me. "I know from him that women don't have visions, and white people don't have visions. Sounds to me like this Sun Bear guy is jiving you and you're just eating it up. I don't believe in all this traditional business anyway. It's just another way honkies have of keeping us in our place, and out of theirs."

For some reason his laughter and derision woke me up enough to be really irritated. I had known Benjamin was political and radical. Otherwise I wouldn't have interviewed him for my book. I had not realized just how much he hated "honkies" which, I assumed, included me. That dislike was bothering me more at the moment than the comments he had made about Sun Bear and visions.

"If you hate white people so much, how come you kept calling me?" I asked.

"Oh, dear one, I don't mean you when I talk about honkies. You're a woman. I'm talking about a man, *the* man. I like women, and I like you," he said, taking my hand and kissing it elegantly. He did have a style I enjoyed, at least when he felt like having it. But I was seeing as clearly as I could that he also had an extremely chauvinistic attitude about women.

"You don't think much of women, do you?" I demanded.

"You are feisty tonight my dear," he replied. "I thought we were going to call a truce and have a pleasant evening."

He was right. That was our agreement. I momentarily drifted back to the warm, safe place, then I got angry again. I decided I would not talk to him anymore.

We sat in silence for few minutes that seemed to stretch into hours.

"Okay," he said finally. "I'll tell you what I think about women if it will make you stop freezing me away from the table."

He proceeded to tell me he loved women, but, as he said it, I knew he was lying. He didn't even like women. He said he thought they were magnificent and noble creatures. I felt as if he were describing wild mares. He told me about his mother, his sisters, his ex-wives, always sounding respectful about their wonderful qualities. It quickly became clear to me that he felt these qualities were noteworthy only in the bedroom and the kitchen. Since no kitchen was available at his friends' place, it was apparent he was trying to lead up to an assessment of my skills in his other favorite room.

I was getting increasingly less enthusiastic about that possibility. The man obviously was a chauvinist pig. I don't know how I failed to see that in all the phone conversations. I guess I hadn't wanted to, or maybe his pills were some kind of truth serum making him speak the truth and me see the truth. Also, he was a flaming egomaniac who represented all the double-standard bull against which I had rebelled far too recently.

When I was making the perilous journey through the prolonged adolescence expected of "girls" in the early sixties, before the sexual revolution was declared and supposedly won by default, good girls didn't, and nice girls did. What nice girls did was have sex. What good girls didn't do was anything that was fun, including sex. I'd been a good girl to an age that would be almost embarrassing to admit today.

When I was recruited by the sexual revolution, I'd become a fierce proponent of its dogma. I'd also become very angry about the stupidity and hypocrisy of the double standard. If only "nice girls" did "it," but all men did "it," who did they do it with? Nice girls were either horribly overworked, or a lot of good girls were also good liars, or a good percentage of men did "it" with someone or something that was strictly taboo.

One of the double-standard notions I'd found most enraging was the one contending good girls were supposed to abstain until they got married. Then by some wave of a godfather's wand, pun intended, they were supposed to become insatiable nymphomaniacs who would spend the rest of their lives pleasing the man who rescued them from their boring "goodness." If I had to explain the double standard to someone from another planet, I could not do it in a way that conformed to the logic so prized in our culture.

Now here I sat at dinner with this pig of a man who obviously thought I was a nice girl.

I wasn't feeling nice. The feistier I got, the more charming and seductive Benjamin became, which made me even angrier. We were almost getting loud enough to draw attention from the manager when, in another about-face, Benjamin totally changed his behavior. He again apologized, and agreed he had been acting like a pig. He promised we would drop the subject of sexuality, of men and women, totally.

He ordered a bottle of cognac and for the next hour he kept

refilling my glass whenever I took a sip. This made it difficult for me to track what I was drinking, or how it was mixing with everything else in my body. He waited until I was in that warm, safe place again, and then began telling me why I should not go to the Bear Tribe. Softly but persuasively he planted large seeds of doubt in my mind about my decision, my actions, my motives, and about Sun Bear and his group. He was clever in his criticism, using his best courtroom style to get across his points without ever giving me room for rebuttal.

What charm and seduction could not accomplish, fear and doubt did.

I agreed I would go back to his friends' house.

The excess of the evening took its toll on him as well as me. We both stumbled into separate twin beds when we got there.

That night, not surprisingly after what I had consumed over the course of the evening, I had many strange staccato dreams. Some were disturbing, including one of being in an earthquake in Denver. Others were more frightening. Benjamin wove his way through several of the dreams I could not remember clearly. I recollected only some of the looks on his face, and they were nasty. I woke up wanting only to leave that place.

I dressed quietly, packed, and was just opening the door when Benjamin awakened.

"Where are you going?" he demanded.

"I'm leaving."

"How could you think of leaving after the love we shared last night?" he asked.

I wondered if he were truly insane.

"I'd hardly call our conversations last night loving."

"No, but after, when we returned here."

"I may not remember every detail of last night, but I do know I just flopped into bed, quite alone, when we got back here. And so did you. You could barely get the key in the lock," I replied.

"Are you sure?" he asked, wearing a nasty smile reminiscent of my dreams.

"Yes, very sure."

"Are you really that sure?" he asked again.

"Yes, I am."

"Well, my dear," he said, smiling strangely, "remember this. There is more than one way for a man to penetrate a woman. And

n require a physical touch. Now if you insist on
come and give me a farewell kiss."

e. He got out of bed and came to me. On his face
vile as those in my dreams.

o my eyes, with no warmth left in his, he said, "It
r. You can go now. The gift has been given."

ugh someone had thrown a stone against my stom-
up my bags and left, going until I found a phone and
he friends. They were happy to put me up until my
or Reno.

5

THE EARLY DAYS

On the flight from Denver to Reno I felt all my anxieties, doubts, and fears coursing through my being like a river that has finally escaped a dam. I was really doing it: changing my life, making a commitment to a spiritual group, to a spiritual path. I was ready to foreswear all the the selfish, hedonistic tendencies that had heretofore kept me from such righteous action . . . almost. I had the stewardess bring me some vodka and orange juice while I contemplated my courage, and wondered for the hundredth or so time that morning whether I truly was crazy to be doing this.

I really had no idea what to expect when we landed in Reno, other than the pleasure of seeing Sun Bear's and Morning Star's beautiful faces again. I understood from our calls and letters that many things had changed with the Tribe since the preceding summer. Apparently when Sun Bear returned from his speaking tour, he found that one or some of his subchiefs had put psychedelics in the tribal medicine pouch, a clear breach of the rules to which tribal members agreed.

Sun Bear told his tribespeople that the psychedelic trip was all right for Timothy Leary and those who follow him, but that it wasn't part of Sun Bear's own medicine. Some of the Bear Tribe people felt it was part of theirs, so they left the tribe to do their own things.

The organization of the Tribe had faltered in Sun Bear's absence. While he was there, his charismatic presence kept people working in the gardens and orchards, taking care of the Tribe's animals and vehicles. When he was away, there was no comparable force to hold things together and keep them running. The subchiefs he left in charge were overwhelmed by the influx of new people and new ideas that had come to the Bear Tribe in the spring and early summer. They tried to make the tribe work, but they had no role models of what a tribe or community could or should look like in this period of history. They had Sun Bear's stories of what tribes and medicine societies used to be like, and the stories of some of the other Native people who worked with the Tribe, but no one knew how to make these stories fit the 1970s and people who had grown up in the most radical segment of a society that prided itself on the concept of rugged individualism rather than community spirit.

As I've since heard Sun Bear put it, there would be thirty people at the dinner table, and three working in the gardens. No one wanted to be branded "authoritarian"—a heinous epithet in the sixties—so no one would say "you don't eat if you don't work," even though that concept has kept communities alive throughout much of history. Consequently, a few people worked and many more ate, until the money Sun Bear and others donated ran out.

Upon his return to California, Sun Bear visited the Tribe's base camps and tried to help his tribesmen work things out. Eventually, when things continued to deteriorate, Sun Bear concluded that his first full-scale attempt at starting a tribe of teachers had been a failure. He then went out into the hills and asked for a vision about the future of the Bear Tribe. Because of something he saw in the clouds, and because an eagle flew around him, he apparently felt the Tribe would hibernate for a while and then emerge again like a phoenix. He wished the people in California good luck and went back to Nevada where Nimimosha, another woman with whom he had had some sort of relationship, had been running the trailer court in which they had an interest.

It sounded to me as though Sun Bear was somewhat depressed about what had occurred in California, and that he was having financial trouble because he had invested his life savings in his vision of a tribe. I, however, had been secretly happy to hear I wouldn't have to share him with 200 or so people, but with just the small group who had come with him to Reno.

When my flight landed, I immediately saw Sun Bear and Star. They were beaming, but that warm glow that I felt emanating from them in New York seemed to be missing. For only a moment it occurred to me that I might not be the only one with doubts and fears about my being there. I chased the thought away because I was not yet ready to see either of these people as human beings. I wanted them to be the mythic, heroic personages I had perceived the previous summer. If they were merely human, I had even greater reason to doubt this move.

After hugs and greetings, enthusiastic on their part, restrained on mine, we got my luggage and then headed to the car, a beat-up former police car. We began to drive to the trailers near Sun Valley where the people who had accompanied Sun Bear to Nevada were living. As we drove, Sun Bear kept trying to get me interested in the countryside. He would point out the hills, and how the sun reflected off them. It all looked dry and somewhat desolate to me. I was glad. If it had been lush and beautiful I could not have stood looking at it in the depressed mood I was in.

I was overwhelmed by actually being there. I couldn't believe I had done it—left New York and all I knew to come out West. Why? I really could not think of any good reason. I looked at Sun Bear and Star sitting in front. Why wasn't the glow there? Had I been temporarily insane last summer?

"Don't make any decisions right now sister," Sun Bear warned, once again displaying that annoying capacity to know what I was thinking.

When we got to the trailer where they were living, no one else seemed to be there. I was happy for that. I really didn't feel like meeting any people right now. I just wanted to think out a plan for going back to New York. Sun Bear took me to his room in the back of the trailer and said, "You are sick sister. The dark ones won the first test. You have an evil within you placed there by the one they were using. That is why you are having strange thoughts now. Tell me carefully what you have done over the days since you left New York."

Oh great, I thought, there's no better way to impress this man than to tell him about my strange time with a purported world-class hedonist.

"What do you want to know?" I asked, stalling for time.

"Come on, sister. I know you're not coming from a meeting of the ladies auxiliary and temperance union. I'm not going to judge what you've done. I just want to know exactly what kind of medicine I'm dealing with. Was this man you were with native?"

"No, he's Asian-American."

"Where is his family from?"

"Someplace in Indonesia."

"That makes sense. Did he say anything about medicine?"

I finally remembered he had said his grandfather was a shaman of sorts.

"Okay, good," said Sun Bear. "Now, can you remember when you began to feel different in any way?"

I remembered Benjamin's saying a man could penetrate a woman without a physical touch. I asked Sun Bear what that meant.

He told me he'd explain more later, but that basically, because of the receptivity of their nature, women could take on some medicine, or spirits, that weren't really theirs, and could then carry them around for a time or transfer them to someone else. Once again I had no idea what he was talking about, an occurence that was to become so commonplace over the next months that sometimes I felt as though I were in a foreign country.

I told Sun Bear about feeling someone had hit me in the stomach with something at the time Benjamin said that the gift had been given.

"Why did Benjamin or his grandfather or whoever want to do this to me?" I asked.

"Sometimes there are negative forces that work to keep someone from their path or vision, particularly someone who will do a lot of good in the world. But the 'gift' was meant for me. You were merely the one bringing it. They were not able to stop my vision with the drugs; or by making some of my people seem crazy; or by taking some land bases away; so they tried this. They know I am vulnerable now, and they know the strong connection between us. By sending you here full of suspicions and doubts they hoped to shake my own faith in my vision. If I had not seen the sickness in you, it could have worked," he said. "I am that weak now in my own beliefs. Luckily, they were not able to use a really skilled medicine person on you. Benjamin is powerful, but his power is diluted by the alcohol and drugs. He did not hide the sickness well enough. But, sister, you probably don't understand much. It doesn't matter now. What matters is getting the sickness out of you. For that, we need the help of the Earth Mother."

What had struck me in what Sun Bear said was that there was a strong connection between us. That mattered more to me than all this talk about medicine.

Sun Bear took me out in the car again. We drove until we were in those hills he'd pointed out to me. Once he found a spot he liked, he had me stand still while he lit some herbs in a shell. Then he took a big feather and began to waft the smoke toward me. As I sensed the smoke begin to touch my skin, I felt a funny sort of tingling all over. Sun Bear seemed to be saying some words to himself very softly. Suddenly, the spot on my stomach where I felt like I had been hit with a stone began to hurt again. I tried to cover the spot with my hands, but Sun Bear removed them, and continued wafting the smoke. Then he put down the shell and began to sort of scoop around me with the feather. That made my stomach hurt more, and I began to feel as if I had a fever. I got hotter and hotter until, quite unexpectedly, everything stopped: the heat, the pain, Sun Bear's talking, and the moving of the feather.

"It's good," he said. "I got it. You'll probably feel tired for a while and then you should feel better. Want to rest here on the earth for a time so you won't have to talk with other people?"

"You mean lie down on the dirt?" I asked.

He nodded.

"But I'll get dirty," I said, "and what if there are bugs?"

"I can tell you haven't been hugging trees," he said, laughing. "You will get dirty and there are creepy crawlers, but you can wash later and the crawlers won't bother you here today."

For some reason, maybe because I felt really tired, I believed him. I lay down on the earth, and a truly warm, safe feeling enveloped me, much nicer than the one from Benjamin's "wonderful little pills." I drifted off to sleep almost immediately. I didn't wake up until Sun Bear gently shook my shoulder and told me it was time to go meet my new brothers and sisters.

My new brothers and sisters were decidedly cool in their reception of me, which came as a shock. I expected them to admire my courage, and appreciate the talents I was bringing to the community. Despite Sun Bear and Star's efforts to convince these people

I was okay, they could not overcome the Westerners' innate distrust of New Yorkers. I was seen as an interloper, a snob, and a cosmopolitan bitch who would be afraid to get my hands dirty. Boy, was I glad none of these folks knew what I had said to Sun Bear about lying down in the desert.

Living there were Mountain Woman and her three-year-old son, Squirrel; Wild Flower and her boyfriend, Strong Oak; and Los Angeles Louie and his two-year-old twin girls. He was a fairly recent arrival, and was considered a real city slicker—hence the name—until I arrived.

Personally, I thought everybody there, women included, looked like the mountain men I had seen in the western movies I had begun to watch while thinking about leaving New York. I disliked westerns but watched them to expand my knowledge of the West and of Indian life. Later I realized that this was like learning about African-American culture by reading *Uncle Tom's Cabin*.

In trying to talk to my new brothers and sisters I judged them to be shallow, closed anti-intellectuals, interested only in what I called "playing Indian." Later I regretted ever thinking that phrase because it floated in the stratosphere, haunting me, for many years to come. I felt then, and verified later, that all the people there, particularly Strong Oak, were convinced I was even worse than they had expected.

Battle lines were drawn. It was me against them, with Star trying to mediate and Sun Bear watching from the sidelines to see who would win. It would be years before I understood that anyone trying to enter a community had to run the gamut of the existing members on some level as part of the initiation process. Given our competitive culture, the new kid in the class always has to prove herself.

In my first few days there I was asked to do or help with every dirty or unpleasant task anyone could think of. I realized they were doing this to make me leave, which would mean they won. I was determined to win so, no matter what they asked, I had to do it and not blow up or walk out. It became a matter of pride. I scrubbed floors, cleaned the bathroom, defrosted the refrigerator, and helped to clean a storage trailer that had last seen sunlight about the year of my birth. While I felt like Cinderella in the grasp of a group of evil stepmothers, I kept working and did not complain. Naturally, the attack was stepped up.

I must have slipped at some point and said that the one thing I didn't want to do was take care of the kids. Any civilized person would have made that statement. These were not your repressed, quiet, and well-behaved little toddlers. These were kids who had tremendous energy and were not afraid to express it in any way they wanted to. They were also "alternative" kids who had been raised with few stable limits, or consistent discipline. In my opinion then, you needed three adults to care for one of these children for an eight-hour period. Of course I was asked to take care of all three of them by myself for a whole day while everybody else went into Reno.

I'd been a baby sitter in my teens, and I did sincerely like children, but I was rusty at best in knowing what to do with them. The trials those three put me through that day, and for a few weeks in the future, made the hazing of the adults look like child's play. I later learned, with Star's help, that all the kids really wanted was love and reasonable limits; a lesson that would later serve me well with all the counter-cultural children—from one month to eighty years old—I helped to grow up in the Tribal community. But that day Squirrel and the twins, Samantha and Pamela, ran circles around me. It felt as if they were thirty children, into every inch of space available in the trailer, particularly if it contained anything harmful to them. By the time I got them to sleep all I wanted to do was take a bath and go to bed for twelve hours.

Just as I was preparing to run water into the tub, Sun Bear came in smiling.

"We had real good medicine in town today," he said. "I met my friend Jimmy in the Cal Neva. He's a rancher. He told me a truck must have hit one of his cows because he found it dead on the road this afternoon. He knows I've got a bunch of people to feed, so he offered me the cow. Strong Oak and Louie and some of Nimimosha's friends are taking a truck to the ranch to get it. When it gets here you'll get your first lesson in butchering. It's a good thing it's so cold. We'll just have to gut, bleed, and skin it tonight and then we can take care of cutting up and packaging the meat tomorrow. It's good medicine."

I cannot begin to express how horrified I was. It did not sound like good medicine to me; it sounded like a nightmare. I had watched New York butchers cut steaks from some quarter of beef, and that had almost made me retch. I could not conceive of dealing with a whole dead cow. Cows were big. I knew that even though I had seen them only from a distance.

At all costs, I wanted to get out of helping with this job. I told Sun Bear I was tired from watching the kids, and that I really needed to clean up and get some rest. He told me that if I ever wanted the folks in the Tribe to accept me, I better forget the cleaning up and resting for a while. He advised me to find the oldest, dirtiest clothes I had. Then he told me he was going to give me a really important present, and went into his room.

The idea of a present intrigued me. I briefly fantasized about something romantic, or about one of those medicine pouches he kept discussing. Sun Bear returned and handed me a brown pocket knife.

"I gave this to a brother at Medicine Rock. When I found it on the ground the next day I took it back because it was obvious he didn't appreciate the gift. A knife is a very important tool for anyone who is going to be self-reliant. I want you to have this one."

Luckily, I had not spent too much time fantasizing. I did not yet know that this was about as romantic a gift as Sun Bear would ever give me. Sun Bear showed me how to open the knife correctly, then got out a whetstone and demonstrated how to sharpen it. He told me to get it good and sharp for working with the cow. Then he brought out some bigger knives (which looked like machetes to me) and had me help sharpen them. I still have that pocket knife today, although it has spent as much time with my medicine objects as in my purse during periods when I've been doing a lot of air travel.

Star later told me that Sun Bear had come back to the trailer, rather than go to help get the cow, because he realized what an important lesson butchering would be for me, and he wanted me to be prepared. While we were working on the knives he spoke to me about the sacredness of all life, and about how everything was connected in the great circle of life. He told me how Native people would pray before they went out on a hunt, asking the deer or buffalo to give over one of their relatives so that the life of the people could continue. He told me Natives would tell the animals that someday they, too, would give their bodies to the Earth Mother so they could help the circle of life continue. Sun Bear instructed me to treat the cow with respect, with thanksgiving for the gift of meat she was giving me and my people. He suggested I pray while I worked with the butchering.

I understood most of what he was saying, and it did make some sense to me. But my understanding was intellectual and, therefore, limited. His instruction had soothed some of my apprehension. I could see the point in butchering the cow, but I was not convinced I would be physically capable of helping. I was also not sure whether I would be able to pray. I still had my conditioning, telling me prayers were something a minister made to God, or children said at night because their parents made them do so. Would I be praying to the cow? Was that a form of idolatry? Since the people and cow were not yet present, I asked Sun Bear that question.

He explained to me that Native people think of God as the Great Spirit, and that spirit is within everything: the cows, deer, buffalo, trees, sage, rocks, corn, potatoes, and people. Because everything is connected, Natives would speak to that sacred essence within all of their brothers and sisters on the earth, whether they were cows or stones. I would not be saying the cow was God. I would be talking to the god part within the cow. When he finished explaining he looked at me and asked with a smile if I was still afraid of going to hell.

Of course, I denied that allegation just as I heard a truck pull up outside, and wondered if hell, in the form of a cow, was coming to me. I could feel my shoulders tighten and my stomach knot up as I resigned myself to having to help with the task ahead.

The cow was big, and the job was bloody. I was glad on several occasions that I had merely had a small dinner with the children. Since I was only expected to help lift the cow to the scaffold we had hastily built in the near hills behind the trailer court, and then to help pull the skin away from the flesh, I was, for the most part, able to keep myself dissociated from the task at hand. Dissociation was a trick I had learned as a child and perfected as a teen to get me through unpleasant situations. From this very objective place I was able to treat this experience as a live lesson in the anatomy of a cow, and be interested in what a heart, liver, lungs, and intestine looked like. I tried to remind myself to pray, or at least thank the cow for its gifts, but doing so was quite foreign to me then. I was a long way from learning what it was to make your every step a prayer.

I got through that night. I don't know how. I was glad there were few mirrors in the trailer because I really did not want to know how I looked. I took a long bath before I went to sleep.

The next day I found out it was going to be Strong Oak and me who would cut up the cow the rest of the way in the cold storage trailer. I bundled up and went out there with him. Neither of us was happy about working together. I had even volunteered to take care of the children if someone else would do this. It galled me to have to take instructions from him about the job at hand. I felt myself superior to this shabbily dressed, bearded, and arrogant mountain-man hippie. I knew he was the general in the battle to get rid of me. I did not like having to admit he could teach me anything.

In fact, he proved to be a good teacher, and I a fast student. We were equally surprised. We worked side by side cutting and wrapping and, by lunch time, we had most of the hind quarter ready for a freezer. To my great shock, I was hungry for lunch. Butchering a slightly frozen cow makes you work up an appetite.

By late afternoon we sent the boxes of meat into a storage locker Sun Bear had just rented for the occasion. Then Strong Oak showed me how to remove the brain from the head because he wanted to try brain-tanning the cow hide. He knew it worked with the deer skins he had tanned, but he had never tried it before on a cow hide. I asked if I could help with the tanning process and he readily agreed. We stood outside smoking my "tailor made" (as opposed to hand-rolled) cigarettes feeling like compatriots. That cow had given me a lot more than meat.

This was the beginning of my acceptance of the people in the Tribe, and theirs of me. I felt relief all the way through dinner. Then, just as my shoulders began to relax, Sun Bear said it was time for me to meet Nimimosha. That announcement served as an invitation for my shoulder spasms to come back and bring a guest.

I did not want to like Nimimosha. By now I knew she had had a lengthy relationship with Sun Bear, one that had spanned eight years. Morning Star really seemed to like her, which confused me. How could you like your mate's former mate? I knew intellectually that it was possible, but I didn't really believe it. How could a former mate still be friends with her ex, and his current woman? And where did I, as the auditioning next mate, fit into all of this? I felt like a soap opera commercial as I asked myself these questions.

I went to Nimimosha's trailer prepared to hate her. I was thwarted by the woman herself. It is hard to dislike Nimimosha. Her name means something between "favorite auntie" and "woman with a heart of love." She truly likes just about everyone, and knows how to make them at ease around her. It almost worked with me, but I was still wary. Able to come up with nothing else, I blamed her for being too good to be true.

Meeting her did, however, lift one concern from my mind. Living with her was Darrell, a man to whom she had been relating for quite some time. They obviously liked each other in a serious sort of way. To me that meant she was no longer active competition.

I must admit I was quite disgusted with myself over all this competition business. Throughout my life I had always had a couple of really close girl friends to whom I could lay bare my soul. I had spent years in consciousness-raising groups learning to trust my sisters. I believed sisterhood was and should be powerful, and that women should support each other in as many ways as possible. Yet here I was acting and thinking like a sterotypical sister-hating woman because I thought I had found my true love, my knight in shining armor. Other than the magical friendship with Star, I was not interested in befriending any of the women I was meeting because I thought they were all there trying to land Sun Bear, just as I was. Strange what the concept I had then of love could do to an otherwise reasonable woman.

Few men of power, from kings to clergy, seem to want only one woman in their life. Sun Bear certainly did not want any such limitation. I knew this from the moment we met, but some part of me was convinced I could be the one to change it. I could be the "Harriet" who would turn Sun Bear into a faithful "Ozzie." I would be the woman who would make this man of power, this medicine man, into a domesticated version of his feral self. I was so hell-bent on changing Sun Bear that I did not notice or care about the changes this self-proclaimed mission was making in me.

When I took Nimimosha off the "active" list, the only person who stood in my way to having Sun Bear was Morning Star. I didn't know what to do about her. I sincerely loved her, as I still do, and had to admit she had a prior claim. So I tried not to step on her toes, and tried not to feel confused about why she kept encouraging me to be with Sun Bear. How could I compete with someone who was so cooperative?

I spent my first weeks with the Bear Tribe trying to figure out why I was there. Was it because I thought I was in love with Sun Bear, or because this was my spiritual path? If this were love, how could I get Sun Bear to notice I was his soul mate? If this was a spiritual quest, why couldn't I forget the love business? While I was intent on my questions and concerns, Sun Bear was just as intent on his, which were to get me to understand anything about the earth or about the "medicine" he kept telling me about. He took me for rides in the hills, pointing out aspects of the scenery. He has really sharp eyes. He could identify a bird before I even noticed that one was there. He could tell the difference between similar-looking plants at a great distance. If a rabbit was hiding behind a bush, he knew it. He kept telling me what he saw, urging me to see. But I was still city-blinded and, truth to tell, nowhere near ready to appreciate the gift of seeing he was offering me.

6

THE SECOND TEST

After several weeks with Sun Bear and his small group in Nevada, I was still full of doubts. I was ready to pack it up and go back to New York, tail dragging, about once each day. Fortunately I still had enough sense to keep the doubts to myself most of the time. Otherwise, I would have tried everyone's patience beyond endurance, not a wise thing for the new kid to do.

I was not the only moody person in our little group. In fact we all seemed to be taking turns being emotionally volatile, even Sun Bear, who had by now convinced me the image of the silent, stoic Indian was a white man's myth. Sun Bear had a good sense of humor, and a "he he he" laugh that fell somewhere between a chuckle and a giggle and made his face light up with impish delight. He also had a quiet temper, the kind that makes for cold shoulders and withdrawal to neutral territory. Being a human doubt machine, even a restrained one, I was frequently the target of his icy anger. In a perverse sort of way I enjoyed that, as it was one of the two ways I had found to get a rise out of this spiritual being I wanted to be a human man, my man. I was beginning to understand why so many male saints were supposedly celibate: no woman had the patience to put up with them.

When Sun Bear was the man of vision, the speaker, the teacher, he had a definitely untouchable quality about him. He looked human, but he gave off an energy that was somehow other-worldly. Any man absorbed in his work has a touch of this energy, and so do women in a self-possessed state. Such people feel to me as though they are enclosed in a glass box allowing them to

65

see the rest of Creation but not be touched by it. This box allows them to ignore the subtle yet complex web of relationships that govern so much of most women's lives. Sun Bear in this state both challenged and infuriated me. I wanted to shatter the glass and shake or pinch him to make sure we both were still members of the same species. I frequently did so verbally. He'd sometimes respond but most often he'd depart, leaving me even more determined to somehow shatter the box around him.

As I met more people of power I realized that Sun Bear stepped out of his box more often than most of them. His passion for living and his sense of humor made him more often human—and vulnerable—than he would otherwise be. Sun Bear the man realized that he'd lose something very precious if he always took Sun Bear the man of vision too seriously.

While I was trying to shatter his box, Sun Bear was just as determined to get through to me with his ideas of how life should be. His dreams kept corroborating his initial impression that I belonged with the Tribe. In fact, they were beginning to show him I was to be a very special medicine helper to his vision. I do not understand how he could have accepted such a revelation given my state at that time. His faith in his visions had to be truly strong.

On the occasions when I was restraining my doubts and he was feeling good, he'd keep explaining his vision, the concept of vision, and what medicine was. I listened and I resisted hearing or understanding. Instead I would cuddle close to him as he talked, hoping to get his mind on other matters. I was afraid the more I went along with his visionary part, the less chance I would have of awakening the man. I could accept neither myself nor him as being both spiritual and human beings. I saw the two as mutually exclusive.

Sometimes it felt to me as though we were two people appearing in the same movie but reading from totally different scripts. I did not appreciate the humor of the undetermined director.

There were times during these weeks when Sun Bear reflected upon the events in California and got depressed because he felt his vision had failed. Star explained to me that these periods of depression had only come on him since he had seen the Tribe faltering, and that it was best to leave him alone when he was in them. While I believed her, I found it difficult not to personalize his depression. I'd feel guilty about my "lack of faith" or I'd be afraid that I still carried Benjamin's "gift." I would talk to alleviate the guilt. My chatter would affect his depression. It would turn into cold anger at me.

After a time, even Star had mood swings, and began to burst into tears for no apparent reason. Like most negativity, each of our bad moods was contagious and soon everyone was having their snappy, doubtful, tearful, angry, or depressed states. This was not what I expected a new Tribe to be like. I had come here to find my spiritual path and purpose as well as my true love, a large order in itself. But I had also expected to find a prepackaged utopia, a community where love and peace prevailed and no one had any personal problems. In that I was just like the thousands of seekers who would come later to the Bear Tribe community I helped found, and who would express to me their dissatisfaction that life there did not measure up to their very divergent ideas of perfection.

The current emotional turmoil became irritating enough that Star decided to go to Sacramento for the weekend to take a break from the stress, and to see some Tribal friends living there. She asked if I'd like to accompany her and meet people who had been at Medicine Rock and other camps. Since I was not thoroughly enjoying myself in the Tribe's Sun Valley trailers, and since I'd never seen Sacramento, I eagerly accepted the invitation.

Sun Bear had left early that morning to go to the casinos and gamble. I was beginning to think he had a gambling problem, but Star and Nimimosha explained to me that Native people have a different attitude toward gambling than white people. It is seen as an entertaining way to test your luck and your medicine. Since many Natives don't have the same sense of possession white people do, they don't mind if they lose sometimes. They almost get a sense of freedom from it. A lot of Indians gamble at pow wows, but that is against Sun Bear's medicine, so he needs the casinos to sharpen his gambling skills.

When Sun Bear returned from the casinos, we told him our plans. He said it was good we were getting away because he knew how negative he seemed right then. He said he was under attack again, and it was taking all his energy to stay as positive as he was. Turning to me he said several tests awaited me during this trip. Hearing that made me reconsider going. I did not like these tests, or flunking them as I felt I had in Colorado. I was not a person who could philosophically accept an occasional failure.

"I'm staying here," I announced to him after a few minutes of deliberation.

"Sister, you can no more avoid your testing than I can mine right now," Sun Bear said. "You need to learn the lessons that will come from these tests. You might be able to put them off by not going, but you won't escape them."

Even while I railed against it, I knew what he said was true.

Star and I left the next morning. I had never driven through the mountains of the West before and I was totally enchanted with them. They were so much bigger and more spectacular than the Allegheny range in the East. Where the Alleghenies seemed old and settled, the Sierras were bursting with young, raw energy. I felt at home riding through them, their intensity evoking a sense of peace with myself and the world. I would later recognize that I am a mountain person, one whose spirit soars when I see the pine-studded, rock-crowned majesty of the earth's highest points. Now I just enjoyed the first real feeling of relaxation I had had for far too long.

It didn't last long.

After we chained up to cross Donner Pass, Star and I decided to stop to have some coffee and warm up. When we were sitting across from each other, eye to eye, Morning Star told me she was carrying Sun Bear's child. I had suspected as much when her formerly stable good nature began to shift, but the reality hit me like a bucket of water melted from the surrounding snow drifts. I was happy for her because I knew how devastated she was by her son's death, and by the fact that Little Eagle now was staying with his father. I knew a baby would heal those wounds as nothing else could.

I also knew I had to exit the picture. Lusting after her man was one thing; causing interference with the father of her child was quite another.

When next she said she was planning to leave Sun Bear and the Tribe when spring began to turn to summer, I was rendered speechless.

"Why?" I choked out. "You belong here with Sun Bear and your child. I'm going to leave."

She explained that I wasn't the only reason for her decision.

She did admit that the passion I had for Sun Bear disturbed her. More important to her now, however, was her feeling the Tribe as it was would not be a good place to raise a child.

"I want a nest before I have this baby, where she will be warm and safe and loved," Star said. "I don't want to be on the road pregnant or with a small baby. My time of traveling with Sun Bear is over. Yours will soon begin."

Even though she'd just said the words I had longed to hear, I felt terrible. Tears sprang to my eyes. In my single-minded determination to get Sun Bear I felt I had hurt this wonderful, generous, loving woman so badly that she was going to leave the father of her child. I wanted to make it right, and the only way I could think of to do so was to depart.

"If you leave him," Star cautioned, again showing that telepathic ability, "he'll be really depressed. And it won't change my mind. Neither of us want to see him fail. He really has seen that you'll help him build a foundation for another Tribe. The two of you have work to do together in a way that I don't think any of us understand right now. You can't help the energy between you. I knew it was there from the moment you opened your apartment door.

"I know the man who will provide the physical fathering to my child. He's an old friend and I will be seeing him in Sacramento this weekend."

I could not detect anger in Star's talk, or resignation. She just seemed to be acknowledging that life was changing and moving, and that she was willing to flow with those changes. She was moving away from Sun Bear the visionary and teacher, although she would have part of the man with her, and I was to fill the space she vacated. She assured me she did love me and that the special tie between us would not be severed by time or space. I doubt I believed her then, but it has turned out to be true.

I reiterated that I'd be quite willing to leave and let her be with Sun Bear, that passion cools at a distance, and that I respected the need for children to have fathers. She assured me her friend Marty would be a more present father than Sun Bear the visionary could ever be. That, too, proved true. The glass box can make any person absorbed by their work—whether entreprenuer, executive, doctor, lawyer, machinist, or gardener—an unconsciously absent parent.

We spent a couple of hours at that rest stop, talking it through. By the end I felt more comfortable with Star's decision than I had thought I could be. The rest of the ride to Sacramento we both were absorbed in our thoughts.

· · ·

When I walked into one of the apartments used by tribal people in Sacramento, I knew trouble was brewing. It wasn't the people present there. In their California mellow style, they were very warm and accepting. It wasn't my vague uneasiness about the smell of medicine weed in the air. It was something I didn't have words to describe, and it frightened me.

To soothe myself I warily accepted the offer of some "good weed" to smoke. I wasn't really very fond of marijuana. Instead of making me mellow, it usually made me "head trip" even more than normal. I was hoping this time would be an exception, but I was careful not to inhale much just in case it wasn't. It must have been strong stuff because it got past the barrier of my noninhalation, relaxed me, then turned me into a philosophical "Chatty Cathy" doll.

"Be mellow," I kept urging myself, knowing I was fighting a losing battle. If there's one course left out of the survival school called New York City, it is "Mellow 101." I was intellectual, I was philosophical, I was goal oriented, and I was sticking out like a bruised thumb.

Star noticed and came over to suggest quietly that I sit it out for a while and listen to what the other people were saying. I sat, placed my upper teeth gently into my lower lip, and listened. There were about twelve people present, divided into three conversational clusters. One was talking about the old days at Medicine Rock, and how good they were; another was discussing the psychedelic landscape one of its members had recently explored; the third was making plans for a benefit concert they hoped would put the Tribe back on its feet. In their own ways, it seemed each person present truly had been touched by Sun Bear and his medicine.

After a while a tall, lean man with a mass of curly black hair came over to me and introduced himself as Sammy Fish Hawk. He said he'd heard I was a journalist from New York. It seems he had been a San Francisco insurance salesman before he had heard Sun Bear speak, left his job, and gone to live at Medicine Rock. Because he had writing aspirations, he had been given the responsibility for doing publicity for the Tribe.

"Looks like I'll have some help now," he said, putting his arm around my shoulder. "And I like the looks of the help."

Even though I found him attractive, I was somewhat offended by his come on. In my own mind, I was now Sun Bear's woman, and this underling was taking undue liberties. Then I thought about Sun Bear and Star, and decided what was good for the gander might cheer up the goose.

With the best come-hither look I could manage, given the heady effect of the medicine weed, I told him I was sure working side by side with him would be a very rewarding experience.

He smiled seductively and I was back on the familiar ground of flirtatiousness. I really enjoyed verbal foreplay, particularly with someone whose intellectual skills matched mine. It was challenging to see how far I could take it without its leading into anything too physical.

"Men are only interested in one thing," I had often been told as I grew up.

Just in case it was still true, I was going to mentally work them close to death to be sure they deserved to get that thing. Given Sammy's former profession, and the wicked twinkle in his eye, I knew he would be a worthy and entertaining opponent.

After a while Star came over and said she wanted to go find Marty. She added that she might not be back until tomorrow.

"Don't worry," said Sammy, "I'll be sure this lovely new sister doesn't get bored or lonely."

Good to his word, Sammy took me on a tour of Sacramento, then to a Japanese restaurant that was reputed to be a favorite of the young governor, Jerry Brown. Sammy was sophisticated, chivalrous, and a good storyteller. I laughed a lot at his stories of the early days of the Tribe. He said his only issue with Sun Bear was over psychedelics. Sammy liked the fast entre into altered states these substances provided. I was not as enthusiastic a proponent. In my few experiences with them, I had been disappointed more often than pleased.

My first trip, orchestrated by a friend who was an old hand at such journeys, was outstanding. It shook me out of my rigid view of the world, and showed me the immense possibilities and intricate interconnectedness of this energy we call life.

My other trips were mild bummers. They showed me the limitations and separations of life and people. I remember walking while high in the streets of New York and seeing everyone as seriously deformed in some way. For months after I could not shake the feeling of hopelessness this view engendered.

After I told Sammy about these experiences, he claimed the problem was that I had taken LSD, which is a synthetic chemical, rather than mescaline, which is a natural distillation of brother peyote, a plant very respected in Native culture. Sammy told me I was really fortunate today because he just happened to have two capsules of really good, really pure mescaline at the apartment.

I said I couldn't take one because it was against the rules of the Tribe. He pointed out I was not a member of the Tribe, then implied that if I did not take this "sacrament," he and the other California tribespeople would never really be able to trust me. Ah, the snake of peer pressure raised its ugly head again, and I, who always feared being "odd woman out," knew its fangs were about to strike and its venom to paralyze my courage and good sense. It did, and I agreed to go along with the mythical crowd. Something at the bottom of my consciousness said I was making a really big mistake, but already it was too late.

Sammy continued being charming until I had swallowed the capsule, and then his demeanor began to change. He ceased being solicitous, and, in fact, left me alone in someone's bedroom while the drug took effect. I was nauseous, I felt terribly alone, and I berated myself for the foolish act I had just committed. I could think of nothing worse than being alone with my overactive mind throughout an entire hallucinogenic episode. I was not sure my sanity would survive. I shed a few bitter tears of self pity.

I decided I would venture out of the room and at least find someone to whom I could talk. The apartment seemed deserted. I felt as if I were in the third circle of someone's fiendish idea of hell. Little did I suspect it would get a lot worse before I ascended back into some semblance of normal reality.

I sat in a chair contemplating leaving the apartment. I had no idea where to go if I did, and I was afraid if I wandered the streets I'd have another replay of "Night of the Human Monsters," seeing people deformed as I had that time in New York City. I tried to stop or at least control the progress of the lavender and char-treuse worms that were crawling along the rug toward my foot, but it was no use. I was way beyond the point of mental discipline.

I heard the front door open. I looked to see who it was. Sammy had returned and with him was a striking woman in her late thirties or early forties, dressed in a blouse and skirt that had an Indian flavor. I could not tell if the woman herself was Native. She and Sammy were laughing and touching in a comradely way. Although I had seen him take a capsule, he did not appear to be under the effects of any drug. My first thought was that he had duped me, giving me a psychedelic—heaven knows what—and taking some harmless powder himself. My second thought was that he was *really* kinky and I had been set up for a night of perversity, to be followed by my crazed person being sold into some sort of modern white slavery. I knew such things happened. I'd seen the headlines in the supermarkets. I hoped Sun Bear would be able to save me.

They stopped laughing when they saw me.

"Did you get restless, my dear?" Sammy asked, trying to seem concerned. "You looked so tired I thought you'd like to nap for a bit. I went to get Gayla because she is a wonderful guide for journeys. I just knew you two would like each other."

It did not feel like "like at first sight" to me. For one thing the woman's face seemed to be merging with that of a vulture, not the world's most pleasant-looking bird. For another, she seemed to have this black glow around her.

She smiled and came over to embrace me. I felt cold wherever her body touched mine. It was so bad I actually began shivering.

"She's cold Sammy," Gayla announced. "Get a blanket, prefer-ably the one I gave you recently."

Wondering if small pox blankets still existed, I tried to focus on Gayla's face. I must not have succeeded because I still saw black feathers coming out of her ears.

"Hello, sister," she said to me, "and welcome to our little circle here. I know we will be good friends. But you don't look well. Sit down here and we'll cover you up."

Powerless to focus, much less resist, I let them lead me to a chair.

I honestly don't remember the details of what was said or done over the next few hours. I felt as if I were in a small dark place with only a speck of light visible ahead of me. I kept struggling toward it. Every time I would almost get there, something would drag me back down. I felt bruised and battered deep within my being. I experienced some overwhelmingly unpleasant physical sensations. I shivered a lot, feeling a lump of ice deep within me. Then I would get extremely hot, feeling as if I were burning with fever. Sometimes it felt like someone was giving me electric shocks on different parts of my body.

Through it all, Gayla kept talking to me. Her voice droned on and on.

I felt in total despair, worse than that I had experienced in New York. Everything was a void around me, black and formless. Nowhere could I find anything solid on which to depend. My past was meaningless in this place. The future was doubtful. I thought of death but feared it would be just an extension of the void. I felt helpless and powerless. I tried to pray, but words would barely come together. Finally I asked the Great Spirit that Sun Bear talked about to help me if she could.

"You do agree, don't you sister," I remember Sammy asking once when I was again capable of understanding words.

I shook my head from side to side, trying to clear my mind.

"Don't interfere," Gayla hissed at him. "Let me do my work."

Later I heard her say, "You know I am your sister, your teacher, and your friend, don't you little sister?"

Again I shook my head trying to clear it.

"Don't be stubborn," she said. "You will not win. Not you or that man you call teacher. I am the real teacher. I can teach him things he will never learn otherwise, and I will teach you. Just admit I am your teacher little sister, and all will be well. Sammy, tell her how good it is to learn from me."

Sammy began to tell me what a wonderful teacher Gayla was, how much she was spiritually superior to Sun Bear. He told me how happy he was since he had renounced Sun Bear and his silly rules and given his allegiance to Gayla. He promised I would be happy if I did the same; I would come out of the place of despair and doubts. He said he knew how depressing it could be to think and analyze too much, and that Gayla would help me stop.

"It's easy, little sister, and it will get better and easier," Gayla said. "I'll take all those spiraling thoughts from you. Then we'll be truly sisters and truly telepathic. My thoughts will be yours, and my thoughts are powerful. You'll really be able to help Sun Bear then because you won't be divided within yourself. You can help make him a teacher who will have total devotion from all his students. And you won't need to tell him I'm helping you. You can take all the credit. Then he'll really love you."

This woman was offering me all I thought I wanted: love, understanding, clarity, spiritual power, and Sun Bear. But, I didn't want to take it, not if it meant I'd have any connection with her. I did not know why I felt so strongly about this. I was still cloudy from whatever drug Sammy had given me. I just knew she and everything she offered felt wrong in the center of my being. Listening to her I even became nauseous again. In fact, I barely bolted from the room to the bathroom in time. The next day I wished I had left two seconds later.

While I was in the bathroom I thought I heard her yelling at Sammy, blaming him for my lack of cooperation. When I went back to the living room, Sammy was there alone. He walked over to me, put his arm around my shoulder, and steered me toward a sofa. I couldn't believe it when he tried to kiss me.

"You timing stinks," I told him, pulling away.

A moment later Gayla came back, apparently realizing there was no chance Sammy could succeed where she had failed. All pretense of friendliness was gone.

"I've wasted almost a whole night on you," she said, "and you won't see the truth. There are ways to force you. Would you like another gift to take with you?"

My arms closed over my stomach, which had knotted at her words. I tried to bring myself back to full consciousness.

Gayla kept saying it would be better if I made the decision myself; she did not want to force me to do anything. She made it clear, however, that she did not intend to let me go until I had renounced any loyalty I felt toward Sun Bear, and acknowledged her as my teacher. I kept shaking my head and saying no.

Eventually she raised her hand, made some sort of strange movement with her fingers, pointed the hand at me and said, "I am your mistress. Accept this now."

At that point I stood up and heard myself say, "No. You are a mistress of the darkness. I am here to work for the light."

I don't know where the words came from. I don't even think

I fully understood what they meant. I certainly can't explain the power within me that allowed me to say them calmly, yet with force.

Gayla got angry. The black field around her grew and resembled the sky when it needs to rain but no moisture comes. She raised her arms and they looked like wings. Her face blurred into that of the vulture again. I felt as if she would fly toward me and peck at my eyes. I raised my arms to my head then lowered them again, saying "no" firmly once more. The clouds and the bird disappeared and it was Gayla looking at me once again. On her face was a scowl that reminded me of the one Benjamin wore when he spoke of his gift.

"You may not acknowledge me now," she said, "but you will. I will return in whatever forms I need to in order to claim you and the one you call teacher."

With that she reached for Sammy's arm, and they both left the apartment. I locked the door and jammed a chair under the doorknob. I didn't care who I shut out. I really wanted to be alone. I threw the blanket they'd given me off the couch, went and found my coat, pulled it over me, and fell into a restless sleep just as the first light of day showed through the window. Sometime later I thought I heard the front door open once again. I pulled my head out from under the coat, and peeked at the door. It was closed and the chair was in place. As I prepared to cover my head again I glanced at the chair where I had been sitting most of the night. Someone was in it. It seemed as if there were lace or cheesecloth between me and the person so I couldn't see clearly. I could make out that the figure was a woman and she seemed very old. Her face seemed as weathered as the hills in Nevada. On it was a bright and wonderful smile.

"Good morning," she said, getting up and moving toward me with a step much sprightlier than I would have expected in someone so old. She came over to the sofa, bent down, and embraced me. Even up close, the cheesecloth haze was still there, blurring her features. She took the coat and began to cover me up again.

"Sleep now," she urged in a voice resonant with love and wisdom. "You've had a long night. Sleep, and I will watch you. Dream of your future. Perhaps you'll see why you might someday be a granddaughter in whom I will take great delight."

• • •

I woke up the next day to pounding on the door. I knew I had been dreaming, but my abrupt reentry to waking reality made me forget what the dream had been about. I had no idea what time it was, and only a vague recollection of where I was. I felt terrible. My head throbbed louder than the pounding. I moved the chair, opened the lock, and saw some faces I didn't know.

"Looks like you had a bad night," one of the women said after the group had entered. "Did you have a fight with Sammy or did he give you some of that bad stuff he likes so well?"

I said both had happened. She introduced herself as Blue Lake, and made it her job to help me out. After a bath, some food, and a massage of my feet—of all things—I felt decidedly more human. The apartment was so active during the day I couldn't understand how Sammy had cleared it out last night. Blue Lake told me he had thrown everybody out as he usually did whenever he had what he considered a hot date. She confided that Sammy did not really understand what community spirit was. That was about the kindest thing I could think of to say about him.

I was hoping Star would return before Sammy did because I never wanted to see him or Gayla again in my life. The previous night already had become a terrible memory, even though I was still vaguely shrouded in a drug-induced fog. I thought Gayla was the most evil individual I had ever met. I asked Blue Lake what she thought of Gayla. Blue Lake had never met her, although she thought she might have heard her name mentioned once.

When Star finally came back to the apartment, I ran to embrace her. She did not understand my ebullience but, looking at me, knew something was wrong. She introduced me to Marty, a pleasant-looking man of medium height and build, then asked if he would mind waiting there while she and I took a walk. When I finished telling her about the events I remembered from the previous night, she said it sounded awful, and that she was glad nothing like that had ever happened to her. She was puzzled because she had met Gayla once at some large event, and she knew Sammy well. Star had no idea there was any sort of relationship between them. She acknowledged I had had a very bad trip, and wondered whether I was clearly seeing the line between

normal and alternate reality. I was certain what I remembered
was real.

We spent that day with Marty. We talked at length about the
early days of the Tribe, and they took me to see the areas surrounding Sacramento where the Tribe had had bases or gardens.
Marty was a nice, decent man, and I could understand Star's
fondness for him. But, given the choice between him and Sun
Bear, I couldn't comprehend why Star did not take me up on my
offer to leave. It would be many years before I'd understand the
reasons.

The next day Star insisted I go back to Sammy's apartment to
get over my fear. She said I would be seeing him again and had
better face him now rather than build things out of proportion.

Reluctantly, I entered the apartment. To my great surprise Sun
Bear was there, talking with Sammy and some of the other people
I had recently met. When we entered he got up to hug and greet
us. While we were embracing he quietly whispered in my ear,
"Congratulations. You passed this test."

I breathed a sigh of relief and felt myself relax a little. I felt I
had passed some sort of milestone the other night, but it was
good to have Sun Bear verify that feeling. I believed then that if
I did well on one test, there wouldn't be any others.

I didn't stiffen when Sammy came over to hug me hello. He
acted warm and friendly toward me, as though the other night
had never happened. When I quietly asked him how many people
he had subjected to Gayla's journeys, he looked at me quizzically,
and said he didn't understand what I meant. He continued by
thanking me for the pleasant evening we had shared, saying he
hoped we could do it again soon. Then, in a statement that almost
floored me, he apologized for not returning after he gave me the
capsule. He said he had gone to a friend's place, fallen asleep, and
assumed I had also. He was so sincere I didn't know if he had had
a memory lapse, or been, despite appearances, so drugged-out he
didn't know what had happened. Maybe he was just a superior
liar. He said he was sorry I had obviously had a bad trip when he
had had such a restful one.

By the time I left the apartment with Star, I knew I could face
Sammy again if I had to, although I never wanted to be alone with
him. Star and I had arranged to meet Sun Bear at his favorite
pancake house. I knew I'd feel freer to talk outside of that apart-

ment. After we got settled and ordered, I told him all about the other night. He nodded as I related the events, and said a loud "Ho" when I finished.

I was almost used to "ho" by now, although I still wondered every time I heard it if that's what the old movie Indians meant to say instead of "How." "Ho" is an all-purpose Native exclamation that means a combination of "it is good," "I agree," and "amen."

"You did good, sister," Sun Bear continued. "I'm real proud of you. Gayla is a sneaky one, and I doubt any of us have seen the last of her."

I sincerely hoped he was wrong on that, but suspected he wasn't.

"Why did she want me to renounce you and acknowledge her?", I asked.

"You won't believe it yet," he said, "but you are a powerful lady. If you are working with me, your power will be channeled into my vision of preserving life on this planet. If you had acknowledged her, your power would be used against that vision."

Once again, I comprehended the words, but not the underlying meaning. My confusion was all over my face.

"You'll understand that in time," Sun Bear said. "Don't worry about it now. However, I hope after this you understand why I don't want people to use drugs and alcohol. When people are 'high' it's much easier for other forces to work on them. When the Europeans came here, they brought alcohol which had been a sacrament in their old religions. They gave it to my people, who didn't understand it, and so misused it. Alcohol almost destroyed a lot of Natives. Now the young descendants of the Europeans have taken psychedelic plants and substances, which are a sacrament to some Native people, and are misusing them. This will lead to more destruction. I don't want that to be part of my Tribe."

While I certainly would not deny that day that drugs made it easier for other forces to work on people, I felt Sun Bear was personally criticizing me. Consequently, I didn't want to acquiesce. Instead I counter-attacked by saying, "What I did wasn't wrong. I am not a member of the Bear Tribe."

"It's about time you were," he replied.

Realizing I had been outmaneuvered again, I lowered my eyes, thought for a few minutes, then said, "You're right." It felt good finally to voice the decision I had been making mentally for so long.

"Good," he replied, his grin acknowledging the victory. "I'd like you to take your oath at Pyramid Lake outside of Reno if it feels like a good place to you. It's a very ancient holy place. We'll go there when you and Star get back."

He then asked Star if she was planning to stop at Eagle Wing's place in the Sierras. When she said she was, Sun Bear told her to ask Eagle Wing if he would take me through a sweatlodge ceremony. Sun Bear said it would help me get rid of the experiences of the other night.

•   •   •

I watched with both anxiety and excitement as Eagle Wing started the fire to heat the rocks for the sweatlodge. It was early morning, just before first light. We were in a clearing in the forests that surrounded the house where he, Little Eagle, Corn Maiden, and her children now lived. Mist settled on the forest floor giving the whole scene a primeval quality. Eagle Wing was as gentle a man as I'd expected Star's former husband to be. He had treated me warmly, and truthfully answered my many questions about this "sweat" we were to enter.

The sweatlodge itself looked like a small dome, covered with blankets and black plastic, the modern equivalent of the buffalo hides of the past. Eagle Wing built the fire in a special way, although I did not then understand it. Within the wood was a good number of large rocks. I waited quietly, watching the fire blaze like a bonfire when first lit, then die down to small, steady flames. The fire was hypnotic, as was the smoke mixing with the morning mist. I began to feel calm and strangely different, as though I were being transported back to an earlier time when humans routinely watched and honored the fires that warmed them, cooked their food, and helped them with ceremonies. It felt right when Eagle Wing made an offering of tobacco to the fire, then asked all of us to do so.

After Eagle Wing took stones from the fire and put them in a pit in the center of the lodge, our small group of humans—even Little Eagle—filed in. It was already hot enough to warm my morning-chilled bones. Eagle Wing closed the door of the lodge.

It was pitch black inside, except for the red outlines of the rocks. Eagle Wing put some herbs on the stones. They yielded smoke that smelled pungent yet sweet. He made prayers that struck me as sincere—humble yet eloquent. Then he poured water on the rocks and steam seemed to explode out of them. The intensity of the heat and the sound of the steam caught me by surprise. I sharply inhaled with a little whooshing sound, and then began to cough from the steam I had swallowed.

"Breath slowly and evenly," Eagle Wing suggested as he poured more water on the rocks. Star began to sing a chant in her clear, melodic voice. The lodge became so hot I felt the steam was burning my skin. When I thought I'd have to ask to leave, Eagle Wing opened the door flap. Blessedly cool air rushed in, along with morning light. He left the door open for a few minutes, and offered drinking water to everyone. I gratefully accepted.

He closed the flap in a while, and poured more water on the rocks. The chanting and praying began again. The heat built, the flap opened. The process was repeated, four times in all. At one point I even made a halting prayer of thanks, still feeling quite clumsy in my efforts to do so. I thought I would not be able to last throughout the ceremony, but I did.

Now, after the many hundreds of sweat ceremonies in which I've participated, it is difficult to remember all the words that occurred during my first. What I do remember clearly is the moment when Eagle Wing referred to the steam as the "breath of the grandfathers" and, for a minute, I left the narrow confines of my mind and felt my body expand until I seemed to become part of every dancing molecule inside that blessed dome.

7

THROUGH THE DOOR

One night, shortly after my return from Sacramento, Sun Bear and I were having a cozy evening in his room. I was feeling very close to him, and he seemed to be returning the feeling. We were talking about traveling, and he was regaling me with tales of the places he would take me to see, and the fun things we would do. I had gone out to Pyramid Lake with him that day and very much liked the vibrations there. We planned on my taking my oath to the Tribe within the week.

"The earth changes are coming in our lifetime sister," Sun Bear said. "You of all people should know that. You've had visions of these changes yourself."

I told him I didn't know about that: I still wasn't sure whether I'd been having visions or experiencing some kind of psychological disturbance.

"Sometimes you really frustrate me," he said. "If you saw a boulder sliding down the mountain toward you, I think you'd stand there analyzing its path so long it would squash you flat. You have so much talent and visionary ability, yet you deny it every chance you get. I don't know how I'm ever going to get you moving on your path. Sometimes I'd like to shake you just so you'd feel there is something to you besides your head."

While he was talking, something strange was happening to me. When he mentioned the earth changes I began to get a splitting headache; when he spoke about vision the headache felt as if it pierced my eye, blurring my vision; when he said "moving on your path," I stood up; when he said, "shake you," I moved toward him, feeling mild anger at his threat.

Then everything changed in a way I cannot explain. I literally saw red, and I lunged toward him, making a gutteral scream of rage. I went directly for his neck, putting both my hands around it and starting to squeeze. Normally I didn't have much strength in my hands and arms, but on that night I did. Sun Bear, who is strong, pushed and struggled against me for a few minutes before he was able to get out of my grip. Coughing, he fought to grab my wrists, but I kept slipping away from him.

"Touch me and you die, you dirty bastard," I shouted in a voice that did not sound like mine at all. "I hate you and all you stand for. All you lousy spiritual humans are the same—sick and demented. You think life has meaning. It doesn't. Nothing has meaning. It's every man for himself and women be damned. Grab what you can when it's there because there's nothing else. Don't be taken in by all that crap you say. I'm speaking the truth now. All you tell yourself is lies."

At this point I was raised up on my knees on his bed, probably looking like a "Far Side" rendition of Elmer Gantry. My lips were drawn back in a sneer. My arms were waving as I spoke. Sun Bear had stopped trying to grab my wrists when I had begun talking. Seeing that, I motioned him toward me with my hands. When he came close, I went for his throat again but, expecting the move, he caught my hands while they were in motion. He brought them behind my back, then made sure he pinned me by lying across my chest. I began kicking and screaming, using every curse word I'd ever heard, and some I had not. My voice was deeper than it has ever been, and I was constantly surprised both by my strength and by the words coming out of my mouth. I had no idea why I was doing what I was, but I could not stop myself.

Shifting his weight so I was still pinned but he could see my face, Sun Bear spoke to a spot somewhere above my eyes, "Let this woman alone. You have tormented her long enough."

At those words the strength in my body doubled, and I tried with all my might to throw him off me. Barely, he hung on. I began to kick at him but he twisted out of range. Horrible words of violence and hatred poured out of my mouth. I felt as if I were splitting apart. Something told me that getting rid of this man was the only thing that could put me back together.

He continued talking softly to that spot in my forehead, which infuriated me.

"Look me in the eye, bastard," I kept shouting.

Sometimes his words were in English, sometimes not. Occasionally I heard words I didn't know coming out of my own mouth. I kept struggling and screaming, wishing he would let me alone so I could kill him or leave this place or somehow get rid of the sensation of being pulled apart. Time lost any meaning. We could have been there five minutes or five hours. Part of me could not keep track of what was happening, and the headache increased until I felt my head would explode. Despite all that, I know my body kept fighting. It felt as if it were fighting for life, but whose I was not sure.

"Sister," Sun Bear said, looking me in the eyes, "I can't do this alone. You have to fight too."

"I am fighting," I replied.

"You're fighting the wrong being. I'm trying to help you. There is a spirit, a force, controling you now, and we need to get it out of you."

"Dream on visionary," I replied, hearing that deep voice come out of me. My struggling intensified. "You're only human, medicine man. Eventually you'll wear down."

Sun Bear kept speaking both to me and to whatever force he saw. Eventually, I began to believe there might be something within me that wasn't me, and that Sun Bear was my friend, not my enemy. I started to want to get rid of this thing. As that desire dawned, my struggling became fiercer and the headache became much worse. I felt as though my head was being blown apart.

"Sister, you need to tell it that it can no longer live within you. You need to command it to get out."

My body convulsed at his words.

"I know how much I'm asking," he continued. "And I know you are strong enough to do it."

I tried to frame the words, but it seemed as though I no longer had control of my mouth.

"You can do it sister."

I tried again but almost blacked out from the pain in my head.

Sun Bear kept talking softly to me, finally suggesting that he would tell it to get out at the same time I did.

Summoning all my strength, finally, I said in my own voice, "Get out of me." My body convulsed once more, then I lay limp, barely breathing.

Suddenly, with a loud crash, the door of the room fell inward.

"No," I screamed, fearing the spirit was coming back to me again.

"It's all right," Sun Bear said, rubbing my back. "It's gone now. That was just its way of saying goodbye."

I felt totally exhausted. The headache was still there, although it was diminishing. Every part of my body hurt. My throat was sore. Yet I felt a lightness and peace within me.

I looked at Sun Bear. He appeared to be as exhausted as I was.

"I know you don't understand," he said. "But I'm too tired to explain now. Let's both sleep and we'll talk later."

For once, I had no doubts about what he said.

· · ·

The next day I kept examining the door. It was a trailer door that rolled open and closed on a track. It had not been broken before and I could see no reason why it would fall off the track in the middle of the night. It was made of thin wood and had cracked from the impact. Sun Bear saw me examining the door and assured me something real had happened.

How could I believe him? How could I believe I had been controled by some force and then exorcised? I didn't believe in spirits. I didn't believe in possession. These concepts were foreign to my worldview. I found it almost impossible to comprehend the possibility that I had had a spirit within me. It made me feel dirty and, even worse, out of control. If a spirit or force had been controling me, even for a minute, it meant I was not the mistress of my own life. If I wasn't who was? I had a hard time returning to a belief in the fatherly God of my childhood, and I did not yet really understand the Native concept of God as verb, as a moving, creating force within and around all of life. Anyway, any god that would allow such an obviously vile spirit within me certainly couldn't be all that powerful. The whole situation absolutely confounded my mind, a lifetime first, and one that made me downright mean.

While I felt as though the entire foundation of my life had been shaken, Sun Bear seemed jubilant. He watched, trying to surpress a grin, as I walked toward the broken door once more. I returned and sat down frowning more deeply. I was broadcasting "bad mood" so loudly that everyone else had left the trailer.

"Would you like to talk about it," Sun Bear asked.

"Considering how happy you are, I'm not sure I would."

"Okay. We don't need to. I know what happened," he replied.

I took the bait and asked him please to explain the incident to me. The grin vanished, and Sun Bear spoke to me seriously and gently. He told me there had been a spirit within me that left last night, knocking off the door in its anger, and that everything should be easier for me now. He asked if I had ever had any strange, "spooky" incidents as a child.

I thought for a time and remembered a couple of things. There used to be an old mirror in a great aunt's house and, whenever I passed it, I would see faces looking out at me. They scared me. I also believed that something bad lived in the back of a dark old closet in our apartment, and I never wanted to go in there alone to get my clothes. I would cry if I had to. Sometimes I would see shadowy shapes slipping by me in the twilight. When I figured out no one else saw them, I stopped talking about them.

Warming to the task, I remembered I could never stand seeing scary parts of movies. I'd run out of the "Wizard of Oz" crying hysterically at the wicked witch. Once I saw "House of Wax" in 3-D and had nightmares about it for months. As I got older I avoided seeing frightening movies or television programs because they really bothered me, both waking and sleeping. Although I still consider such avoidance good sense, I realized I reacted more strongly to such images than other people seemed to.

When I'd drink too much and get depressed in New York I would sometimes think of going to turn myself in at a church, any church. I never understood why, but it was a strong urge. Even as a child I had desired to keep my thoughts in control of my life because I was afraid of some part of me that lay just beyond them.

Sun Bear kept nodding as I spoke. When I slowed down he said, "Enough. What you are saying backs up the pattern I've seen since you have been here. There are forces I call 'rider spirits' that sometimes come into children, particularly girl children with great receptivity, or any children who are born with the potential to find and fulfill important visions. These spirits basically try to keep them from finding their visions. Usually they make the person do stupid or self-destructive things, like drink a lot or take drugs or hurt themselves or take foolish risks."

He continued by telling me that these were basically bother-
some spirits, rather than vicious ones. He made it clear that
people who had them were not possessed by them; rather, they
were plagued by them. The strange thing about rider spirits is
that they could turn out to help a person, instead of hurting him.
By having to fight this self-destructive, self-deprecating energy,
the person with the rider spirit would sometimes become a much
stronger individual than he would otherwise have been. If he
became strong enough, the spirit would see it had no chance of
stopping him, and would leave of its own accord. If that didn't
happen, the spirit would usually succeed in its mission and the
person would become too weak to even know he could have his
own vision of life.

Sun Bear said not every child who saw shadows or was afraid
of scary movies had a rider spirit. In fact, they were rather rare,
and he wouldn't have been certain that was what was bothering
me, except that I had had all the "symptoms." He continued by
telling me the only time these spirits could get really nasty was
when it was clear they should admit defeat and leave their host.
Because of my decision to leave New York, to leave Benjamin so
quickly, to say no to Gayla, and to consider stopping using any
alcohol or drugs, it seemed as if I were rapidly becoming strong
enough to shake my rider.

"When we were talking last night I could see you almost totally
comprehended 'vision.' Understanding vision is the first step
toward finding vision. Your rider saw that too and knew it would
have to leave soon. It got mad at me for helping you," Sun Bear
explained.

"It was a strong spirit. I had a couple of close calls there last
night. But it's over, sister, and things will be easier. We just have
you to fight now, you and your mind."

After last night I did not want to fight my mind. I wanted to
worship it. In my shaky state I was sure such mysterious "forces"
would not bother me again if only my mind were strong enough.
Without my usual intellectual confidence, I felt like a jigsaw puz-
zle I couldn't quite fit together. I did not like the feeling.

Trying to regain control, I began asking Sun Bear a lot of
questions about what he had just said. He answered most of them
curtly, probably realizing my ploy. When I asked why these spirits

most often came to girl children he said it was because women embody the receptive.

"I suppose that means we're supposed to be passive receptacles for anything that comes into us, human or otherwise," I said contemptuously, happy to replace my confusion with righteous anger.

"That isn't what receptive means to me," he replied.

It would be years before I would first share then build upon his understanding of the absolute strength it takes for the surrender preceding true receptivity.

. . .

It took me a few days to settle down from the spirit experience before I felt ready to take my oath to the Tribe. It was a beautiful sunny, crisp high-desert winter day. A few clouds were scattered throughout the sky. Pyramid Lake, one of the remainders of the vast inland sea that once covered this now-arid land, seemed to sparkle both with life and mystery. Sun Bear, Morning Star, and I walked alone along its shoreline. I had asked Sun Bear if my oath could be witnessed only by those two people whose love and belief had brought me to this point.

I felt the way I imagined an innocent young bride would feel: full of hope, yearnings, and expectations that could not be put into words. I thought of a friend who had gone into the convent, and envisaged myself in a similar situation. I was about to commit myself to a whole new way of living: a communal, tribal way foreign to the society I knew. I was going to pledge myself to try and build a loving family relationship with these two people I did love, with the ones back in Reno I liked, with the ones in Sacramento I hardly knew, and with people who were yet to come. How fortuitous was my ignorance about the difficulty of building loving relationships, and about some of those people yet to come!

I had traveled to the Bear Tribe out of love as I understood it then. I was taking this oath out of love as I understood it at that moment. With all my heart I yearned to be able to build the relationship to which I was about to commit myself; yet, being a child of this culture, my tools were so pitifully weak.

To me, then, love and lust were hopelessly entangled, and both were feelings to be hoarded for that special someone. Love was a commodity to be traded for the best advantages I could manage: security, position, prestige, riches, affection, warmth, purpose, and procreation. Love was a substance to be measured out with care and calculation. This was before the days when the concept of "the limitless abundance of unconditional love" flowed easily through the lips of as many people as it does now. I doubt I had ever heard the term "unconditional love," or that I would have believed it possible even if I had. In my experience, love was very conditional, yet some part of me fervently hoped it could be otherwise.

In addition to pledging myself to this loving family relationship, I was also about to commit myself to living my life without violence, negativity, or possessiveness—to the best of my ability. I considered myself a pacifist so I had no intellectual problem with living without violence. Luckily, I was so naive then about the pervasive cultural violence that inevitably had seeped into me that I did not realize how hard that part of the vow would be to keep. The angry words, the nasty thoughts, the kidding punches on the arm, the whacks to a child's behind, the folded newspaper on a pup's hind end—all of these are symptoms of the deeper violence we've been taught is the normal way to live.

To live without negativity seemed a tall order. It is. Years of working with people has taught me that the only way past most negativity is through it. Negativity can be surpressed, but it will always rise up again in another form. That day I just hoped I could live without negativity for at least the few hours surrounding my oath-taking. I harbored the same desire concerning possessiveness. With the feelings I had for Sun Bear, I could not in any conscience say I would not be possessive with people. But I cockily thought I would have little trouble giving up possessiveness of knowledge or material goods. Later I would realize that divesting myself of my thoughts, my theories, my experiences could be more painful than letting go of someone I really loved.

Equally frightening to me was the vow I was about to make to abstain from alcohol and drugs. Drugs were not my concern. I had not used them enough to consider them an important crutch. Alcohol was. It was the magic potion that eased my mental meanderings and provided a valve for emotions I otherwise feared expressing. Giving it up was so anxiety-producing I had sneaked off downtown last night and had a double scotch. It was to be my last drink for eleven years, until both the Tribe and I grew to a different level of understanding.

I had talked at length to Sun Bear about my fears and hesitations. He was quite impressed with the amount of thought I had put into the oath-taking. His concern was with people who took the oath much more lightly, not even thinking about it enough to come up with misgivings. He appreciated my desire to take the oath with as much consciousness and integrity as I could manage. He assured me few people could go from lives in the dominant society to life in the sort of tribal society he envisioned just by vowing to do so. He knew change took time, although he has never grown easy with this fact. He reminded me the words "try to live" were in the oath, and, as long as I kept trying, I would be living up to my commitment.

Eventually the primitive beauty of the lake worked its magic. I calmed down enough to find a cove that felt like the right place to me. By this time the sun was beginning its descent to the West.

"Will this spot be all right?" I asked Sun Bear and Star.

They both said it felt good to them. Sun Bear laid down the Bear Tribe's medicine bundle and, one by one, showed me each item in it and explained its significance. He took out the tribal pipe, smudged it, made offerings with it, and then shared it with Star and me. He spoke very solemnly of his vision then asked if I was ready to make my commitment to it.

I pledged myself to try and build a true love relationship with my brothers and sisters, and to try to live my life without violence, negativity, or possessiveness. I foreswore the use of alcohol and drugs.

"Sister, you have a new name," Sun Bear said.

I steeled myself to hear "Motor Mind" or "Gopher Mouth," two of the many names I feared I would be given.

"Because of where you come from, and because of the qualities I see within you, I am giving you a special name in the language of my Ojibwa people. You are Wabun, the East Wind, the Woman of the Dawn."

I vacillated between relief, elation, and the realization that I was being given a name that carried with it awesome responsibilities I could not yet begin to understand.

Later, Morning Star would tell me her name in Ojibwa is Wabun Annung, which translates as Morning Star, or Dawn Star.

We felt our names forged another connection between us. Over time I would learn the major qualities of the East are clarity, wisdom, and illumination, and that it is the Medicine Wheel position to which one comes for mental healing. How appropriate!

I got my wish that day: I was able to put aside my doubts and negativities for the hours surrounding my oath-taking. My shilly-shallying ceasefire was pleasant, but brief. When we got back to the car after the ceremony, Sun Bear saw liquid under it and tried to open the radiator cap to be sure there was enough water left. The cap was tight and he was wrestling to get it off. Like most humans, nothing could irritate him more quickly than a problem with his car. He got annoyed, and I quickly followed suit, complaining that everything had taken so long I'd never be able to get my celebration dinner ready at a decent hour.

We took turns being cranky much too frequently during the next month. By this time, it was becoming clear that the schism in the Tribe over the use of drugs would not be healed. Sun Bear could not compromise his medicine, and some people in the Tribe would not compromise what they saw as their medicine. I was firmly on Sun Bear's side on this issue, especially after my Sacramento experience. Aside from the physical, medicine, and moral issues, I though it was stupid for any alternative group to endanger itself by having drugs around. I began to lobby for ceasing the use of medicine weed for that reason if for no other. Eventually my lobbying was successful.

Soon after I took my oath, Sun Bear decided to resurrect *Many Smokes,* his magazine that had had a hiatus while all his energy was going to the Tribe. *Many Smokes* had started in 1961 as an inter-tribal newsletter in Los Angeles when Sun Bear was actively working there with the many Native people who were relocating to the cities in search of employment, which was then, and is now, extremely difficult to find on reservations. Being away from their traditional tribal culture was as hard for these Natives as trying to build a tribal culture proved to be for non-Natives. Being in an urban environment seemed to breed a hopelessness that could often lead to alcohol abuse. In the fifties and sixties Sun Bear was involved with other Native Americans working to build a renaissance of interest in the traditional ways in the urban Indian population. *Many Smokes* originally was a newsletter about that renaissance.

There was a two-and-one-half-year lull in publication, from 1963 through 1966. When Nimimosha began working with Sun Bear, she used her journalistic and artistic abilities to turn that newsletter into a magazine, which published until 1970. I began *Many Smokes* again in 1972 and, with a name change to *Wildfire* in 1984, it has been publishing since.

I was quietly thrilled about *Many Smokes. Finally,* I had my own magazine! I got to use all my Columbia Journalism knowledge and added to it skills most journalism majors never get: layout, ad sales, making negatives and plates, offset printing, mailing list management, distribution, and wholesale and retail sales. *Many Smokes* became my craft project. I saw it through sometimes from idea to finished magazine. Then I went out and sold it. In many ways the magazine became the bridge from my past to my future. When everything else was confusing me or depressing me, I'd turn to *Many Smokes.*

Many Smokes also became my teacher. In researching stories for it, I learned a lot about Native American tradition, history, and current affairs. While Sun Bear and most of the other Native teachers I met taught by example more than words, my work on the magazine gave me the words that kept my mind occupied and happy.

In addition to *Many Smokes,* I learned to do an incredible variety of work in my early months with the Tribe—things I'd never imagined I would do. Following up my early cow caper, I became a fairly proficient skinner and butcher, thanks largely to the road kills Sun Bear and I found while traveling. A road kill is just what you would think: A poor animal who meets an untimely end blinded by or attracted to car headlights.

When I used to see the remains of animals hit by cars in or by the road on the East Coast, I would get sad or depressed. Sun Bear had a better method, one very much in keeping with the Native belief in honoring all of life by not wasting anything. When he'd see a dead animal, he would stop the car, make a prayer for its spirit, and then see how long it had been since the animal was hit. If it was smelly or stiff, we would take any feathers or fur still usable for medicine, then put the remains away from the road, on the Earth Mother, so the body could go back to her, or be eaten by some other animal without danger of the scavenger being hit. But if the body was fresh enough, and of an edible species (and

Sun Bear considers almost everything edible), we would get it to a safe place and skin it out, keeping all usable parts.

Over time I feasted on road-kill deer, antelope, porcupine, raccoon, possum, squirrel, wild rabbit, turtle, snake, goose, quail, pheasant, and ruffed grouse. After I got over my initial nausea, I enjoyed most of these gifts from the animal kingdom. I used to tease Sun Bear that I couldn't tell the difference between goose and grouse because, in those prenutritional awareness days, he told me to fry everything up in grease and it all came out tasting like greasy fried meat. No, everything doesn't taste like chicken, although rattlesnake does. I even learned how to make jerky as a way of preserving even more of our gifts from nature.

Another new experience for me was driving and maintaining cars. Coming from D.C. and Manhattan, I thought of driving as the sport of cabbies. I didn't realize it was something regular people did. I did have a license but I had rarely used it. Out West, I had to drive because of the space between places. Even though Sun Bear liked driving, I had to relieve him sometimes. Reluctantly I learned this motor skill. Usually driving recycled vehicles, I also had to learn about car repairs, changing flat tires, and chaining up for driving on snow- and ice-covered roads. It seemed that most chaining up situations would occur when I was with another woman. I kept wishing my New York feminist friends could see how well I dealt with that particular equal opportunity.

At the Tribe I also got to perfect my culinary skills, and learn how to whip up an intimate dinner or breakfast for ten on an hour's notice. I even learned how to bake bread from scratch, something else I had never imagined myself doing.

Over time I became more experienced in child care, and grew to like it, even if the twins were there. I remember my joy the day Squirrel learned to say my name, and smilingly called out to me. My housekeeping abilities improved through use. Five or ten people in a place generate a lot more disorder than one.

I learned about possible problems with electrical lines, sewage, and septic systems, thanks to the trailer court. I became a carpenter's assistant upon occasion.

I began my herbal training, learning the correct way to identify, locate, speak to, and pick necessary plants. The absolute necessity of correct identification was forever drummed into my mind when someone thought they had brought home wild onion on a night when I was hungry. It went into a stew which entered then exited my body in short order. While I never knew positively which poisonous plant was the culprit, it was most likely naturalized lily of the valley, often mistaken for wild onion.

I became a gardener, helping to start, then plant, the small garden we had in Sun Valley that year. Seeing my first sunflower push its head through the soil brought me as much joy as Squirrel did the day he learned my name. Sun Bear eventually made a hiker out of me, and I now could see the subtle beauty in the hills I had once thought arid.

To my surprise I even became a reluctant craftsperson, helping make kid's toys first, then graduating to leatherwork. Somehow I managed to get my ten thumbs working together, and a few items turned out pretty well.

I learned about the I Ching and how to throw it; and that some people know more about astrology than what they read in the paper. Sun Bear tried to educate me about gambling, but I was not a good learner. I could neither adopt the Native view that gambling is a way of testing your medicine, nor release the conservative view that it's a fast and nerve-racking way to lose money.

The biggest lessons of those early days were about community, and about relationship. Both struck me as very trying areas of life, and intimately interconnected. The split in the Tribe over drugs was a real difference of philosophy, and one that seemed to grow more irresolvable with time. Added to that was the stress of financing a community. Sun Bear really had spent all his savings on the California bases. He didn't have more to give. Several other individuals had also exhausted their monetary resources supporting the Tribe. Without financial backup, some of the camps seemed to be having problems with figuring out ways to take care of basics, such as food. I was very surprised when I figured out that some of these people were actually angry at Sun Bear because he didn't have more money to give. It was my first experience of dealing with the human desire to find a big daddy (or big mama) who is responsible for everything, and I didn't like it.

Judging from what was happening on several of these bases, it appeared that having communities located on donated land did not seem to be working well. If there were any sort of disagreement between the owners and the Tribe, or if something strange

"got into" the owners, the land could be taken away, with no
compensation for any buildings or improvements. And it had
begun to seem to me as if there were always disagreements if you
had more than one person doing anything.

One of the reasons Sun Bear had revived *Many Smokes,* and had
begun to go to pow wows and shows to sell merchandise, was so
he could make money to get a good land base for the Tribe in the
future. Some of the other tribespeople—those I had heard discussing it in Sacramento—continued to plan a benefit concert for the
same end. They had lined up several musical groups and planned
to have it at the University of California at Davis. When they ran
out of money to complete the benefit planning, Sun Bear ended
up taking a personal loan to help them out. Even though he was
discouraged about the Tribe, he wanted to give it every possible
chance to work.

In all their planning, the benefit organizers, led by Sammy Fish
Hawk, had *somehow* failed to check the UC Davis schedule. Consequently, they *accidentally* scheduled the concert for the weekend
before spring finals. This oversight meant the benefit bombed.
This failure, added to all the preexisting problems, turned the
tribal schism into a permanent split.

Now Sun Bear's thread of depression about his vision failing
wove its way through everything else. He went back to Reno more
discouraged than ever. Some of the tribal bases changed their
names and philosophies and continued, for a time, with community living. Other people went on to explore other teachers or
teachings, or went back to the society or lives they had left. It was
a disappointing and sad time for many people.

Our circle in Sun Valley grew smaller. Always one to root for
the underdog, these events tied me to the Tribe as nothing else
could. No one—human or otherwise—was going to destroy Sun
Bear's vision, not if I had anything to say about it, and it seemed
I did. At times I felt like a one-woman cheering squad trying to
convince Sun Bear he had to go on. It hurt me to see his pain,
and I was powerless to help him. I'd listen when he wanted to talk
about the negativities that had succeeded in driving the Tribe
apart. He told me that now, when his vision was far from reality,
these energies were attacking him personally, trying to ensure he
wouldn't have a second chance to fulfill that vision.

Sun Bear took to spending more time in the casinos, escaping from the Tribe's problems, and testing his medicine in a way a lot easier than trying to fulfill his Tribal vision. One night, concerned about his mood when he left the trailers, I went to find him downtown. As I approached the coffee shop in the Cal Neva, his favorite casino, I saw him sitting with a dark-haired woman, smiling, and laughing. From my vantage point, the woman looked like Gayla. I left before they saw me.

Back at the trailer, I was assailed by all the doubts I had had since I arrived. What was I doing here? How could I work toward a true love relationship with a disappearing tribe? For that matter, how could I work toward a true love relationship with anyone? I certainly didn't seem to be doing so well with Sun Bear, or the other people there. How could I get rid of my negativity when even the chief seemed negative? And what was the relationship between us supposed to be?

I still harbored the fantasy that he was my true love. He kept talking about my being his medicine helper. There was a lot of energy between us. Both of us acknowledged that. But it felt as if I called it "apples" and he called it "oranges," and there was no compromise without grafting our concepts together and creating a whole new species of relationship, something we were both too stubborn to do then. I didn't trust him because I couldn't understand him. He claimed both to trust and understand me. While for many years I furiously denied he did either, in truth, he probably did.

Sometimes we were friends; sometimes we were adversaries; yet, always, we could work together on anything that had to do with his vision. It was most remarkable. We could be hissing and spitting like treed cats, but if someone walked in, or we had to go somewhere, we were immediately as civil as we could be. It seemed as though something wanted us working together, and how we felt about it was immaterial. Our relationship definitely did not live up to my ideas of how true love should be. But every time I'd be ready to give up on it, there would be a magical moment when he'd take my hand, or smile at me and I'd feel warm, whole, and complete. At those times, I felt as though we had been together since the dawn of time.

After the benefit, Morning Star was back and forth between Reno and Sacramento fairly frequently. Usually Marty was with her. I was always glad to see her because I believed she understood my problems with the relationship. She also seemed to sense some importance in my staying with the Tribe, so she would try to help me work things out. When Sun Bear's depression would affect me too greatly, and I'd think about returning to New York, Star would advise me to stay for one season of the garden and then see how I felt. I tried to decode this growth analogy I was sure Star was making, but I didn't know enough about gardening—or the earth—to do it.

Even though I knew it was coming eventually, I was stunned the day Morning Star announced she was going to move to Sacramento to prepare a home for her child. Sun Bear was stunned too. I wanted to convince her to stay, but I knew it would be impossible. She was as bullheaded as I. I would miss her greatly.

Over time, Wild Flower, Strong Oak, Mountain Woman, and Squirrel had become valued friends. Thankfully, they were planning to stay on. Still it seemed as if the place would be very empty without Star. Star assured me other old Tribe people would return, and that new people would come. Yet it would never be the same for me. Without Morning Star, I did not see how the promise of those golden days in New York could ever be fulfilled.

Feeling sad, discouraged, and lonely, almost accidentally I stumbled out into the garden. I figured as crummy as life seemed, I might as well have dirt all over me too. In the hot noon sun of Nevada on a summer day, I was digging rows in which to plant some tomato seedlings. I was also shedding some tears into the ground. I felt a little dizzy from my mood, the heat, and the exertion. I half sat, half fell backwards so that I was sitting on the earth, looking up toward the sun. When I brought my eyes down again toward earth I saw in front of me the same figure I'd seen that night in Sacramento. I caught my breath in surprise and said, "Who are you? What do you want?"

She smiled, and, for that moment, the world was right.

"You are where you should be my dear," she replied. "Help the man named Sun Bear. He is one of my beloved grandsons."

8

THE POW WOW TRAIL

The first few years of my life with Sun Bear would have made an excellent travelogue. He is definitely a nomadic Native. For someone like me who had lived on the East Coast, where a long trip is the train ride from New York to New Haven, these years were like a safari to the moon. Within the first six months I had been to various parts of California so many times that the trip was beginning to feel like the commute from Manhattan to northern Jersey. By the autumn I had seen many parts of Nevada, Utah, Baja California, Colorado, Washington, Idaho, Montana, and Oregon. In the winter we began our cross-country traveling, and I filled in the map.

When I first began traveling with Sun Bear the only states of the contiguous forty-eight he had not visited were Vermont, New Hampshire, and Florida. We went to the New England locations in my second year with him, but it took a couple more years before we got to Florida. In the early 1980s, we explored Hawaii. By that time I, too, had discovered America by going to all forty-eight continental states at least once.

Our style of traveling was quite different from my refined East Coast model. We weren't on planes or trains in those days; we weren't even in a motor home. We went everywhere in the recycled cars, rebuilding them as we went along. When we started selling in earnest at pow wows and shows, we accommodated our inventory in the trunk, the back seat, and, later, in a car top rack, with boxes carefully wrapped in tarps and plastic. When wind and rain played havoc with the rack, we eventually traded it in for one of those cartop carriers that look like fast-food sandwich boxes.

Sun Bear's students have a standing joke now about those of them that used to think roughing it meant being in an economy motel with only a black and white television. I laugh heartily at the joke because I used to be one of "them." Our accommodations in those days were quite a shock. They were not economy motels, or even economy tents. We didn't have room for camping equipment with all the inventory. Most of the time we slept wrapped in sleeping bags, either out on the ground or in the car. I swear, I had a strong back until I subjected it to two years of intermittent sleeping with inventory boxes piled in the back seat. Sometimes, when we felt flush, we would stay at an eight- or ten-dollar motel. Once we got one in Mexico for four dollars. It's hard to believe now that eight-dollar motels existed in the 1970s. These were not quality inns, but were the kind of places you hoped you wouldn't find stains on the walls or the sheets. I remember one where we changed rooms three times because the first two had so dangerously strong an odor of propane.

I became obsessed with finding rooms with a bathtub, which I usually needed badly. In between such splurges, I usually washed my body and hair in service station restrooms. Most eight-dollar motels had just showers—finding one with a tub was a worthy challenge. The owners or managers would occasionally lie about their accommodations, knowing you'd never get your money back once they got it. I got in the habit of having them show me the tub. In one motel, the young man running it swore they had tubs. When we got to the room, there was only a shower.

"Where's the tub?" I asked.

"Right there," he said, pointing to the shower.

"That's a shower stall," I stated.

"Yes, miss," he agreed, "it's a tub you stand up in."

I laughed, paid him, and took my bath standing up.

In case you're wondering what has happened to the eight-dollar motels, they are still around almost two decades later. You just pay thirty-five dollars and up for them now.

Our early travels were unique gastronical adventures. Remember these were the early 1970s, and general nutritional awareness had not advanced to its current state. Sun Bear and I also had not yet been somewhat converted by the variety of vegetarians, fruitarians, Pritikin plan people, Fit for Lifers, food combiners, macrobiotics, and assorted food advocates who have since come through the Bear Tribe community. Sun Bear's idea of a good restaurant dinner then was a hamburger steak with onions, and mashed potatoes, whether instant or real. True to my cosmopolitan background, I preferred a good coq au vin, but French restaurants were far apart in the West in those days, so I settled for fried chicken with french fries, hold the grease.

We were constantly on the lookout for the perfect "Ma and Pa" restaurant, the kind that made home-tastin' food at reasonable prices. Alas, we never found it. We sometimes talked about writing an underground guide to good greasy spoons, coast to coast, only we didn't find enough worth mentioning. Don't ever believe the old saw that says a place is good if truckers or the police eat there. I think some greasy spoons keep such vehicles permanently parked in their lots just to fool unwary travellers. I kept trying to convince Sun Bear to pick a better grade of restaurant, urging him to get rid of the "back of the bus" mentality that kept me poised on the precipice of ptomaine. I slipped over that cliff on more occasions than I want to count, which resulted in my becoming somewhat expert on the natural treatment of food poisoning.

His restaurant tastes did change a bit in later years when we had land and food for the Tribe, and he felt justified in occasionally spending enough to eat in a natural or ethnic or good (not grand) restaurant. Yet I feel even today that it would be better if good places gave Sun Bear the old "lady's" menus that come without prices.

My nickname for Sun Bear in those early days was El Cheapo, which was an apt description of his spending habits. We were on the road to make money to buy land to rebuild his visionary tribe. Almost every cent we made went back into inventory of some kind: books, jewelry, beadwork, leather work, kids' toys, posters, and postcards. Sometimes I felt our only stipulation for stocking an item was that it was heavy and/or bulky.

The greasy spoons were a luxury, not our constant fare. Most of the time we would eat in campgrounds or in the car as we drove. Aside from road kills, some of our favorite treats were boloney sandwiches, cold hot dogs, and milk and cookies, followed by copious amounts of caffeinated coffee, "the black medicine." My stomach can't decide whether to churn or yearn remembering these menus of exotic items that rarely pass my lips these days.

Traveling in the early seventies, the "back of the bus" mentality sometimes turned out to be a necessary defense mechanism for both of us. There were places then—and I suspect there are now—where Indians, and white women traveling with Indians, just were not welcome, equal rights notwithstanding. Such places won't kick you out, which would be illegal; they'll just keep you waiting until it's clear you could starve, or your fellow customers give you a look that declares you'd make a nice doormat. Not all experiences of racism were in little cafes either. I remember one very posh hotel that "lost" the reservation a well-known author had made for Sun Bear, who was to speak at a symposium the author was sponsoring. The hotel manager made it clear that another room couldn't be found for Sun Bear and I—until the white male author intervened. I complained in writing, and later we were offered a free weekend at the facility for any "inconvenience" we had experienced.

Not all racism came from white folks either. I had a good taste of it from some Native Americans who didn't like non-Natives at pow wows and other events, particularly white women companions to Indian men. Some of these Natives did not mind volunteering their opinions of me to me. While I could certainly understand their rage at the system, I resented being judged a part of something I rejected myself. These encounters left me with a bitter taste, and a better understanding of what nonwhites have had to put up with. I left several such unasked-for confrontations in tears of frustration, or in deep sadness.

At that point in my life I had no idea of the complexity of the relationship between Native and non-Native people in this country. Now I have some idea, and know there are no simple answers. My foremost feeling then was one of intense shame for the treatment whites had inflicted upon red people. Like most people who go through the stage of new found social awareness, I wanted to exonerate myself from the sins of "my fathers," even if they had been mining coal in Wales while the West was being "won." I didn't know how. I wished I had been born Native because I saw that as the only salvation. I still had "the noble savage" complex that has always complicated Native/white relations. I even lied a couple of times and claimed a remote Indian ancestor, not an outlandish thing to have in this country. Once someone printed my claim and it really surprised my father, who thought he knew his relatives better than that.

Later I realized I wasn't helping anyone by feeling shame for deeds I did not do. Rather than wear myself out with guilt, I tried to learn from, and respect, the Native keepers of this continent, like Sun Bear. Later still, some of these keepers told me I had the responsibility to take what I had learned back to my people because everyone—red, white, black, yellow, and all shades in between—needs to work for the good of the planet now. Otherwise, we run a good risk of species or planetary annihiliation.

For each one of the Natives I met who were abusive about my racial background, I met scores who treated me with warmth and kindness. Some of these people opened their hearts and their homes to me, and thus taught me a great deal about themselves, their culture, and how to have a better relationship with the earth and all of her other children.

When I'm not writing or teaching, I'm fairly shy, particularly if I'm in an unfamiliar situation. I was in such situations constantly in my early years with Sun Bear, so naturally I kept my mouth closed and my ears open. I didn't know it at first, but that is the Native peoples' idea of the correct orifice positioning for a young person around his or her elders. Because my mouth wasn't flapping with a hundred questions, and my ears weren't closed to the answers, I gained acceptance from people who would later be my teachers, acquaintances, or friends.

When I say someone was my teacher, it doesn't necessarily mean we were involved in what I would have considered previously a formal teaching relationship. I learned a lot simply by being in the presence of some people, or by watching how they did things, or by listening to what they told me. For example, the woman who initially taught me about Indian dancing never set up specific times to do so. Rather, she would have me sit with her while people were dancing and she'd talk about what was happening. After a time, she'd ask me questions just to see if I had been hearing correctly. I would bring gifts for her whenever I thought we'd be sitting together because I wanted to somehow return the energy she was giving to me.

With others, the teacher/student relationship became more formalized, yet not in the ways I would have expected. I can't ever remember going up to someone and saying, "Will you be my teacher?" or "I'd like to learn all you know about plants," or "Sun Bear told me to ask you all about your prophecies." Rather, the teaching situations just seemed to happen, sometimes over the course of many years. Admittedly, being with Sun Bear placed me in the position where this learning could occur. Sometimes I've considered the possiblity that my education was being orchestrated by some unseen mentor.

During my first year traveling, I met several people who were to be important teachers, even though I was still fighting the idea I was in the right place to learn. One was another white woman, then in her seventies, who lived with "the Old Coyote," a Blackfoot man who had an Indian store in Los Angeles. Joan had been with Bill so long she looked like an Indian, and she certainly acted like one. Sun Bear had known these two since the early days of working with the Native Renaissance in Los Angeles. The Coyotes basically ran an informal Indian Center out of their store, which was also their house. They always had a meal, some clothes, a bed, and a kind word for any Native people who were feeling lost in the vastness of city life.

Joan taught me about generosity, hospitality, and true compassion, which often has an element of what, today, we call "tough love." She also showed me how much strength of spirit it takes to be a true servant of the people. Joan never complained about having to put together her twelfth or thirtieth meal of the day. She truly enjoyed being able to feed her people. She would have given you the blouse off her back, and the skirt and slip to go with it—not out of any sense of guilt but because she liked to share what she had. Joan was a willing servant, but was not in any way a martyr, which really set her apart from many women I knew. She did what she liked in her life, and she liked what she did.

Had I met her in New York I would have been horrified by the "stereotypical female roles" she fulfilled. I probably would have tried to "liberate" her and, thus, lost her as a teacher. Joan gave me another view of womanhood: One in which the traditional female role could be fulfilled out of choice, and with a dignity and grace I had not believed possible.

Because of our frequent trips to Los Angeles, and because Joan and the Old Coyote still traveled to pow wows, I got to see her in many situations over a good period of time. While the setting changed, Joan didn't. She was still the same crusty, kind woman, whether in her home or after ten hours of being in the sun. Unlike most women I knew, she didn't have a different mask for various situations. She was Joan. You liked her or you didn't. I did, and by accepting her I accepted a previously rejected part of myself—one I had to reconcile with in order to go on with my learning. The intimate dinners for ten on an hour's notice would have been impossible otherwise.

Without Joan's gentle example, my feminist prejudice against "traditional roles" would have kept me from being able to experience the matriarchal foundations of Native culture. She began to show me what it means to care for your people for this generation, and all generations to come. Joan was a good teacher and friend to me until her death. I now have a moose foot pouch that was hers. The Old Coyote gave it to Sun Bear to bring to me when Sun Bear helped conduct Joan's funeral. It's a Native custom to give a dead person's possessions away to his or her friends. Joan's death helped me understand why. Every time I look at that pouch I remember the good times and the needed lessons I experienced with this wonderful woman.

Ruth Drafall, a clan mother from an eastern tribe, reinforced Joan's lessons, particularly those about feminine strength. I would consider Ruth a medicine woman, although I never heard her refer to herself in that way. She was gratified to have been chosen a clan mother, a position given only to women who have proven themselves to have stability, compassion, fairness, deep love, and a fierce sense of protectiveness toward their people.

Ruth has all those qualities, along with physical and spiritual beauty, grace, courage, and directness. You never have to guess where you stand with Ruth. She tells you.

When she first met me out West, where she was then living, she thought I was in pretty sorry shape. It was obvious to her that I was sincere about wanting to do well in my new life, but that I had little idea of what I was supposed to be doing. She was right. I was suffering from a severe case of culture shock, and I was also deadly serious about getting things right. This often made me the target of friendly jibes from Native people who thought my solemn attitude could use some lightening. Not understanding the Native sense of humor, it took me a long time to figure out when I was being kidded.

At the first pow wow I attended, one of Sun Bear's "uncles" came over to invite us to dine with his family. Sun Bear had instructed me previously that turning down a meal invitation, or food that is offered at a meal, is a grievous insult to Native Americans. Thus, I accepted readily.

"What are we having?" Sun Bear asked.

"Oh, the usual," uncle replied, "dog stew."

My stomach turned over, and I got green around the gills. I worried all day about how I could get out of both insulting the family and eating something I knew would make me vomit. I'd keep asking Sun Bear if his uncle really meant it and he'd tell me some tribes did eat dog and that he had done so when he was hungry during the Depression. He assured me it didn't taste bad.

We got there and the menu was steak, potatoes, and vegetables. I felt foolish, and promised not to get myself worked up again. That lasted until we got to the next pow wow and a different "uncle." I was sequentially afraid that each tribe would be the tribe that really did eat dog.

At the pow wow where I first met Ruth, an uncle came over while she was standing by our booth. She watched the exchange. Then the green tinge came to my skin and she knew just how much of a tenderfoot I was. When he left she asked, with a small smile playing around the corner of her mouth, whether I had had much dog stew. I told her no with a serious face. She burst out laughing.

"It's unlikely you will at the dinner table. Dog stew is a sacred meal only served after certain ceremonies," she said. She came around the booth, put an arm around my shoulders, gave me a squeeze, and said, "Little sister, you seem like you're having problems. I'm going to help you out."

I was very grateful to have her help. When Sun Bear and I weren't storming, he was a kind and gentle companion and teacher. But when we got into discussing my doubts, he could get into silent states that would last until I was ready to scream. At those times, which could occur during pow wows, I really needed someone to talk with. I hoped Ruth would be around a lot. Frequently that summer I felt as if I were in a Berlitz total-immersion course in Native pow wow culture, and I was failing. Consequently, I kept pretty quiet. I didn't like the taste of my shoes. Ruth's offer was definitely the best one I'd heard in a long time.

Beginning then, Ruth took me under her powerful wing. I felt as if I had a kind aunt watching out for me—sometimes. To say that Ruth can be formidible is an understatement. She is a power-house, and widely respected. I was smart enough to know that being with her was a situation in which I should shut my mouth, open my heart, do a lot of dishes, and try to anticipate ways to be helpful.

Ruth was always a firm teacher, but a fair one. The first time I started to discuss my doubts about what I was doing, she made it clear that they were my problems and she didn't want to hear about them. Sun Bear's vision had chosen me as his medicine helper and Ruth was going to make sure I knew what my job was, and how to fulfill it. She made it clear it was a great honor to be selected to be a servant to the medicine. While she did not under-stand why the Great Spirit had chosen a white woman to help Sun Bear fulfill such a big vision, it wasn't her place, or mine, to question either the Creator, or someone else's medicine.

Over time, she showed me the difference between being sub-servient and serving; between being passive and receptive. In the former cases you see yourself in an inferior position; in the latter, in an equal but different position. As my education went on, she made it clear my responsibility was to take care of as much of the earthly, physical level of business of Sun Bear's tribal vision as possible. That would leave Sun Bear free to work with his medicine.

She did not see women as inferior beings in any way, nor did she see the task I had as demeaning. She believed life worked better when mothers took care of the family and clan mothers took care of the tribe. That, she assured me, was how things had worked on Turtle Island for many thousands of years before that "Columbus guy took a wrong turn."

If Sun Bear was going to build a new tribe, Ruth was deter-mined his female medicine helper was going to know what a clan mother was, and how she should act. A few years later Twylah Nitsch, the Seneca woman who is the founder and clan mother of the Wolf Clan Teaching Lodge, joined the effort to teach me about this position. Although I don't think she and Ruth have ever met in the flesh, they are sisters of the spirit. Between them, I learned not only about clan mothers but also about how to straighten out all aspects of my personal life.

The first year I met her, Ruth also undertook my education on crafts, insisting I learn to make my own moccasins so both my hands and feet would connect me better with the earth. She taught me how to respect the animal kingdom by cutting spiral laces for any craft project, thus using more of the leather than I would otherwise. While I was a swift learner about most things, craft projects were not my forte. Ruth insisted I keep trying, telling me that the more my hands worked the less my head would.

I always tried to stay on my toes around Ruth, or else found myself taking a backward fall. When she had me in shape to be helpful to her and to Sun Bear at ceremonies and other spiritually oriented events (which did not happen in my first or second year of knowing her), I then had the opportunity to watch her straighten out other young people, both Native and non-Native, who had missed some lessons in life etiquette. She could be sweet as syrup one minute and hard as nails the next—both attributes, she assured me, of all clan mothers. She was especially tough with those of the hippie bent who wanted to learn about Native culture but still thought anything was okay as long as they were going with the flow.

I remember one event where some young mothers decided it would be fine to let their toddlers play without supervision, while the mothers sunbathed by a river. Ruth found one of the babies wandering close to the riverbank, retrieved her, and purposefully set out to find the mother.

When she got near the group, she asked the toddler, "Who is your mommy?"

The girl, charmed with Ruth as all children are, pointed to a pretty young woman. Ruth called her over. Hesitantly, she came. Ruth pleasantly asked her if she were having fun. When the woman said, "Yes," Ruth began to blast her about her lack of responsibility. The woman interrupted Ruth to point out that in the old tribal days, children were everyone's responsibility.

Ruth asked the woman where her tribe was. The young woman said these other women were like her sisters.

"But all of you were here. No one was watching the children," Ruth said, "That would not have happened in the old days."

"But you found her before she fell in, so everything is cool," the woman replied.

Ruth did not agree everything was cool. She let loose and gave that woman and her friends a necessary earful about their lax ideas of motherhood, and about the bad examples they were setting for their men, and for their children. I doubt any of them has ever forgotten what she said.

Ruth definitely did not need an assertiveness training course to know that women have the sacred responsibility to speak out for life, for children, for the elders, the sick, the helpless ones, and for the earth. She, along with Twylah and some other teachers, have succeeded in instilling me with that responsibility.

Louisa Papineau was another woman who had a great need to speak out for the earth, and for her people. She lived in a small town in Oregon with her four daughters and, occasionally, her son. The girls were spread over the adolescent years while John, her son, was in his early twenties. He was a very angry man who drowned his rage in alcohol and expressed it through radical politics.

I met Louisa early in my first year of riding the pow wow circuit. She, too, was an old friend of Sun Bear's. All Louisa's energy was directed to one goal: getting back a piece of land that had traditionally been a spiritual site for her people. The land now belonged to a large timber company that wasn't very sympathetic to her efforts.

She wanted it returned so it could become a traditional camp where the young people of her tribe could learn about their own heritage. Louisa was a master teacher about her tribal tradition. She knew the entire history of her people, and felt compelled to preserve it. Her ears perked up when she heard about my journalistic background.

Louisa supported her family through doing crafts. She produced some of the most beautiful beadwork I've ever seen. She tried to teach me but, where leatherwork was difficult for me to do, beadwork was almost impossible. The only beaded project I've ever done, in which I feel pride, is the turtle-shaped pouch I made and lightly beaded to contain my goddaughter's umbilical cord. I did my absolute best in making that because having such a pouch helps a person always feel connected during her earthwalk.

The first time I met Louisa, at her tribe's annual celebration, she let Sun Bear and me use a tepee she had received through a trade for some of her beadwork. The tepee was a wonderful boon because it gave me the feeling (if not the reality) of privacy. Sleeping in the round engendered a special feeling of wholeness. I loved looking through the smoke hole at the myriad stars above.

That first summer I couldn't believe how many stars were visible out West, and how many of them zoomed around. In city life, the man-made light obscures the stellar expanse, allowing us humans to consider ourselves larger than we really are in the overall scheme. In the country, with a thousand lights twinkling overhead, it's difficult to harbor such notions.

It was Louisa who began to teach me to have an understanding of the gestalt of the contemporary pow wow. If I had just walked into a pow wow in those days, I might have come away with a pretty skewed idea of them and of Indian culture. Pow wows could have seemed like carnivals or fairs where the major activities were competitive dancing for prizes, stick games and other gambling, eating, buying, selling, and trading. At a lot of them, drinking was rampant. In fact, Sun Bear and I often would make gas money by gathering up the beer and soda cans left behind on the grounds. Thankfully, we'd have a hard time doing that today because many pow wows have outlawed drinking.

What a casual observer of pow wows could not know was that they are a major and important reunion for many Native families, clans, and tribes that are spread apart on different reservations, or in cities. Pow wows are a time when people exchange news, ideas, plans, songs, dances, crafts, food, and visions. It is my understanding that pow wows helped keep the Native American culture alive when many other Native gatherings were frowned upon by the government. Since the Wounded Knee massacre of 1890 (and probably before), the U.S. government became nervous when Native people got together to dance, so they outlawed sundances and discouraged most Indian ceremonies. From that time until the Native renaissance in the 1950s and 1960s, pow wows were the only large cultural events many tribes had. It wasn't until 1978 that the Native American Religious Freedom Act was passed, allowing Native people to dance and worship as they wished.

While I began significant learning relationships with Joan, Ruth, and Louisa that summer, they were far from my only teachers. I believed, even then, that I could learn something from everyone I met, so usually I did. Some Navajo women taught me that, in their culture, it was only the women who took care of the earthly matters such as trading. Given the choice of making a deal with Sun Bear, a Native, or with me, a white woman, they choose me. They felt it was only proper for the woman to take care of such things. The Navajo nation, even today, is close to its matriarchial roots. Many of the women still own the sheep, the trucks, and the homes, called hogans. It is also the Navajo women who took the lead in preserving their culture and land in the government-orchestrated affair called "The Navajo-Hopi land dispute." Navajo women are consumate traders. They know the value of their work, both in jewelry and in rugs, and they do not undersell this value.

Going to both the Navajo Fair and the Crow Fair were unique experiences on many counts. For one, English is the second language on both reservations. For another, both tribes have learned to work with the dominant culture without being assimilated by it. Being on either reservation is like being in another nation, with a different language and culture.

At the Crow Fair I saw one of the biggest giveaways I've ever seen. A giveaway is an event at which a person, family, or tribe gives some presents away to honor an experience. At pow wows, the giveaways honor the pow wow itself. Family or individual giveaways could honor a Vision Quest, a marriage, a birth, or a death. Part of the reason for a giveaway is to allow participants to share in the joy or memories of the celebrants.

It's easier to understand the giveaway if you understand that traditional Native people place a different value on material goods than white folks do. If you admire something that belongs to such a Native, they are likely to give it to you. Life is transient. "Things" belong with people who enjoy them. Consequently, giveaways often seem very generous to those of us used to setting limits on the amounts spent on Christmas gift exchanges. The Crow Fair giveaway took my breath away. They gave away Pendleton blankets, Stetson hats, beadwork, moccasins, money, food, scarves, shawls, and even horses. They gave away to friends, relatives, tribesmen, acquaintances, strangers, and passers-by.

I was so inspired by the concept that I tried a personal giveaway myself at the Fort Peck Oil Discovery Celebration the next week. The Assiniboine people at Fort Peck were quite poor, but very decent and hospitable. At every pow wow, part of my job was to find kids who wanted to make some money selling *Many Smokes,* our magazine. It sold for fifty cents then, and the kids got to keep ten cents for every copy sold. Sun Bear used to tease me about being "Wabun Hood" and my sales staff being "my merry men," although girls were some of my best salespeople. At Fort Peck I had one super salesman, an eleven-year-old named Eric. I watched him sell and sell, and then take every cent he made and give it to his mother. That was unusual. Most kids sold enough to buy whatever they wanted, but Eric was doing this selling to help his family. At the end of the weekend I presented Eric with a belt buckle he had been admiring, my giveaway to him for the memory he left with me.

Another person who remains a fond memory is Stan, a Canadian Indian and prize-winning dancer. He taught me to dance the owl dance, and to overcome some of my self-consciousness about being a white at pow wows. We met at a Northwest Coast pow wow and spent a lot of time talking at the booth. I kept enviously eyeing the dancers because, by this time, the drum had gotten into my blood.

Stan asked me why I didn't join in the friendship dances, which were dances in which everyone could participate. Having been impressed by Louisa with the proper way to approach dancing, I explained I didn't have the right clothes to wear, not even a shawl. He left and came back later carrying a wing-tip dress, which is a long cloth dress with ribbons and a contrasting calico underdress. Sun Bear was walking behind him.

"Sun Bear bought this for you," Stan said, "and he's ready to watch the booth. Find a place and put the dress on."

I happily obliged. When I emerged all decked out, the master of ceremonies announced an owl dance, a graceful, paired Indian dance. Stan invited me to be his partner. I told him I didn't know the steps but he assured me he did. He led me out to the circle around the drum. After that initiatory experience, I enjoyed joining in the friendship dances when I could get away from the booth.

One of my favorite dances that year was a Bear Dance held in California. A Bear Dance is a traditional dance of purification; a way of getting rid of the old, and making way for the new. After the proper preparation, a person dresses in a bear skin and dances around the circle of participants. The participants all have wormwood switches, because wormwood is a cleansing plant. As the bear comes around, they strike him gently with the switches. With each blow, they let go of some negative thing they are thinking or feeling. When no more blows come, the bear goes to the nearby river and washes himself off. As he emerges clean, all the negativities people switched to him float away downstream. The Bear Dance was sponsored by an elder woman who had seen in vision that it was her responsibility to keep this tradition alive. Such cleansing of negativity is something that could sure help a lot of people in the mainstream society.

No tale of the pow wow circuit would be complete without mention of stick games, also called hand games, which are a uniquely Native form of gambling. Because traditional Natives look at possessions differently than whites do, the same holds true for gambling. In Native gambling, winning or losing money is tangential to the true purpose of such games: testing your medicine. Now, as I've mentioned, Sun Bear never participates in hand games because he can't use his medicine in this way. But he had watched them enough to explain what was happening to me.

There are two teams. One of them gets a pair of sticks. One stick has markings. The team with the sticks tries to hide the marked one somewhere on the person of one team member. The other team leader has to point to the person with the marked stick. If she chooses correctly, her team gets the sticks, plus a marking stick to signify their victory. When one team gets a certain number of marking sticks, the game is completed. Both teams have drums, and both teams have power chants. Once I heard some of those chants and they stayed in my mind for days. Some teams also use other methods of exercising their power. Sun Bear warned me to protect myself around stick game areas, but I didn't believe him until I was standing too close to a team once, and felt as though bolts of lightening were striking me throughout my body. I had accidentally been caught in a medicine crossfire. I was much more careful after that.

I valued Sun Bear as a teacher more and more as the summer slipped toward autumn. When we started traveling, I had clung to him as the only familiar landmark in a sea of strangeness. Clinging doesn't become me. As I met more people who became familiar faces, I eased up. That allowed him to give to me more freely. The best teaching Sun Bear gave me then was the benefit of his eyes. He saw so much more of life than I did—from mountains, trees, and rocks to rabbits, birds, and zippies. Over the summer, as we traveled, he kept telling me what he saw.

"Where?" I'd say as he asked me if I saw the hawk circling overhead.

He'd point to the right where a hawk would be circling over the edge of a cliff. Unfortunately, he usually would point the steering wheel in the direction of his hand and I'd miss the hawk or eagle in my panic that we were about to drive off the cliff.

Eventually I began to be able to see more myself, and there were even a few times when I'd see something before he did.

Through our travels, he also had the perfect opportunity to teach me more about the attitude differences between Natives and whites. He'd make me figure out all I could on my own, and then fill in the details. He did that about food and stick games and giveaways and butchering—about everything he safely could.

Sun Bear's mood had begun to improve as soon as we got on the road. It continued on this upward swing for most of the summer. Sun Bear truly likes traveling and all the new things he can see and experience. He also liked the fact that we were beginning to amass the money that would allow us to buy land. Once I got over the shocks and into the pace, I liked the traveling too. It allowed me to see and experience so many new things.

Other than my experience in the stick game area, it seemed for a while as if my "tests" had abated. That made me very happy. I had had quite enough of that spirit stuff. Then, when I was feeling pretty sure I could put all that behind me, I saw Sun Bear leave the booth at one pow wow and go talk with a woman who, from the back, looked exactly like Gayla. I could not be sure because they were too far away. While I was staring, the woman turned around toward me and thrust her arm in my direction. Again, I felt as though I were being hit with lightning or electric shocks. Then, immediately, I got depressed.

When Sun Bear returned, he saw something was wrong and he quickly made some medicine that took me out of my despair. He even apologized for talking to the woman, whom he called Jennifer, and thus exposing me to her tricks.

"She was sweet on me," he explained, "and she is jealous that you're with me. What she did is nothing serious, just annoying. You'll be okay now."

Surprisingly, he was right. The depression lifted as quickly as it had come.

Within a week, I had another weird experience. We were driving in Nevada near Walker Lake, another one of those desert treasures. I was looking at the scenery and enjoying myself when I began to "hear" some strange sounds in my head. They got clearer and louder. From my experiences with pow wows, I knew they were a chant. It was like having someone inside my mind singing this chant I had never heard before.

"This is it," I announced to Sun Bear when the chant had ended. "I have gone totally crazy."

"What are you talking about?"

"I've gone over the edge, bonkers, nuts, insane," I declared.

"What makes you think that?" he asked.

"Now I'm hearing voices chanting inside my head," I replied.

He turned to me and smiled, going perilously close to the edge of another cliff.

"Whatever made you think all of your teachers would be in human form?"

9
DEATH AND BIRTH

Once Sun Bear and I got on the road, we never really got off. When the pow wow season finished, the Indian Show season began. Sometimes the seasons overlapped and we'd divide up the inventory and head off in two different directions. The shows were fun, but I didn't like them as much as the pow wows. They were usually indoors and under flourescent lights, which tend to make me restless and irritable. After three days in a row of standing on cement floors for twelve hours a day, I would use the metal ring-sizing hammer to give myself a foot massage. Any change of foot sensation felt good.

I missed the life and vitality of the pow wows, particularly the beat of the drums and my band of "merry kids" selling *Many Smokes.* But some familiar faces were present at shows, and occasionally there were dancing exhibitions and fry bread booths (an Indian treat, similar to an unsweetened donut, and wickedly delicious). But we would have gone to the shows even without these extras because the shows gave us a way to continue making money to get land and rebuild the tribe.

In late September, I went to visit Star and wait for the birth of her baby. I stayed a week, but it wasn't the right one. Her daughter Autumn made her appearance on earth six days after I left. A few days later both Sun Bear and I went to meet her. Every infant is wonderful, but Autumn was particularly so. In my objective opinion, she was a bright, beautiful, open, energetic baby with the countenance and disposition of an angel. Star was beaming as much as Autumn and I was truly happy to see the healing birth can bring. So was Star. She later became the sort of midwife I wished had brought me into the world: a truly wise woman healer.

Birth and death are close on the circle of life. The day after Autumn's birth, Nimimosha's friend Darrell was killed in a hunting accident. While I had not spent a lot of time with him, I had valued the time we had together. Darrell was a handsome, bright, and energetic man with a lot of good plans for the future. His death devastated Nimimosha, and came as a big shock to me.

Other than people in my grandparent's generation, I had not known anyone who had died before. I don't think it really occurred to me that young people could die. I believed in the actuarial tables, and the media fantasy world that tells us we all live healthy lives until at least seventy years old for men and seventy-five years old for women. Darrell's death seemed obscene to me. He was so young, so vital, and so full of hopes and dreams. What sort of malificent god would cut down a flower just beginning to bloom?

Sun Bear went to comfort Nimimosha while I commisserated with Wild Flower and Strong Oak. When Sun Bear returned, my tears had changed to anger at the unfairness of death.

"Wabun, you waste so much energy being riled up about things you can't change," Sun Bear exclaimed. "Death is as much a part of life as birth. You fear death because you don't understand it.

"Death isn't the big deal white folks make it out to be. You don't stop being, or go to some family reunion in the sky; you keep changing, learning, and growing. We are all part of the Creator, the Great Spirit. That Spirit always is, but not in an unchanging way. The Creator creates and grows too," Sun Bear said. "I get a kick out of all these people who are waiting to get to heaven to be happy and fulfilled. What they don't realize is that they could be in heaven every day they live if they would only take real responsibility for their lives and for the earth."

"Do you mean you believe in reincarnation?" I asked him.

"That isn't exactly it for me. I don't think being in human form is always the highest destiny we can have. I remember being a tree once. That was nice and restful. And I've been several kinds of animal. Some of them were a lot of fun, and some were pretty challenging.

"I'm positive you can find a connection," he teased, "between my animal lives and my name now."

Suddenly understanding why they are called throw pillows, I tossed one at him.

I felt a little better, but still depressed. Years later I would hear a Native story that helped me understand more deeply the connection between birth and death. As I remember it, the story said that at one time death did not exist in the world, but birth did. Everyone lived forever. After some time, the earth began to get crowded, and the people knew something had to change. In those days the women counseled only with each other, as did the men. Each council discussed possible solutions to the problem of over-population. The men finally concluded that birth should be banned so all the people living then could go on as they were. But the women, remembering the sweet, soft skin, the shining eyes, the gurgling sounds of the newborn, decided death had to be instituted so birth could continue. When the two councils met, the women's view prevailed. Death and the changes it brings became a natural part of life.

Years after that first discussion with Sun Bear, on a sunny day in a desert, I would experience death, and come back. I believe that adventure gave me as good a grasp of the subject as one is likely to have while still wearing a human overcoat.

But this autumn, I was painfully aware of the little deaths all around me. Using Sun Bear's eyes, I saw them as I never had before. I watched the California leaves brown, wither, and fall. Even the desert plants of Nevada seemed to draw within themselves. Small animals ceased scurrying around. The sun drew farther away. I felt sadness mixed with a hope I could not explain.

Our little circle seemed to be disappearing too. Mountain Woman and Squirrel had left that summer while we were traveling. I missed Squirrel's shiny face and joyful smile. After vacillating back and forth, Wild Flower and Strong Oak decided to leave also. I felt as if the vision were withering, just like the leaves. Sun Bear didn't agree. He pointed out that Nimimosha, he and I were still there, and that the deaths of fall herald the rebirths of spring.

He was right, and spring came early for the Tribe. When we lighted in Sun Valley long enough for it to happen, people began coming to join us. War Dancer and his friend George were two of the first. War Dancer was a young man from the Flathead Tribe, a champion fancy dancer, who had been with the Bear Tribe for a time in the early California days. George, a friend of his from the reservation, had not been with the Tribe in California, but had heard about those times and decided to check it out.

War Dancer was like a younger brother to Sun Bear, and Sun Bear was glad to see him return. I was happy to meet him myself. I couldn't believe it, but I'd been feeling kind of lonesome with just Sun Bear and myself in the trailer. Our time alone at home had given us the opportunity for some wonderful romantic interludes. Unfortunately, they were frequently followed by unromantic disagreements when Sun Bear would leave the trailer and go off to the casinos. He'd accuse me of never being satisfied with what I had. I'd accuse him of running away from intimacy. In the time until the next interlude, I'd be very aware of how solitary my life seemed.

War Dancer's appearance changed that. Shortly after he and George arrived, a man named Ted Running Deer came from California to join our circle. Ted, who had had a Cheyenne great-grandfather, had worked as a gardener, carpenter, and photographer, so he had some skills we really needed. Soon I realized how glad I was Ruth had given me some clan mother lessons. Otherwise I wouldn't have known how to handle four unruly and often sloppy men. When George told me he didn't know how to cook or do dishes, I told him it was about time he learned. He did. He was the first of my many students in culinary and home economics skills.

Ted didn't stay in the trailer long. When he and Nimimosha met, it turned out they had known each other years ago in California. They had liked each other then, and apparently the attraction was still there. I was glad to see Mosha come out of the depression that had surrounded her since Darrell's death.

Before Christmas that year, we had our inventory items on display in a bookstore in Reno. One of us had to be with them during business hours, so I learned about being a shopkeeper. I also tackled the mailbags full of correspondence about both *Many Smokes* and the Bear Tribe that had piled up while we traveled. With Ted and Nimimosha's help, I prepared another issue of the magazine.

I finished up my first year with Sun Bear by traveling with him to the East so he could meet my family and friends. Sun Bear was supportive then, as he is now, of Bear Triber's keeping in active contact with people from their past. The more you understand your past, the freer you are in your present.

Driving cross country in winter can be both beautiful and

frightening. The pattern of snowflakes coming toward a car, especially at night, is lovely, and hypnotic. Icicles growing from the rock faces beside the road are magnificent, and potentially dangerous. I was as speechless at the sight of a herd of hundreds of antelope in Wyoming as at the number of cars in the ditch. The medicine held and our trip was safe.

Of course we stopped a few times along the road to make some wholesale sales, even selling an expensive squash-blossom necklace-set to an Indian store in New Jersey on Christmas Eve day.

On this trip I went through Des Moines, Iowa, for the first time. My reaction to it was the same as my first response to Spokane, Washington.

"What an ugly city," I thought, "I'll never live here."

Try not to ever say "never" about possible locations. I think it issues a challenge to the spirit of the region. I spent eleven years in the Spokane area, and two and a half in Des Moines. I discovered my first impression of both cities was wrong. A small city atmosphere has many advantages, and both cities are set in beautiful natural surroundings, albeit of two very different types.

The East Coast trip went well, and we found the trailers and our small circle in good repair when we got back. I stayed around Reno and worked on *Many Smokes* and on organizational work for most of the winter. We ventured out to an Indian show in San Jose in January. While there I had a vivid dream of an earthquake that reminded me of my New York experiences. That was enough to keep me out of California for a couple of months.

In March of that year, Sun Bear went to South Dakota's Pine Ridge Reservation to report on the Native takeover of the small town of Wounded Knee. Wounded Knee was the site of the horrible massacre of 300 Native people in 1890. It was being occupied now to bring the nation's attention to the plight of the Oglala Sioux people in the area. These people live in grinding poverty and constant high unemployment. When some Oglala people had spoken out against the tribal government's part in these conditions, they became victims of "mysterious" violence.

Wounded Knee succeeded in bringing people's attention to some of the problems of Native people in this country. However, the specific problems of the Oglala people were not redressed.

While he was there, Sun Bear did help in making a documentary about the situation entitled *Spoken From My Heart.*

During the time surrounding the Wounded Knee occupation, quite a number of Native people visited with us in Reno. Listening to them gave me more understanding of the current political and social problems of Native Americans. That increased understanding certainly helped with my *Many Smokes* work.

Shortly after his return, Sun Bear went to a pow wow in California. When he came back he looked strange, but I couldn't figure out exactly what was wrong. When I asked, he pointed to his nose. He had been punched there by a Native man who objected to Sun Bear's working with whites. Sun Bear did not fight back.

"What would that have accomplished?" he asked me. I had to admit it wouldn't have accomplished anything except provoking more violence.

"It evens things out," Sun Bear said. "Quite a few years back I got punched in the nose by a white rancher who didn't like Indians. I didn't hit back then either. But I did take him to court because he was in the habit of punching Indians."

I wanted to put an ice pack on his nose, but Sun Bear wasn't enthusiastic about the idea. I didn't push it. I had learned that we got along much better when I didn't nudge or prod. By this time Sun Bear and I had settled into a more comfortable relationship, though it was not the one I had envisioned. We were good working partners, and, at times, romantic energy was still there. But Sun Bear was unwilling to admit I was his true love, which frustrated me. He readily acknowledged he loved me, and thought I was a good woman and a superb medicine helper. That was it. He wasn't willing to pledge me his troth or forsake all others for me.

While there was a part of me that still rejected the idea of marriage, there was that other part that kept saying, "But it's what is expected. It's what will make you an honest woman." With a primitive understanding of the principle that would later become popularized as affirmations, I had started presenting myself as Sun Bear's wife, both playing with the idea and hoping that saying it would make it true. "Significant others" weren't as common then as they are today, and my emotional neanderthal part shyed away from being on the cutting edge of unconventional relationships.

Sun Bear wasn't happy with my subterfuge, but agreed to go along with it for a time—as long as I realized he did not believe in white man's marriage, and wasn't about to compromise on the issue any more than he already had.

"We've joined our life paths together," he said. "Why do you want to complicate it with papers?"

It wasn't the papers I really wanted. It was his recognition of the fact that we were fated to be among the world's great loves. Often, wanting this made me furious with myself. My desire was so maudlin, so corny, so reactionary—and so deeply embedded in my otherwise forward-thinking consciousness. It truly got in the way of an otherwise congenial relationship. And it got in the way of my relationships with everybody else, particularly women.

In April we drove cross-country again, this time on the southern route. We went through Navajoland and the Pueblo territory, buying as we saw the sights. I felt like a poor kid let loose in F.A.O. Schwartz. I had carte blanche to buy all the beautiful Indian jewelry I desired. I hand-chose each piece of jewelry we carried that year, and sold some pieces as reluctantly as if they were really mine.

We attended a big Indian show in Maryland, near Washington, D.C., and another at the Statler Hotel in Manhattan. It was a successful trip, and another good chance for me to visit friends and family. I also met with the publisher of my first book *The People's Lawyers* and planned some publicity for the time of its release.

In the weeks between pow wows that year I did some radio and television shows and newspaper interviews for my book. They were fun to do. I enjoyed the contrast of getting out of my pow wow jeans and into my publicity skirts. The interviews also necessitated extra baths, always a treat. I remember the thrill of seeing the first copy of my book in print, and of getting reviews, albeit small ones, in *Publishers Weekly* and the *Kirkus Review*.

We went to a number of the same pow wows we had the year before, which gave me the opportunity to spend more time with Joan, Ruth, Louisa, and my other new friends. Because I had quieted down and wasn't in the same "sorry shape" or culture shock I had been in, I made a better student.

We went also to the Sheridan, Wyoming celebration which featured the "Miss Indian America" pageant. It was quite an event, and provided me with many photos for *Many Smokes*.

Again that year my favorite pow wows were in the Northwest. The minute I set foot in that part of the country, I loved it. The Cascades are spectacular, and I felt very peaceful in them and in several other parts of the region. It was almost like coming back to a well-loved and remembered home. I was particularly partial to Chief Seattle Days in Suquamish, which is on Bainbridge Island across from the city named after this wise and eloquent leader. The ferry ride, the land, the salmon bake, the canoe races, and the people all contributed to my enjoyment of the event.

Chief Seattle Days was also quite a contrast to the Omak Stampede, which usually occurred the previous weekend. I called the Stampede "the Bash." Like many celebrations I visited, the Stampede had a rodeo, a carnival, dances, pancake feeds, Indian dancing, stick games, and booths that sold everything from cotton candy to Navajo rugs. By Saturday night it seemed as though everyone in town was in very high spirits, often with the help of alcohol. There was sure to be feeding, fussing, fighting and a few other f's. Omak is a small town in Washington and this is the yearly chance for everyone to cut loose. The residents usually are joined by thousands of guests who are more than happy to cut loose with them. The Stampede is the home of the famed "Suicide Race" in which horses and riders run at full gallop down a steep twenty-five-foot hill and swim across the Columbia River where it is at least eight feet deep. I was surprised how few injuries occurred in the years I was there.

I took time out from our summer schedule to accompany my parents on a short tour of the West, then rejoined Sun Bear at the Navajo Fair. When we arrived back in Reno after the Fair, Anna and Alex, both friends of mine from New York, came to visit and check out the Tribe. Nimimosha and Running Deer who had been holding down the home base alone were glad to see all of us arrive. Shortly after, War Dancer and George, who had been traveling another part of the pow wow circuit for most of the summer, also returned to Sun Valley.

I had known that Anna and Alex intended to come visit, but was happy to see them actually arrive. I had met Alex when I was working in the public relations field, and I knew Anna had done similar work. If they decided to stay, I looked forward to their help with the magazine and our ever-increasing correspondence.

We heard from lots of people who wanted to come live with the Tribe, but we were hesitant to let them do so until we were back on the land.

Shortly after we all arrived, so did Cindy and Joseph, a young couple we had met in Maryland. With them were their two small children. Joseph was a poet and a potter, and I felt that any community had to be a place for the arts to thrive. After the initial personality conflicts that always seemed to occur when new people arrived, we began to feel like a circle of friends. We fancied ourselves a community. None of us actually realized then the effort it would take to forge a group of unrelated people into a workable, let alone loving structure.

The council circle was our form of organization and self-government. We would sit in a circle and pass a stick called the "talking stick" around. When you held the stick you had the right to speak. When anyone else held it, you had the right to listen. In those days we had councils to solve personality conflicts, councils to determine future plans, and councils over such weighty matters as dishwashing and picture placement. This council idea was new to most of us, and we needed some practice with it.

Toward the end of the year our circle was visited by Brad Steiger, a well-known author who was researching a book about the resurgence of Indian culture to be called *Medicine Power.* That visit resulted in a friendship that has spanned the years since. The book itself would bring us connections with a few people who became good friends and supporters—Grandmother Twylah Nitsch being one—and with thousands of seekers who felt the Tribe might be what they were seeking.

When Christmas season came, we reopened our craft section in the bookstore in Reno. I was glad for the extra help our new arrivals gave me. We held Earth Renewal ceremonies on the day of the winter solstice. This day—when Father Sun begins his return from the South to heat again the Earth Mother—is the beginning of the life cycle for many Native people, and a very sacred time.

We felt particularly blessed this year because our traveling had resulted in enough money to begin to search for the land that would give us our foundation as a tribe.

When I made my own prayers on the solstice, I was grateful for the new people who had joined our circle, for all I had learned in the year passing, and for the gentle year of synthesis I had just experienced.

I doubt that I was wise enough then to realize that life's active times are often followed by quiet ones. My first year with Sun Bear had certainly been stormy on the personal level, the cultural level, the political level, and the spiritual level. This year had been a breeze. That should have given me an indication of what to expect in the coming year. It's not that I believe good times are followed by bad. Rather, the Creator within always pushes us to grow, expand, and change.

10

FORK OFF THE ROAD

The dream came first. It was one of those vivid dreams that make me wonder whether I'm awake or asleep. In it Gayla came to live with us in Sun Valley. She was constantly scornful of me, and constantly seductive with Sun Bear. I remembered the time I thought I had seen Sun Bear with her in the casino and at the pow wow. Answering my thoughts her dream form said, "Of course it was me. I told you I would return, in whatever forms I need, in order to claim you and the one you call teacher. Remember the night in his room? He called that force a 'rider spirit,' but you know better now.

"Hear me well," Gayla said, "because the more you think you understand, the more you will suffer. Because he is a man, Sun Bear neither sees nor perceives me as you do. I'm getting impatient with you both. I haven't made enough progress in the forms I've worn so far. So I'm going to change now. Watch me!"

With those words Gayla drifted behind a wall of mist and changed into a much younger, prettier woman. As I watched this metamorphosis, I strained to see her face clearly or to see some identifying mark. As sometimes happens in dreams, the harder I tried to focus, the less I could see.

Twirling to show off her perfect figure, Gayla began to laugh.

"This is wonderful," she said, "now you'll suspect every pretty woman you see. That should endear you to your Sun Bear. Do you think you can compete with me in this form?" she asked grinding her hips suggestively. Then she began to laugh. "I don't think so, serious one. But we'll see, won't we?"

I woke from that dream filled with dread. Even after all the

intervening months, I still couldn't explain what had happened
that night with Gayla. All I was certain of was that I didn't want
to have any more to do with her, whatever she was, or with any
of this spirit business. I had liked the previous year when my
teachers were in human form, and nobody was inside my head
singing in my ear.

The dream also frustrated me because I had not been able to
see Gayla clearly. If she was going to return to torment me, she
could at least have had the courtesy to identify her new form
clearly.

I told Sun Bear about the dream. He listened attentively and
agreed that it must have been frustrating.

"The ones who work on the side Gayla works on usu-
ally don't follow a book of etiquette," he replied to my complaint.
"I don't know exactly what Gayla is, but I suspect she is some kind
of female force that has something important to teach you. I'm
not sure why she seems to oppose my vision, but she sounds
powerful, and she sounds sneaky. Let me know if you hear from
her again. Oh, it wasn't her that came out of you that night. It was
a rider spirit. Sounds to me like Gayla wants to take credit for
everything. Be careful you don't give her more power over you
than she already has."

I didn't like Sun Bear's answer. It made me nervous when he
didn't know everything about the aspects of life that still felt
strange to me. I resented it when he implied I was somehow
giving this force power over me. As far as I could tell, Gayla was
one of the first people I'd ever met and hated in my life. I didn't
see how hating something could empower it. I wanted to question
him more, but he seemed restless, so I let it go.

I vividly remembered the dream again a few weeks later when
we displayed our jewelry at a brunch given for that purpose at the
home of a prominent television actor. He and his wife were
friends of Sun Bear from his Hollywood days, and they were
enjoying helping our cause. They had assembled the wives of
actors, directors, screen writers, and other men of money to
"ohh," "ahh," and buy our Indian crafts.

I checked the women as they entered. They all looked like
Gayla had when she was twirling behind the mist. They were all
as beautiful as she had seemed to be, and they all gave off the

same sort of energy she had. I felt trapped in some sort of twilight zone.

The brunch was great for the Tribal treasury, but devastating to my ego. Every other woman in the room shopped in the size 3–5–7 section. They were all dressed oh-so-fashionably, while I had ceased even packing the few fashionable togs I had brought from New York. Their make-up and hairstyles were all perfectly casual as befitted the hour and the event. I had known the brunch was likely to be a chic affair but, given my resources, I had opted for the ethnic look. I put on the ribbon skirt and blouse I got at the Navajo Fair, combed my uncut, straight hair, and borrowed some lipstick from Joan.

I felt like the "before" in a room full of Elizabeth Arden salon "afters." Of course they were all flirting with Sun Bear. He was exotic, and he was very male. He wasn't minding it, but I was. I did my saleswoman duty, and did it well. The stress took its toll, however, and I took one of the cigarettes graciously out on display and went in a bathroom to smoke it. I'd quit the year before, and did not want Sun Bear to see my fall. Good thing I was in the bathroom smoking. The cigarette made me sick, which seemed an appropriate way to end that morning.

When we returned to Nevada, another young couple had joined us. Morning Glory had been in one of the California camps, gone home, and convinced her boyfriend Larry to return with her. Figuring Gayla would come as someone new to the Tribe, I welcomed Morning Glory. She and Larry were experienced in gardening and in preserving food, so I thought they'd be a good balance for our little group. At that point I was working with a theory that a good community would spring full-blown into existence when we had attracted a certain number of people involved in physical survival, self-reliance, teaching, business, child-care, and the arts. I wasn't sure of the number in each category but I expected that the people would come trained and ready-to-go.

The Hollywood brunch had put us over our financial goal, and we began looking for land. We went to a few locations in Northern California and in Oregon but could not find acreage that looked good and was within our price range. Sun Bear was determined the place have a good water source and land suitable for farming. Most budget parcels were better equipped for desert survival training or raising mountain goats. After a few forays, we were getting discouraged.

On our return from one land-scouting expedition, we received a message to call Louisa Papineau. We did, and she made an interesting proposal to us. She had forty acres near her home that she had inherited from her family. One of her relatives had started to build a house there, then gone to Los Angeles. The land was flat and suitable for farming. An irrigation stream ran through it.

Louisa said it was ours to use if we would help publicize her land fight.

Sun Bear was hesitant from the start. It was, after all, another donated land base. But he agreed to go and see it. It was beautiful land, with everything Louisa had said. All that was missing was a source of potable water, but there was a public spring nearby. The house frame was solid. There were even mountains in the distance and a river within a few miles. Running Deer, Nimimo-sha, and I all loved it. Sun Bear had to admit it was much nicer that any of the other pieces we had seen. But still he was hesitant.

He liked Louisa, and agreed with the work she was doing. But he had been disappointed so many times before he really had qualms about living on anyone else's land.

"I don't believe in owning land," he told Louisa and me. "That isn't the way of our people. No one can own the earth mother. But I do want a stable land base in the name of the medicine society. With that, the vision will grow and my people will have land in which they can put roots."

Louisa certainly agreed. Similar sentiments fueled her land fight. However, even though she wanted to, she could not sign the land over to us because of family restrictions on the inheritance. She asked Sun Bear if her word as a traditional Native would be good enough.

"You know I trust you Louisa. That isn't my point. Give me four days to think it over," he asked.

Sun Bear continued to vacillate. He knew it was good land, but he was concerned that something could "get into" or interfere with even as fine a woman as Louisa. He had seen it happen before. I did not share his vacillation. I thought we'd never build a real community so close to a city, particularly a gambling one.

There were too many distractions. I liked Louisa's land. It didn't make me feel as much at home as land farther north, but it seemed a good location.

On the third night after we left Louisa, I dreamed for the first time of that old grandmother I had seen in Sacramento and in the garden. It was wonderful to see her again. In the dream she told me Louisa needed my help in her project. The Grandmother also said that Louisa's project was one that would truly assist her. What she did not say was that we should move to Louisa's land.

Telling Sun Bear the dream, I interpreted it as though the Grandmother had said to move there. I was that sure taking Louisa's offer was the only logical and right thing to do. Sun Bear looked at me skeptically as I gave my interpretation.

"Are you sure that's what she said?" he asked me.

"Pretty much so," I hedged.

"Well, you've convinced the council circle we should move. Now you have spirit support for our relocating. It looks like we'll move there," he said.

I was elated until he continued.

"Wabun, I have a strong feeling this is a fork off the road of my vision. But since you obviously need the lessons waiting on this fork, I'm going to take it."

The council made its plans for moving and building. Sun Bear and I would stay in Sun Valley, going to shows or working on the magazine, until we could move equipment and inventory to the new land. Everyone else except Anna, Alex, Cindy, and the kids would go start building.

It was almost spring, and the members of our circle had the resurgent strength that comes at that time of year. Plans moved quickly. Nimimosha packed her things, sold her trailer, bought a tent, and headed up to join the others.

The day after she left, a woman arrived to join us. As soon as I saw her, little bells jangled along all my nerve endings. Her name was Trudy, and she had met Sun Bear when he was at a California pow wow alone. She had helped with the booth, and he had invited her to join us whenever she could. He had somehow forgotten to inform me of the invitation.

Seeing her, I could understand why his memory had lapsed. She had come from Los Angeles where she made her living designing and making moccasins for the Beverly Hills set. She looked the part. She was tall and fashionably slender. She had those dark, sultry Mediterranean looks that made me think she had Indian blood. She wore tight-fitting jeans, with a matching short jacket, a silk blouse, and brand new cowgirl boots. Her thick dark hair was casually coiled in a beaded barrette.

How I wished Sun Bear would come home with a road-kill deer for her to butcher! But I had the feeling she'd find some way to get out of it. Like most average women, I felt immediately outclassed by someone who is beautiful. I was sure such women lived in a rarefied world of luxury, privilege, and chivalry I could only imagine.

Within minutes it was clear Trudy had come here wanting to relate to Sun Bear. This was my worst nightmare coming true. The word nightmare made me remember the Gayla dream. In a flash I knew this had to be the form Gayla had assumed. Now that I thought about it, she did look like the woman in the dream.

To my disappointment, Sun Bear arrived without anything to butcher. But he had a wide smile when he saw Trudy. When he turned away, I would have sworn she scowled at me. With that, my torture began.

Trudy was everything I felt I wasn't: delicate, feminine, sweet, subservient, naturally coquettish, capable of vast adoration, and experienced in the psychic arts. No matter how I acted, she was sweet to my face. From others, I heard this was not the case behind my back. Her sweetness infuriated me. Her subservience to Sun Bear enraged me. Her lack of intellectual depth increased my feeling of contempt toward her.

She was the woman I could not be, and the kind of woman I abhorred. She was the heroine of every romance novel, living only for love and her man. She knew nothing of feminism, nor of psychology and the daemonic, or shadow, energy she so oozingly represented. What's more, she didn't seem to care. She had her man, her clothes, her cosmetics, and her tarot cards. What more, she'd ask me, could she need?

She was inordinately attracted to Sun Bear, and he to her. I watched, feeling helpless, as she wove her web around him. When she took her oath to the Tribe, Sun Bear named her Spider Woman. In Southwestern Native myths, Spider Woman is one of the creating forces of the universe. While I thought Black Widow Woman would have been a better name, Spider Woman—in its common rather than mythological usage—seemed appropriate enough.

After hearing about it for two years, I knew Sun Bear believed people could be capable of loving more than one person. Overcome with jealousy, I certainly could not agree. I thought, once again, of leaving and returning to New York.

Occasionally I would try to tell Sun Bear that Spider Woman was the person I had seen in my dream, but he didn't seem very interested in my opinion. We definitely were not in one of the more friendly periods of our relationship.

Sun Bear took Spider Woman up to help with the new place, feeling that the more space between us, the better. At first I was happy with his decision. It meant I would not have to see her hated lovely face for a while, and that Sun Bear wouldn't get to see it either. Then reports started coming back to me from Nimimosha about Spider Woman's behavior. To put it mildly, she was not proving to be a unifying force in the community. As soon as Sun Bear left, she threw herself at Running Deer. Then she started in on Larry, then on Joseph. She seemed determined to have every man, available or not, on her string.

After I heard from Nimimosha, I couldn't wait to pass the word on to Sun Bear. But Mosha phoned late in the evening, and I fell asleep before Sun Bear returned. That night I dreamed of a web around Sun Bear. The web got tighter and tighter, choking the energy out of him. Then a voice I didn't recognize told me that Spider Woman also means Changing Woman, and that I should keep very aware of what was happening with Sun Bear's vision.

Because of that dream, I decided to keep my own council about what Mosha had said. Instead of complaining about Spider Woman, I tried to engage Sun Bear in speaking about his vision and medicine, something he had not been doing very much lately. Try as I might, I could not get him interested in talking about either of these areas. That really worried me.

He stayed around Sun Valley for a while to go to a show at which we had a booth, then he went back to the land to see, he said, how things were going. But I heard the only thing he really checked out was Spider Woman. She, of course, stopped flirting with anyone else as soon as he appeared, and denied allegations that she had ever done so. She claimed such talk was just the result of women who were jealous of her. And the men seemed hesitant to come forth and tell the chief they had been coveting his new love.

What hurt me most was that Sun Bear seemed to be treating Spider Woman in the way I had always wanted him to treat me. He seemed entranced with her; he was devoted, romantic, and even jealous. Before she came, I had begun to believe it wasn't my fault Sun Bear couldn't express himself in those ways; rather, I had convinced myself that these were qualities foreign to his nature. Now I watched him giving her everything I longed to have. It wasn't fair! I had done so much for him and his vision; she had done nothing. Yet she was getting all the goodies, and I was getting only reassurances that I was a good woman and a great helper. When my jealousy overcame my control, I wasn't even getting that.

I really wanted to leave. It was too painful to watch Sun Bear with Spider Woman. I would have left, except I had given *my* word to Louisa that I *personally* would help her with her land fight. Aside from that, I had pushed hard for this move to the land, and I was really curious to see how it affected the Tribe. Would being on the land make a community function better? If I left now, I would never know. I was looking forward to learning more about gardening and preserving food this summer. That would be hard to do back in New York. In addition, I really liked most of the people living with us now. If it weren't for my having to see Sun Bear fawning over Spider Woman, I had to admit I didn't really want to leave.

In order to stay, it seemed like the only logical thing to do was withdraw my interest from Sun Bear. That was about as easy for me as giving up drugs is for an addict. I was hooked on my idea of what our relationship should be, and a little thing like cold reality wasn't going to change my mind.

I kept hoping Sun Bear would see how Spider Woman acted around other men, or realize how uninterested he had become in his own medicine. It didn't happen. He seemed blind to her faults and to the effect she had upon him, as blind as I was to the real relationship I had with Sun Bear.

As it has the habit of doing, even when we are busy creating emotional chaos, life went on. The frame of the house was filled in, everything in Nevada was packed, the trailer was sold, and the move to Louisa's land was completed. We went to shows and pow wows, and even sponsored a very successful craft show in Sacramento.

When I actually got to the land, our new dwelling was quite a shock. It didn't have plumbing! I had known we couldn't afford a septic tank and a well, but the reality of living without a shower or indoor toilet was a lot harder than the idea. It was even worse than the pow wow trail because it was going to go on longer. We had an outhouse and what we, like our grandparents, euphemistically called "honey buckets." These we dumped in our own land-fill, strategically located a safe distance from both the house and the irrigation ditch. At council we decided to rotate this task, a decision that pleased me. It meant Spider Woman would have to take her turn. I kept hoping she'd trip.

Obviously, Spider Woman did not engender loving thoughts within me, but I succeeded then in keeping them under control. I had plenty of work to help me. Besides the magazine, the mail, and working with Louisa, there was community and property building. At this point in the Bear Tribe's development, community building consisted largely of meeting together in council whenever a problem arose. With Spider Woman's help, problems were a daily occurence. She seemed to thrive on subterfuge and emotional chaos. Because Sun Bear claimed not to believe people's allegations about her, it was impossible to come to any consensus about how to deal with her. She had virtual immunity, and she used it to the fullest. Circles that went round and round accomplishing nothing seemed to take up far too much of my time.

Even though the move was complete, there was still a lot of building to be done on the land. We wanted a chicken coop, a root cellar, and a building for food and tool storage. We also wanted to grow, gather, and preserve as much of our food as possible that year. It seemed as if every person in our council circle—which then numbered thirteen adults and two children—had a different fantasy of what self-reliant country living should be, and we were trying to fulfill them all at the same time. That resulted in physical as well as emotional chaos.

There were bright moments for me in this largely gloomy time. One was when Ruth came to visit, and blessed our new home and gardens. Another was when Sun Bear discovered one of the old ranchers in the area was married to one of his grade school teachers. That meant more acceptance and help from the old-timers in the region. They had previously been referring to our building efforts as "The Hippie Hilton resort."

A week or so after that connection, another farmer brought us some geese as a "good-will gift." Those critters definitely turned out to be a mixed blessing. There were six of them and they were full-grown so we had to let them wander. Geese are very territorial and they adopted the land from the house to the irrigation ditch as their territory. That meant we no longer went barefoot in the yard. The geese were particularly protective of the path between the house and the outhouse. They would run full-bore, honking and flapping, toward everyone who attempted to use it. If they caught you they would try to demonstrate how the term "goosing" originated. Basically, they were cowardly creatures and you could stare them down, but they terrorized the kids and anyone who forgot their existence at night. We eventually moved their territory to the other side of the ditch. It was that or invite them all to be the main course at an early Christmas dinner.

We built a sweatlodge and began to use it regularly. That seemed to be a really positive addition to our community life. Nimimosha brought up the horse she had pastured in Nevada, and a rancher agreed to let us use two of his horses in exchange for our pasturing them. We got a pony for the kids. The horses were nice, and Sun Bear, Mosha, and Running Deer shared their riding skills with the rest of us. The pony turned out to be as gentle as the geese, and we eventually gave him to a rancher with more training skills.

I learned a lot about natural food preservation that year. We sun dried as much as we could, laying the fruit in shallow card-board boxes, which we could bring in at night to avoid morning mist or rain. Whenever possible, we went into orchards or fields and bought less-than-perfect produce, or got permission to pick fruit or vegetables left because it was too expensive for agribusiness to harvest things that need to picked by hand. Using hand picking, we harvested enough potatoes for ourselves and all of Louisa's relatives for the winter. I liked that job because Spider Woman was working with us. There is no way to hand pick potatoes in an already-picked field without getting covered with earth. It becomes embedded under your nails and in every line and crack of your body, particularly if you are dressed only in shorts and a halter, as she was. It was obvious she didn't like being dirty, but she couldn't complain without showing Sun Bear what a cream puff she really was. I was gratified to see that she could indeed sweat, and that the perspiration made little rivulets in the dirt on her face, just as it had on mine. I knew it was mean-minded of me to take pleasure in such things, but I did. Being around her gave me a better understanding of the soldier-at-war mentality.

A couple of times that summer we went to shows or pow wows and took Spider Woman with us. Sun Bear wanted to, and I figured it was either have her drive me nuts or drive the community apart. I choose the personal problems. At least with her along I knew what she was up to. These events gave her a chance to fine-tune her ability to flirt with every man in the vicinity behind Sun Bear's back. I couldn't understand how this man, who could read most people's thoughts, could be so dumb in regard to her. Sometimes I fancied she drugged him. I would have been happy to find out that she had, simply because it would have made sense out of his otherwise unexplainable behavior.

Traveling with the two of them gave me some sympathy for every chaperone who has ever lived. I didn't just feel like a third wheel, I was one. I tried to bury myself in selling, in reading, in working hard, in talking to my friends, and in seeking out any of my teachers. Whenever Spider Woman saw me talking to someone, she would later go out of her way to charm the person. Thankfully her methods did not work on Joan, Ruth, or Louisa.

The first time Ruth saw Sun Bear with Spider Woman she asked, "What's going on there?"

"He's in love with her," I replied.

"I doubt that," Ruth responded. "But she sure does seem to have some kind of power over him."

I wanted to ask her to do something, but I knew how inappropriate that would be. She came back later and told me to try to talk with him about his medicine as much as possible. She said she wouldn't interfere, but that this whole thing was a really important lesson for him as well as me.

"You're holding up pretty well, sister," Ruth said. "I'm proud of you and I'll pray for you. Remember how important his vision is, and how important you are to it."

It was the first time she had called me sister, and I was touched. Even on the rare occasions when Spider Woman tried to be helpful to me it was usually a disaster. Feeling like a cow around her, I wanted to diet that summer. Spider Woman, who fancied herself an herbalist as well as a beauty consultant, suggested I begin by using a tea that is purported to help. Neither of us knew for sure, but she thought that she had heard the tea could be poisonous if prepared incorrectly. She told me to boil it all day to be sure to take the poison out. I know now that what I had then was a concentrate, not a tea. I chugged down an eight-ounce glass. To say it almost killed me is stretching the point only a bit. I lost a lot of weight in the next twenty-four hours as I got rid of the poison in every way I could. Spider Woman, knowing her part in this illness, was very solicitous until I recovered.

For some reason, that episode heralded a new time of testing for me. This time I got one illness after another. If I didn't have ptomaine I had inexplicably high fevers, the kind that come woven with dreams. These dreams usually were not pleasant. The recurring themes were the destruction of the earth, and the failure of Sun Bear's vision. Some of them made my New York experiences seem tame. Gayla entered my dreams in many forms, always taunting me. Spider Woman would also appear, usually accompanied by Sun Bear. Sometimes one of the three would tell me I was a fool to be committed to a vision that would never see the light.

There were days when I'd be lying there not knowing if I were dreaming, delirious, or awake. I would feel jolts of something that felt like electricity come into my body, the same as they had at that pow wow when I thought I saw Gayla. I would tremble when I felt them, and I would try to make them go away. I was convinced they were malevolent spirits sent by Gayla.

Nimimosha was always kind, and particularly helpful when I was ill. She'd sit and talk with me, bathe me with cool cloths, and make me soup and tea. She would offer to take me to a doctor but I would refuse. I'd gone to one when I started having the fevers. He had said it was a flu; rest, take aspirin, etc. I thought it was more than a flu, but I didn't believe it was a problem for which modern medicine has an answer.

Whatever the cause, I felt this bout of testing was trying to steal what little clarity or wisdom I had left, and thus destroy me. I didn't really understand why I was a target for whatever these energies were. I certainly did not see myself as being powerful enough to warrant all this attention. It was clear to me that I was fighting for my life. At the moment, I appeared to be losing. That made me very angry. Eventually the anger gave me the strength to fight even harder.

When I was feeling better, I once asked Nimimosha if she had had any similar experiences during the time she had been with Sun Bear. She said that a couple of times people—usually women—had thrown some sort of medicine on her when they figured out she was relating to Sun Bear. She'd tell Sun Bear when it happened, and he would do something to get rid of it. She'd never had anything like my seige with Gayla. She felt I was going through it because I had some special work to do that Gayla opposed.

"But what is it Mosha?" I entreated.

"I wish I knew, Wabun," she replied. "I think if you understood it, all this negative business would stop. All I can figure out is that it probably has something to do with women, and something to do with emotions. And that's just my feeling, not based on anything in particular. I know you are a special sister, and I know you're strong enough to get through this, whatever it is."

I appreciated her vote of confidence. Eventually, I began to get stronger physically, but I was under no illusion that I'd put a stop to whatever had been happening. The dreams still came and so did the jolts. And Spider Woman was still charming Sun Bear and wrecking havoc with the Tribe. I seemed impotent to stop her. Morning Glory and Larry were the first to leave. They came to me and apologized, but said they could no longer take Spider Woman's games. Anna and Alex followed. War Dancer and George took to staying out on the pow wow circuit for longer and longer periods of time.

Did this make Sun Bear question his devotion to Spider Woman? Not that I could see. In fact, using some formula that seemed inverse to my reality, the fewer people around, the more time he allotted to her.

Honestly, I could not comprehend his actions. He certainly wasn't acting like the man I had met, or the teacher I wanted to learn from, or the visionary I loved. In fact, in my opinion, he was doing a great imitation of a moonstruck idiot, and I didn't like him that way at all.

"What did you just think?" I asked myself. I realized the irony then. Here he was acting toward Spider Woman the way I had wanted him to act toward me, and I didn't like it! Would I have changed my mind if I had been the object of his attention? I don't think so. I had fallen in love with a man with a great vision, with a real purpose to his life and actions, with a sense of vitality, and a love for challenge that comes only to those who know their true path in life. I had become enamored of this visionary and then, listening internally to all the stories I'd been told about men and women and love, I had tried to turn him into a caricature of Prince Charming, the eternal wimp. Spider Woman had succeeded in uncovering the Prince. Seeing Sun Bear in this role filled me with disgust at her, at him, and at me. I wanted the visionary back!

Following Ruth's advice, I would frequently try to engage Sun Bear in conversations about his medicine and vision. He'd answer as though by rote. The only time I'd get a spirited response would be if I brought up my doubts. At this point I was questioning why he would want a woman as his medicine helper, as this practice was different from any I'd heard of from other Native people.

He assured me that this form of apprenticeship came from a tradition older than most of them remembered.

"There is a sacred medicine that comes from male and female working together," he said. "The Old Ones knew how to build and strengthen this medicine, and how to use it to bring harmony and abundance to the earth. I only know a part of the medicine, but it is something very important to learn at this time. I know it's hard for you now, but I really want you to stick it out. We are supposed to work together, to create together. And our creation will affect many people."

The way he'd been acting lately, I didn't believe we'd have any creation, much less one that would affect many people. I stuck it out, but I told myself I did so because of my commitment to Louisa. So many people had left that those of us still there had our hands full with farming realities. I'd not put in nearly the time I intended to on Louisa's struggle, and I couldn't contemplate leaving unless I had fulfilled that commitment.

While Nimimosha, Running Deer, Cindy, Joseph, and I tried to do everything we could, Sun Bear continued to go off with Spider Woman. Sometimes they went to shows or pow wows, but sometimes they just went off traveling. I couldn't believe it. Here his vision was falling apart again and he just went off like some lovesick kid.

I knew there had to be a solution to the problem, but my own jealousy was clouding me so much I couldn't see it. During that summer I explored a very shadowy side of myself, one that could even wish ill upon another human being. I was flabbergasted when I found out such a part existed at all. Then I began to take a morbid sort of pleasure in exploring it. What evil thoughts were hidden in that crevice? What kind of curses amused me? How much ill did I really wish? What kind? If I went into that cave in my mind, could I actually imagine hurting another person? How? How did jealousy feel inside me? What had I done wrong to deserve all this?

I went off alone for these reveries. Sometimes I would find myself singing chants I knew were bad. I was revolted these could come into me as easily as healing chants. Some very strong force inside me always stopped me before I could direct these thoughts or chants at anyone. For that I am very grateful.

During these daydreams I often thought about how much I hated Spider Woman. I blamed her for taking away my chance for the happiness true love could bring. Even after my revelation about Sun Bear the man versus Sun Bear the visionary, part of me still believed that what I fantasized about him was true love. In this area my logic and ability to analyze deserted me. I felt like a starving child, constantly being teased with a cake I could not reach. I wanted that love all the songs told about. I wanted that love I saw in the movies. I wanted love that would make me whole, complete, fulfilled, and ecstatic. I wanted it, and Spider Woman seemed to be getting it. How could I not hate her?

Deep inside, I blamed everything on Gayla. Somehow it seemed to be her I was fighting most of the time, even if Spider Woman appeared to be my opponent. Fighting Gayla felt like battling a shadow. Sometimes I'd suspect everything and everyone of being connected to her. Then I wouldn't trust anyone, not even Mosha.

Over time, Spider Woman's thin veneer of liking me began to crack. When I'd ask Sun Bear about his medicine, she would scowl at me if he wasn't looking. Her scowl looked like Gayla's, at least to me. I wasn't surprised at that or at her new animosity.

I doubted anything could surprise me. I felt as if I'd been in darkness so long I'd never see the light.

One day I watched Spider Woman trimming Sun Bear's hair and was reminded of the story of Samson and Delilah. I remembered my dream about the web and was convinced Spider Woman was trying to drain Sun Bear's very life's energy from him. I told him of my concern.

He replied, "As the gift Benjamin gave you was for me, so Spider Woman's lessons are really for you."

At that point, all I could do was hope I'd survive long enough to learn them.

11

BURST OF BLUE

I was glad to see the little deaths of early autumn that year.
They matched my mood. I felt as if I were browning and
withering along with the leaves. To get away from the scene of
my discontent, I suggested Nimimosha and I go to a show in
Redding while Sun Bear and Spider Woman helped the others
hold down the fort at home. I managed not to say "for a change."

There were a few new faces at this show, and I was strangely
attracted to a couple of them. One belonged to a big, tall, mixed-
blood man. The other belonged to his pretty, dark-haired wife.
They were selling some very unusual turquoise and silver jewelry
which had been designed and made by his clan. I spent a lot of
time talking with them on set-up day. I felt they had something
to teach me. Nimimosha agreed, and covered the booth for me
as much as possible. Their names were Richard and Joyce Rainbow, and he belonged to a California tribe. They told me how
they prayed over each piece of jewelry as they made it, and prayed
at shows that each design would go to the person it could help
most. Their concept of jewelry was interesting, but that's not why
I was attracted to them. There was something more.

Saturday night they invited us to their camper after the show,
and I found out what it was. That night, and much of the early
hours of the morning, they taught us about a rainbow meditation
the Great Spirit had given to them. They had taken their names
from that vision. While in the last few years I had been learning
about Sufi things, and then Native American spirituality, I had
never studied general metaphysics. I had listened to Spider
Woman talk about her tarot and astrology readings, her

143

channeling, and her psychic impressions and, considering the source, I rated it all as gibberish. What Richard and Joyce taught was all new material to me and, because I had a burgeoning respect for them, I listened carefully to what they had to say.

It was a most magical night. The Rainbows taught us to visualize white light and rainbow light, and showed us how to use these to protect ourselves while doing psychic work. I told them I wished I had known how to do that when I was too sick or too scared to go get a smudge bowl, put in sage and sweet grass, light them, put out the flame when they were smoldering, and then cleanse myself with their smoke. Then the Rainbows guided us in the rainbow meditation. This is a beautiful visualization in which you deeply connect yourself with the energy of the earth, the sun, and the sky. You then send rainbow healing all around the Earth Mother, and out into the universe. The Rainbows did this meditation daily, and they sometimes taught it to people who were really interested.

Seeing that I was having some sort of problem, they encouraged me to do this meditation frequently and to share it with others. What a gift they gave me that night! I spent part of the next day and evening going over the meditation with them, wanting to be sure I had it right. Again they encouraged me to use it and to share it.

I began to do so immediately when I got home. The visualization had brought me so much peace and joy I was hoping it would infuse some of these qualities into the community. Apart from that, the Rainbow meditation gave me a concrete way to send my energy to the earth; a way I believe really helps with her healing. I led the rainbow meditation in the sweatlodge one night, and I felt a connection with life and the earth I never had before. Louisa even commented she felt something special during that ceremony. With variations that were given to me over time, the rainbow meditation became the Rainbow Crystal Healing Ceremony that has touched many thousands of people at Medicine Wheel gatherings and other events. In my turn, I have taught this ceremony to people who are now passing it on to others.

Meeting the Rainbows and learning this meditation were real turning points in my life. The meditation unblocked a channel for a part of my energy that had become obstructed by Spider

Woman's arrival. Seeing this, Sun Bear suggested I go to another craft show, this time accompanied only by Spider Woman. I was not thrilled by the suggestion, but I realized he was correct in saying I couldn't solve my problem with her by avoiding it. Seeing me reconsider my original answer of "no way," Sun Bear pushed on by pointing out that it would help the community if Spider Woman and I could come to some sort of understanding and equilibrium. With great reluctance, I agreed.

As the weekend approached, I regretted my decision on a daily basis. From the increasing tension I felt from her, I suspect Spider Woman did too. But we had both given our word, the booth fee had been paid, the inventory was in the car and the car-top carrier, and neither of us was going to lose face by backing down.

I had decided that while I had to work with her, I did not have to talk with her. I had vowed to myself not to say an unnecessary word to this woman, my nemesis. Apparently, she had made a similar vow. Both lasted for about an hour. Then the silence screamed between us. We began by talking about our current impasse. We'd done this many times before and now, as then, it got us nowhere.

"You're so damn beautiful," I finally sputtered, "you could have any man you want."

"You've got to be kidding," she said. With that began the first true conversation we'd had since her arrival. She admitted she could make herself look pretty by society's standards, but she told me she was anything but beautiful. She enumerated her faults. Her hips were too narrow, her buttocks sagged, she had the beginnings of varicose veins, one breast was smaller than the other, and they were both too small anyway. She had little crows feet by her eyes, and an incipient double chin. Her fingers were stubby, and her legs were too bony. While I could see none of these faults, she insisted she had them. I thought she was beautiful. In her opinion, she was a mess.

"On top of all that, my looks are my best feature. I'm not bright like you, and I can't learn how to do a lot of things quickly. I can draw, sew, and cook. I'm not well read, and I don't know another language. All I have is my looks, and they are beginning to fade. What will I be when they are gone, if I haven't managed to land a man by then? Ugly, and alone. The only reason Sun Bear likes me is because I'm pretty. That's the only reason any man has ever wanted me. Why do you think I design my own clothes? So I can cover up my faults."

I was floored. I didn't know what to say. Here was this gorgeous creature whom I thought had everything she wanted—including my man—and she thought she was a mess! I'd never had a real talk with a beautiful woman before. Talking with Spider Woman had surely shaken my fantasy that beauty automatically brings wealth, self-confidence, security, privilege, love, and happiness. This knock-out woman was telling me it wasn't so. I knew she was speaking her truth. But if someone like her couldn't be secure about her appearance, who could be?

Spider Woman's revelation shocked me as much as my own realization that I liked the real Sun Bear, the visionary, more than my fantasy Sun Bear. Not knowing what to say, and seeing that Spider Woman was primed to talk, I decided the best thing to do would be to listen. I gave her nods and "ah huhs," and sympathetic clucks that became more sincere as her story continued.

Spider Woman told me she'd never really had the opportunity to open up to a woman before and that, although she knew I could use it against her, she was going to take this chance. She said that she did like me, but that I definitely got in the way of her hooking—yes, she said hooking—Sun Bear.

"I really do love him," she contended. With my expanded understanding of "love," I believed her. "I only want what's best for him, and I know I can provide him with the best. I don't bother him about all of this silly vision business like you and the other people do. Sure he's a medicine man, but he's also a man. I know how to take care of the man. I wish he'd come away with me alone and forget this silly business about forming a group of people. I could give him everything he wants, and more."

Spider Woman began to talk about her childhood. It was a sad story. As she went on, it was painfully obvious that this was one of the first times the woman had ever opened up this much to another human being.

I wondered why she had chosen me. I finally asked her. She said she wasn't really sure. She said it felt as though something wanted her to tell me all this, but she didn't mind. Spider Woman said it felt good to be able to talk this way with someone. I was not tempted to respond in kind, nor did Spider Woman want me to.

Every time I started to say something personal, she changed the subject. She made it clear she wanted me to be the priestess for her confession, but had no interest in exchanging the roles, at least not today.

The more I listened, the closer I felt to Spider Woman. How could I have ever had bad thoughts about this delicate and vulnerable woman? All she needed was a little compassion and education about what sisterhood really was.

That feeling lasted until we got to the show. As other exhibitors entered and greeted me, she turned on her charm full strength. If they liked me, she was determined they'd love her. If I spoke to them five minutes, she'd go talk to them for ten. It seemed as though she had to have everything I had.

I felt used. How could I be comfortable with a supposed sister who acted like an archrival? I remembered why I'd always given women like her a wide berth. Try as I might, I could not now really picture myself as a friend to this vixen. She didn't know how to be a friend, and I did not really want to be the one to undertake her instruction.

Fuming and fussing, I left the booth and sought out the Rainbows. Feeling vastly put upon, I let down my usual guard and told them all about what had been happening with Sun Bear, Spider Woman, and me. I included the dreams I'd had that summer.

"Whew," Richard whistled through his teeth. "It sounds like you've had a tough time. Has Sun Bear told you about Vision Quests?"

I said he had told me about going out alone to fast and pray upon the earth, crying for a vision that would give you knowledge of your path, and your purpose in life.

Richard told me that was the most common form of Vision Quest, but that there were other ways vision could come to people. He said sometimes vision would come when a person was ill, as it had for Black Elk whose vision is preserved in the book *Black Elk Speaks*. Richard said there were times when vision would follow a period of trials, whether self imposed, or imposed by life circumstances. It was his opinion that all my tribulations may have been preparing me for some sort of visionary experience.

Richard told me that usually people who received vision in unusual ways were ones who already had made a solid connection with the earth and with the Great Spirit. And Richard added that there had to be a reason for the vision to come in a different manner. He told me to hang in. If he were right, I'd be the first to know about it.

Little of what Richard said made complete sense to me, but I felt better just being around him. I wished for the hundreth time that these Native teachers would come to some sort of agreement about how things should be. It confused me when one said vision could come to you, while another taught that you had to seek vision. Whenever I mentioned such inconsistencies to Sun Bear, he reminded me there had been about 300 different tribes on Turtle Island (a Native name for North America) before the Europeans came. Within each tribe there were clans and medicine societies, and within these were individuals who had their own visions about how to do things. A philosophy most tribes shared was that each person had the right to his or her own vision, and that no one should question the vision of another. Consequently, there wasn't one Native way of doing anything. There were many, and that, he assured me, while confusing, was good.

I went back to the booth and tried, once again, to be nice to Spider Woman. I succeeded for the rest of that day.

After the show ended Saturday night, we went back to our room. It had been a long day and we were both tired. We kicked off our shoes, switched on the television and sat watching it for a short while. Then nature called and I went to answer.

The light in the bathroom didn't seem to be working, so I left the door open a crack to enable me to see. I was settling into my task when, suddenly, there was a burst of blue that seemed to emanate like a ball from the television, then fly around the room. While that was happening, all the electricity in the room went off: lights, television, clock. I thought the television had exploded, shorting out the room. I expected to smell smoke at any minute. I jumped up off the toilet, pulled up my pants, found my shoes, and headed for the door, urging Spider Woman to join me.

"Wabun," she said calmly, "this isn't a technological event. It's a spiritual one. Someone really went out of his way to get our attention. The least we can do is sit down and see who it is and what he wants."

Given my prior experience with spirit forces, about the last thing I wanted to do was see who it was or what it wanted.

Besides, I didn't believe Spider Woman. I really thought the electricity was burning within the walls, and this was just her latest attempt to do me in. I headed for the door again.

"I'll prove I'm right," she said. "If I turn on the light switch and the television and everything comes back on, will you believe me and stay here?"

I agreed, certain things wouldn't go back on. But the lights and television did. She turned off the television, and we sat cross-legged on the floor.

"I'm going to cover myself with white light and do the rainbow meditation," I announced. I didn't want to take any chances that this was another visit from a "rider" or from Gayla or any of her henchspirits. Spider Woman agreed and I did both. Then we sat quietly.

"What am I supposed to do?" I asked after ten minutes of nothing.

"Sit and be quiet," Spider Woman said.

I was nervous and apprehensive about this whole undertaking. I would have preferred to go to the motel desk and see if we could switch to a room that didn't have blue bursts coming out of the television.

Then I heard a familiar voice singing inside my head. It was the same voice I had heard my first year on the pow wow circuit. It was the voice that had brought me six chants already that year— three for healing, two for working with animals, and one for thanking the water. It was definitely not the voice I heard singing the harmful chants. I had become used to this familiar voice, and had noted it seemed to be only interested in teaching me how to help people and the earth.

On this night, the voice gave me another chant. Like the others I had received it was made up of simple, repetitive vocal sounds that had a haunting melody when sung out loud. I began to sing the chant and Spider Woman listened until she learned it, then joined in.

While we were chanting I smelled smoke. I told Spider Woman and she sniffed. She smelled smoke too, but she said it smelled more like the smoke of cedar being burned in the smudging ceremony. Whiffs of it floated across the room. Then I heard the tingle of small bells, like the ones Native dancers wear around

their legs or arms. Without saying what it was, I pointed out the
noise to Spider Woman and asked if she heard it too. She asked
if I meant the bells.

This was getting spooky. I wanted to stop but Spider Woman
urged me to sit a while longer. I tried to relax. Then I felt as if
someone were pulling my arms, trying to put them in some particular positions. The chant started in my head again and, all at
once, I realized that something was trying to teach me a dance
that went with the chant. I relaxed and began to cooperate. When
I had learned the arm movements, I was pulled to my feet and
watched as they were moved into several different positions. I felt
what was expected of me, and I began to do the dance. It made
me feel good, as though I were actively connecting the energy of
the earth and the sky with my own energy. Spider Woman
watched, then got up and danced with me.

We sat down again and the whole process was repeated. I was
given another chant, then arm movements, then leg movements.
I danced this dance and felt as if I were celebrating the links
among all parts of life.

Again we sat. I closed my eyes. Then I saw him. I knew who he
was. In the first chant I'd ever heard, my first summer on the pow
wow trail with Sun Bear, he had told me his name. I had studied
about him since, both from books and from information learned
from Native people who knew about the work he had done. I knew
we were close here to his home country. He seemed so familiar
that he did not frighten me. I asked him what he wanted. Using
hand signs, he indicated he could not talk in words I'd understand
unless I gave him temporary use of my mind and mouth. Normally I would have refused, but this whole night had been so
sweetly magical that I gave my silent assent. I felt a momentary
intake of breath when he came in, but it wasn't jarring like the
bolts had been. Soon I was breathing fully again.

"So we meet again," the spirit whispered inside my ear. He
didn't actually speak in words. Rather, he transmitted an understanding to me that I can best explain by translating it into familiar words. "Don't worry. You know I work only for the good."

"You have been a difficult human to work with. Your clarity of
mind is so strong you made us go to extremes. You clung to your
mind whenever any energy, positive or negative, came to you.

You clung so tightly that you couldn't tell the difference between the good ones and the others. You wonder why you have had so many testings. You brought them on yourself because of your love for your mental strength.

"That strong mind wouldn't let you trust anyone, not even Sun Bear, so we couldn't get through to you with love. There is no love without trust. You are too enamored of stability to be capable of ecstatic joy. You left us little choice. We stopped shielding you for a time. But you were too stubborn even to frighten easily. So we had to allow you to go through a situation in which you'd confront your own strong negative emotions. These, we hoped, would break through the barriers your mind had created. Gayla and Spider Woman were the perfect weapons to free you from the narrow prison of perception you had constructed.

"You needed to be freed. Like all humans, you came into this world with work to accomplish. But, unlike many, you remembered this and knew you had a job to do. You've been trying to find your path since childhood. We energies that protect the earth need the assistance of humans. Whenever one begins to search, we try to give him or her all the help we can. But we can't use force. The desire must come from the human, and so must the effort to break out of the small consciousness that binds so many. It's hard for us all—energies and humans—these days when people fear vision so much.

"The earth is sick. The illness comes from the mind of man; the mind working without the heart. Man must heal the disease he has caused or he will sicken and die himself. Male is the mind. Female is the heart. It is time for the heart to help the mind, but first the heart must succor herself.

"Open your eyes and gaze upon the one with you now. In accepting her today, you opened yourself to me. She doesn't know her mind; but she knows something of her heart. Teach her, and learn from her. It is no accident you wear a female form. Learn from it. Accept it. Find your unique strengths. As you heal the breach within yourself, you will know more how to help with the healing of the planet. Daughter, your help is needed.

"I have given you the dance. It is the dance of life. Those who fear life call it by other names. The dance now will always be within your heart, pumping you full of life and vitality. As your heart beats you will remember, and you will forget. It's like the drum. *Tum-tum . . . tum-tum . . . tum-tum . . . tum-tum.* Open, close, open, close, open, close.

"You will share this dance one day and help to awaken others. It is good. Thank you for letting me in. I will leave you now. It isn't likely I'll return in this way. You have the basic knowledge you need. Your testings are not over: to be human is to challenge yourself so you can grow. You have this dance now to help you when tests come, and you have something else—more of yourself. Be at peace, daughter. Remember the dance. All of life is part of the dance."

With my next exhalation, the force was gone. I felt strangely lonely, but totally at peace. I opened my eyes again and looked at Spider Woman. I felt tremendous warmth and gratitude toward her. Without her help, I never would have had this experience. I was surprised by the petulant expression on her face, but I got up and embraced her anyway. She pulled away. I looked at her quizzically.

"Why did the spirit pick you?" she asked. "I have so much more experience with energies and spirits."

"I don't know," I answered truthfully. "But I'm sorry you feel bad."

The next morning we were both tired, having only slept for the two hours left to us after the spirit visit. We were preparing to go find coffee so we could stay awake for the show. I was looking for my shoes. I bent and looked under the bed. Lying there was a white feather. I picked it up and asked Spider Woman if it were hers.

She got very excited.

"It's only very special spirits that leave white feathers after a visit," she said. "Do you know the spirit's name?"

I did, and I told her, adding some of the information I had gleaned from my studies.

"What an honor," she said, her eyes opening wide. We decided to consider the feather a symbol of our new-found peace.

12
DANCING FOR UNITY

Spider Woman and I had one more magic time on our way back to the Tribe. I suggested we stop at some petroglyphs Sun Bear had shown me some time ago. These picture writings were on a sheer rock wall across from a lake that had been sacred to the local Native people. It was a California winter day, misty and cloudy. When we parked the car and began to walk, I started to hear chanting within my head. As I was about to ask Spider Woman if she heard anything, she turned to me and asked, "Do you hear it?"

"I hear a chant," I replied.

"So do I," she said. "Far out. Spirit is speaking to both of us at the same time."

Still not being a true believer, I asked her to sing the chant she heard. To my amazement, it was the same as what I had been hearing. As we continued our walk, the chanting also continued, although the chant changed when we neared the petroglyphs. To me, the chants sounded sad. Later I learned that a battle that resulted in the local tribe losing its land had taken place near the lake. Despite the chanting's melancholy quality, both Spider Woman and I were pleased with the psychic closeness we felt.

With the innocence of a child, she took my hand and squeezed it. She turned toward me and said, "I'm so glad we're friends. You feel like the wise older sister I never had."

Without thinking, I embraced her. Her shy smile became brilliant. I smiled back. At that moment, I could feel the drum the dancing spirit spoke about beating within my chest. *Tum-tum . . . tum-tum.* Before our recent experience together, Spider

Woman and I had been distant, now we were close; later distance would likely return. Seizing this moment when I felt warmth and acceptance towards her, I asked Spider Woman to join me in the dances we had learned. After we had danced, we decided to leave the white feather as an offering to this place. It felt to both of us as though the spirits here needed some token of human concern.

When we got back to the Tribe, Sun Bear was overjoyed to see us both, and to see we were not only speaking to, but also smiling at, each other. He acted like a mother hen who had just succeeded in making peace between two warring chicks. He asked if we'd like to have a council that night to tell people about the show. Smiling at each other because we realized just how much we had to tell, Spider Woman and I agreed we wanted a council. The three of us began to unpack the car. Soon Nimimosha and Running Deer came to help us. A few minutes later, both Sun Bear and Spider Woman disappeared. I realized at that moment that even though some things had changed, others were very much the same.

A few days after our return, Sun Bear went off with Louisa to talk about her land battle at a meeting of a national Indian organization. Spider Woman and I went to another show that weekend. We did work well together on the shows, bringing a good booty into the tribal treasury. The following week the three of us went off together to a show in San Francisco. It had become clear to me by then that what my new-found alliance with Spider Woman meant was that I now knew my character as chaperone: to Spider Woman I was the spinster older sister; to Sun Bear I was the business manager and, of course, the medicine helper.

On this trip Spider Woman began to take it upon herself to beautify me. I suspected she hoped this would help me find a suitable mate, and thus get me out of her picture. I have found that stunning women, when given the opportunity, truly enjoy fixing up the few plainer women who dare to become their friends. One of them told me it was like having a live doll to dress and groom, but that it was a lot more fun because the results were so much more noticeable than a change of clothes on Barbie. More than that, it is an opportunity for beautiful women to share a skill they have perfected. Like everyone else, such women enjoy demonstrating their talents.

The first morning of the show, Spider Woman asked if she could fix my hair and do my makeup. Since my makeup for the past three years had been lip gloss, I agreed, curious to see how I'd look now in societal warpaint. She was good and, after the initial shock, I liked the results. So did a number of men coming through the show. That helped to restore my faltering ego. I was surprised to see I still remembered how to flirt, even if my heart really wasn't in it.

No, my heart still belonged to Sun Bear, whether or not he wanted it. I was sure if I were patient enough he would get over whatever his attraction was to Spider Woman, and realize that I truly was his love. Whenever I would catch myself thinking such thoughts, I'd berate myself for having them. Hadn't I realized I loved the visionary more than the Prince Charming? Yes, I had. Didn't I hold Spider Woman in contempt for similar ideas? Certainly I did. Wasn't I being stupid then for wishing for something I really didn't want? Most assuredly.

Then I'd be overcome with a fantasy of Sun Bear, as Rhett, carrying me, as Scarlett, up the sweeping staircase, promising to banish all thoughts, all objections. But what about all the work I'd done to understand that such fantasies were not only fairytales but also, and more important, society's way of always keeping women in an inferior place? I'd remember all I had learned, often at great personal expense, and would be disgusted with myself. Wasn't I a strong individual, capable of standing alone? It seemed so. Didn't I value my individuality and independence? That I did. Didn't I realize that no one else—mythical Prince Charming included—could change me; that I had to banish my own thoughts and quell my own objections? Hesitatingly, and with a sigh, I did.

I was constantly on the horns of a real dilemma. I'd been repeatedly told by family, friends, teachers, ads, stories, novels, movies, and plays that men and marriage were my only real salvation. I vacillated between wanting to believe it was so, and seeing evidence all around me that certainly indicated it was not. In my fleeting moments of clarity about this mire, I realized I was not obsessed with Sun Bear as much as I was obsessed with the concept of having a conventional relationship. I was obsessed with the concept, but I didn't want the reality. Otherwise I would not have shown the consummate irony I had in choosing to explore this area of life with the least likely potential husband I'd ever met.

That weekend I began to realize that being flirtatious was more fun than being a shrew. So I let Spider Woman dress me up and prayed for more clarity about my feelings, or at least additional patience with the situation at hand.

Patience came, but clarity didn't follow. I appreciated the patience, however, because additional tests soon presented themselves. After the experience with the dancing spirit, the "lightning bolt" night attacks seemed to step up. I continued to use what the Rainbows had taught me and cover myself with white or rainbow light every night, and whenever I felt the "bolts."

One night a particularly strong one struck, making me tremble for quite some time before I stiffened up. I heard a male voice say, "What you are doing won't do any good. I'll take the white light out of you." I covered myself and the house with light, then, just to be sure, I went and woke Sun Bear and asked him to make certain everything was okay. He said it was, although it didn't seem so to me. I hated these nighttime attacks because I couldn't figure out what to do about them. Having had them for as long as I had, I knew they really couldn't do me irreparable harm or they already would have. But they sure did make me nervous, confused, and angry.

I couldn't understand why, if the spirits had gotten through to me, the tests had to continue. When I asked Sun Bear this question, he suggested there might be some areas in which I was still blocking the good energies and spirits that wanted to work with me. Reluctantly, I had to agree that was a possibility, but I certainly had no idea how to change the situation. I asked Sun Bear to tell me what to do. He said this was one problem I needed to figure out myself. He suggested that I might benefit from spending more time with the earth.

Since it was winter and the farm was taking up less of my time, I followed his advice. I really enjoyed the winter walks as long as I bundled up warmly enough. On one of these walks I decided that this day was as good a time as any to begin keeping my word to Louisa. Beginning with that decision, I threw myself into her land fight with all the energy my frustration with Sun Bear evoked—a considerable amount. She had already made some progress in her efforts since we had moved to her land, largely because of Sun Bear's ability to speak on her behalf. Now I was determined to see her make a lot more progress.

I figured that to get the land for her traditional camp, Louisa needed publicity and money. I saw no problem in obtaining either item. Cash could buy publicity that didn't come free, travel, and any legal fees. On our next trip to San Francisco, I began to utilize my public relations skills. I arranged for Sun Bear to speak about Louisa's efforts on public radio, and to the alternative papers in town. That got the publicity moving. Then I called a few classmates from Columbia and got the story on the local news and even on a network news show. I made arrangements for Louisa to be interviewed on several talk shows in the following month.

While we were at an Indian and Western show that weekend, I went around to the dealers and got them to donate merchandise to Louisa's cause. With Sun Bear's help I arranged for an auctioneer to do a benefit auction of the donated items at the same time Louisa would be in the city appearing on radio and television. We even got a large hotel to donate the use of a ballroom for the auction. That took care of the immediate need for money.

A month later, while Louisa was packing for the trip to San Francisco, she decided to take some of the best craft items she had made and add them to the auction items. I urged her to keep these items because they were so intricate and beautiful. She told me, "Good, they'll bring a better price then. The land is more important to my people than these are to me. I can make more crafts. Only the Earth Mother can make more land."

Being in San Francisco with Louisa and Sun Bear was like taking a couple of seven-year-olds to an amusement park. While Sun Bear was very city-wise, Louisa was not. Her ingenuous excitement was contagious to him. He wanted to show her everything. They "Ho'd" and "Ah'd" their way through Fisherman's Wharf, Nob Hill and the cable cars, Golden Gate Park, Fleischaker Zoo and Aquarium, Chinatown, Ghiradelli Square, North Beach, Coits Tower, Union Square, and the Presidio. Since Louisa was dressed in her usual wing-tip or ribbon dress, and since Sun Bear and I were both wearing the ribbon shirts she had made us for the occasion, we drew attention everywhere we went. Louisa loved it. She had an ever-fresh audience for tales of her people and the story of her land fight. I enjoyed watching her captivate most of her listeners.

She talked so much I was afraid she'd be hoarse for her press interviews. When I told her about my concern, she smiled and said, "Little sister, do you know how many years it has been since

I've had so many young people who wanted to hear my stories? Don't worry, I have years and years of words saved up."

These impromptu talks seemed to fire up both Louisa and Sun Bear. They were convincing, charming, and sincere on all the radio and television programs. One host said, "It's a good thing you two didn't meet the pilgrims at Plymouth Rock, or we'd all be back in England, and probably wearing buckskins and braids."

The benefit auction was a success. Because of the interviews, it was well attended, and people were generous in their bids. Louisa figured she now had enough money to carry on her fight at least for the next year, even if she had to hire some attorneys to help. Then it turned out that one of the people attending the auction was a very good lawyer who was more than happy to donate his time to Louisa's cause.

With a big smile she turned to me and said, "Then we'll do what Sun Bear suggested, and use some of this money to have a good, old-time Unity Meeting on the land this summer. We'll get some really powerful medicine people to come and make prayers there. Then there's no way that lumber company can keep from giving us that land."

On our way back home, we stopped in the Sacramento Japanese restaurant sometimes frequented by Governor Brown. Sun Bear had bet Louisa dinner that she couldn't eat with chop sticks. To my surprise, and Sun Bear's delight, the governor himself was at the restaurant that night. In our usual not-so-inconspicuous way, we were able to get his attention, and Louisa had a few minutes to tell him about her cause. He listened sympathetically, and said he would help if he could.

This chance encounter made us realize a little lobbying would be in order. Within a few weeks I had the opportunity to set things up in that regard because I needed to go east on personal business. I spent quite a bit of time in the New York area, and used part of it to get some national publicity arranged about Louisa's efforts. I was hoping that both Sun Bear and Louisa would come to appear on shows and do interviews. However, Louisa wasn't willing to leave home for that long a trip, and she wasn't really anxious to see "The Big Apple."

"I saw one city," she told me on the phone. "That's enough."

I reminded her of the fun she had had, hoping to change her mind.

"Seeing my first city was fun because everything was new. In my second city, it won't be new."

I told her New York was very different from San Francisco. She didn't believe me.

"It's body might be different, but its heart will be the same," she said.

Sun Bear came alone, and we had a good press conference about the situation, which lead to some other interviews. When these were completed, we headed to Washington, D.C. to talk with the press there and to Louisa's representatives in congress. This part of the trip was successful enough that an administrative assistant in her congressman's office drew up a bill that would arrange a U.S. Forest Service exchange of land with the lumber company, then a transfer of the land from the Forest Service to Louisa. It appeared it would just be a matter of time until Louisa had her traditional camp. And that meant I would have kept my word to her. Then I would be free to leave if I were not happy with the situation with Sun Bear and his Tribe.

When we returned home, I was glad to see everyone again. In our absence Cindy and Joseph had had a "mysterious" disagreement, and she had left with the children. Later Nimimosha confirmed my feeling that Spider Woman was the cause of the disagreement. Apparently she had been consoling herself with Joseph in Sun Bear's absence. But she was not about to admit it, and neither was he. I wondered how the consolation prize would feel now that the first place winner had returned. Not wishing to disrupt the tentative harmony Sun Bear and I had achieved on the road, I kept my mouth shut.

Louisa was very happy to hear all about the trip, and to see the news clippings I had brought back for her. While we had been away, she had been busy planning the Unity Meeting for the land. With Nimimosha's help she had issued invitations to medicine people from all around the country. Quite a number had agreed to come.

While Sun Bear and Spider Woman once again enchanted each other, I had my work cut out for me getting food and entertainment donated for the meeting.

When I had procured the things we would need, Louisa suggested that she and I spend a night on the land, fasting and praying for the success of the meeting that was about to happen.

I was honored she asked me to join her. I had frequently been to the land Louisa hoped to get, especially when I needed inspiration for her efforts. The land usually gave me what I sought, as well as a feeling of peace and hope. I was looking forward to a night-long experience there.

Louisa and I both had ceased eating the night before we went to the land. We had agreed to talk until sunset, but then to refrain from talking until the sun rose the following day. That afternoon we discussed our progress, and Louisa's future plans. She showed me where she wanted each part of the permanent camp to go: the tepees, the longhouse, the gardens, the sweatlodge. We decided to camp for the night by the river, where the sweatlodges would be built. We made prayers aloud as the sun was setting, then settled into our own quiet space, out of each other's view.

I spent my first hours watching the shapes of things change as the twilight deepened. Then, when my eyes could no longer see the banquet of colors and shapes so clearly, my ears took over. I heard the wind whistle and sigh through the evergreens; the loud cry of the nighthawk, the strange "whoosh" of her wings folding; the "buzz" of mosquitos looking for a bedtime snack; and the unidentifiable snaps and crackles of the forest floor. An owl flew by *hoo, hoo, hoo*ing. In the distance, the coyotes called and sang.

Then the moon, waxed to three-quarters, rose and bathed the dark landscape in her silvery luminescence. My eyes and ears began a friendly competition, before agreeing to work in concert. I became aware of my skin, and the wind gently caressing it. I reached out my hand and began to feel the moss on a nearby rock. It felt so soft I got goose bumps, and I wanted to touch more. I stood and put my back against a grandmother fir, tall and majestic. I felt the slight movement of the trunk as the gentle wind blew through her top. I sensed the sap, her lifeblood, flowing slowly through the wood. The wind was blowing on my face, the tree was supporting my back, the moon was bathing my eyes, the coyote chorus was filling my ears when, suddenly, the "bolts" began to strike.

They caught me off guard, so I couldn't stiffen up immediately. Nor did I think my usual, "Oh, no, I've got to do something." They were so unexpected I just let them wash over me. And that's all they did: wash over me. Because I was relatively free of tension, confusion, anger, and mind games, there was nothing they could attach themselves to. Make no mistake. They tried to. But now, for the first time, I didn't help them. This time I didn't have to mentally call the white light; already it was surrounding me.

A real battle was taking place between me and whatever force the "bolts" represented. I had the sense I was finally going to win. I knew I was more protected than I had ever been before. The bolts kept coming. I continued to let them flow over me. I prayed to be part of the goodness and beauty all around me and so be impervious to any negativities that attacked. My prayer was answered. The bolts stopped attacking. I was no longer the easy target I had been.

The flow of life, of energy, around and within me continued. It probably was always there, but now I was exquisitely aware of it. It became a rather pleasant sensation that seemed to connect me with all I saw, heard, felt, and sensed. Strong sensations elude words. the best description I can give is that my body began to melt into everything around it. Then, not moving, I began to dance. My heart was the drum, my breath the connector. I felt wonderful; stronger, freer, and less limited than I ever had before. That dance could have taken a minute, an hour, or the whole night.

First light came and blended with the mist rising off the river, making everything look primeval. I felt as if I were witnessing the dawn of creation as light infused the scene around me. When the sun rose, tears of joy replaced words. The mist thinned then disappeared, and everything was bathed in golden light. I made truly heartfelt prayers that morning. Some even had words.

When Louisa came to the river, all I could do was embrace her and hope my eyes could express what my words could not.

"The Earth Mother touched you here," she said. "You are fortunate, and I'm glad. You have been such a help to me in this project that I pray will help her."

I was happy too. I felt more in touch with myself and the earth than I ever remembered having felt before. The feelings the night engendered stayed with me, on and off, for most of the next week. It made the last-minute preparations for the Unity Meeting a lot easier. In quiet moments my mind tried to analyze what had happened that night, but it kept being checkmated by my body, which would respond to this analysis by producing more sensations that defied definition. These events planted within me a seed of respect for my body. Until that time I had looked upon it as a tool of my mind, not as an organism that was as much a part of me as my constant thoughts.

Sure I had had sensations before, but I didn't look upon them as real until my mind could explain them in words. I was very much out of touch with my body. Consequently, I felt few compunctions about abusing it through various excesses. It would be quite a few years before the seed of respect planted then blossomed to the point where I would truly learn to care for myself. Then the best I could do was realize that the more I respected my body, the more I respected the earth, and vica versa.

The Unity Meeting itself was a good success. Almost 400 people attended, including Ruth, the Coyotes, and the Rainbows, along with an Iroquois elder, a Navajo medicine man, a Cree medicine woman, and two medicine men from the Lakota Nation. Louisa's son John showed up and brought some of his radical friends. That caused some tension because they vocally objected to Sun Bear and some of the other Indians there who worked with non-Natives, but with Louisa and so many elders present, they behaved.

There was a lot of prayer and ceremony that weekend, as well as some serious councils around the fire. There were moments of entertainment and fun. The people in the Tribe, with the help of Louisa's daughters, had made enough venison stew for everyone to eat the first night. We barbecued most of a cow to feed people the second night. We also had food people could take to cook for their other meals. We ended the event with a giveaway to the people attending. By then I felt as though there was a foundation for real unity among everyone there, and I definitely believed the land for Louisa's camp would be forthcoming. Many of the medicine people prayed for rain during the gathering and, four days after it ended, the rains came. Native people say that rain coming at the end of an event, or four days later, shows that the Great Spirit is happy with what has transpired.

During the gathering, the Iroquois elder took me aside and told me she had seen how much work I was doing to help Louisa and to help the earth. She told me I was doing very good work, and that I should keep it up. Then she reminded me of the prophecies of her people that speak of the time of earth changes, and of things people can do to lessen their severity. She told me I was very fortunate in learning as much as I had about Native culture and ways, and about the earth. She admonished me that it was now my responsibility to share what I had learned with my own people, the non-Native inhabitants of this continent. I was very honored by this acknowledgment, but did not have a clear idea of how I was to fulfill her instructions. That part of my vision, in slowly unfolding stages, would come later.

I was pleased with the success of the Unity Meeting, and glad I had been able to be of help to Louisa. Now the gardening and pow wow seasons were upon us and I knew that these, along with the community, would take up most of my energy. Fortunately, some of the people from the Unity Meeting decided to stay and work with the Tribe for a while, which meant we got our gardens planted on time.

I decided I'd be happier this summer if I let Spider Woman accompany Sun Bear to many of the pow wows and shows while I stayed home to work with the community. Although the Tribe was once again reduced in size, I was still hopeful that I could help the community aspect of Sun Bear's vision become reality. I wanted to do so. Over time I had been realizing that I understood and shared Sun Bear's feelings that people had to learn to live together in self-sufficient communities. I knew now from my own experience that the lifestyle of the dominant society was too cut off from nature, and from any aspect of human nature except the mental. This set people in constant competition with each other, and with all other species. The closer I became to the earth, the more I realized land-based communities could be wonderful learning places for contemporary people. But it seemed really hard to get together a group of any size that could live in harmony and, therefore, be an example, a beacon to show people another way of being.

It seemed so hard to get a group together that the challenge of it increasingly interested me. After all, people had lived in tribal communities for untold thousands of years. If they could do so successfully, why couldn't we? It seemed to me that most of the communities succeeding then (and there weren't that many) were formed around one or two strong leaders who decreed the actions for the other members. I thought of these as "guru-centered communities" and, while they definitely helped some people, I wasn't interested in seeing the Bear Tribe become one. For one thing, I thought there were enough gurus around. Sun Bear didn't need to become another one. For another, the fact that most community leaders were men rankled my feminist spirit. From what he told me when he'd still talk about community, Sun Bear wasn't interested in becoming a guru. He said that Native communities stressed the sacredness of each person's vision, and the importance of the council circle. Neither vision nor the circle would be strengthened in any sort of authoritarian setting.

If the Bear Tribe wasn't to be guru centered, it seemed as if there were few guidelines to help us formulate a plan for successful community. Trial and error seemed the only option, so we took it. I, of course, was the community thinker and philosopher. I was always watching to see what seemed to work, and what did not. For many years I found a lot more did nots. It wasn't that people didn't want to live in harmony; they just didn't know how to do it. I could understand that: I had enough trouble keeping myself in reasonable accord. People came to the community that summer, and most of them went on. It discouraged me, but Sun Bear would sometimes remind me that everyone had to find their own path, and the Bear Tribe wasn't the path for everyone. I agreed with that, but I kept hoping we could find twelve of us, plus Sun Bear, who could live in harmony. At that point I was certain twelve plus founder was the magic number. After all, it had been used many times in history.

I did leave the community a couple of times that summer. Once was to go to a pow wow I'd missed for the past three years. Sun Bear spoke highly about it, and felt it would be of special interest to me. It was on an Oregon reservation where many of the people kept to their old religious practices. These included a form of dance. I was privileged to be able to attend one of their services during the pow wow. While the dance was different from the one I had been given, it engendered similar feelings within me. It inspired me to begin dancing daily. Nimimosha always joined me. Sometimes other people did too.

Nimimosha and I began dancing daily on July 3 of that year. On July 4, Nimimosha conceived a child. She waited a while to be sure, and then shared her wonderful news with me. Together we welcomed this new being coming to the Tribe, and asked the child to join in the dance with us. We also joked about it being one sure way to increase the size of the community.

A month before we had added a new four-legged one to the community, also kidding about that being a way to increase membership. The four-legged was a three-month-old black half-shepherd, half-labrador puppy. We named her Tsacha, which I had read means "she dog" in a Canadian Indian language. I'd so much missed having a dog around that I hogged Tsacha's time and she became "my" dog. As a young dog Tsacha reminded me of Zachary, the dog I'd given my parents, in the scope of her bad habits, though the forms differed. Tsacha was a car, truck, and horse chaser, a chicken killer, and a goose terrorist. Now no one objected to the last habit, as long as she didn't maul, but everyone objected to the chicken killing. Tsacha wore a chicken necklace for a while and let the feathered ones alone afterwards. None of us ever succeeded in breaking her of the car, truck, and horse chasing. Eventually I let her know she could keep chasing, but it would probably cut down on her life span. She did keep chasing until she was about twelve. Then advancing age slowed her down.

The week after Nimimosha's happy announcement, I accompanied Sun Bear to a show an old friend of ours arranged. On the way back, in the shadow of Mount Shasta, both Sun Bear and I saw what looked like a white wolf standing by the side of the road. It was a magnificent animal. We stopped to get a better look, and I opened my car door just in case. When we stopped, the animal loped over to the car and jumped through Sun Bear's open window. He settled himself on the inventory boxes on the back seat and gave one or two wags of his beautiful tail. He looked at us as if to say, "Well, aren't we going to get moving?" We were miles from any human habitation so we figured if the animal had belonged to someone, he had gotten lost. Besides, it really seemed as though he had been waiting for us.

That big white dog was Shasta, who became Sun Bear's famous medicine dog, and my dear friend. When we got him home he and Tsacha acted like long-lost buddies. He was obviously an older, more experienced animal but he had infinite patience with Tsacha's puppy ways. She developed the habit of chasing him and nibbling on his back legs. He let her. Although they would pounce and fight, Shasta and Tsacha were fiercely loyal to each other. In that way they reminded me of Sun Bear and myself.

13

BACK ON THE TRAIL

By August our gardens were growing nicely. So was the community. People still came and went but we had a core of eight adults that seemed pretty solid and, as I frequently reminded myself, eight was close to thirteen. A few months earlier, Joseph had gone to visit Cindy. They worked through their disagreement, and she returned with the children. On their return they asked to become members of the Tribe. When they took the oath, Joseph was given the name Star Marker because of his interest in both astronomy and astrology. Cindy became Wild Rose because of her herbal knowledge. The children were named Goldenstar and Little Beaver. With the exception of time spent at a couple of special pow wows, War Dancer had taken up residence. Nimimosha and the child within her, Running Dear, Spider Woman, Sun Bear, and myself completed our circle.

Since Spider Woman and I had made peace the previous winter, the emotional chaos that marked much of the previous year had been much reduced, except for the period when Sun Bear and I were in the east working for Louisa. I'd made a large mental note that the community tended to expand and solidify more in the absence of chaos. Relative calm allowed us to spend more council time making plans, and less working on personal problems that usually proved unsolvable.

During our last Earth Renewal ceremonies we had put prayer markers and the concommitant circle of protection around the land. Since then it had come alive under our care. The gardens were fruitful, and so were the wild plants and animals. Even the stones seemed to shine brighter. Our nonhuman relations love it when we pay them some attention. I was responsible for the eastern prayer marker, and I loved to go to the eastern boundary of the land to make cornmeal offerings and sing the chants that kept coming to me. I had received several more chants this year, and my understanding of them was growing. Some chants were literally songs of a place. I would hear them in my travels, and I knew I was to use my voice to sing them aloud. Often I would not remember them later. That seemed appropriate since those chants seemed to belong to the particular area where I heard them.

Some chants were for a purpose: healing, honoring an element, working, or calming an animal. Most of these I would remember. I was consistently amazed that chants came to me, who has the voice of a frog: croaking, deep, and sometimes disharmonious. It is the sort of voice a Christmas choir director once listened to for one stanza of "Silent Night," and then assigned me a nonsinging shepherd role. The fact that I'd never had a musical talent made it very difficult for my mind either to explain away or take credit for these chants.

Although I was only occasionally in touch with the earth in anywhere near the way I had been that night on Louisa's land, the pleasure of these rare occasions was enough to keep me walking outdoors, hoping for more. During my walks I'd keep my mind happy with learning to classify and describe various aspects of nature. I was just beginning to get a sense of place—of connection and rootedness with this piece of land—then it was time for the Omak Stampede and the Chief Seattle Days Celebration. Because both of these events were usually very busy, Sun Bear asked me to accompany him and Spider Woman. Since these were two of my favorite shows, I agreed. We left a week early to do a pow wow in Seattle, then drove on to the Stampede. I was glad I attended this event because I had the opportunity to talk there with a man who is active in another form of ancient religious practice that also centers around dance and drum.

After the Stampede, we decided to drive around the Northern Cascades until Chief Seattle Days began, hoping to wholesale some inventory to shops there. I was in my mountain element, and very much at peace with myself and the world. Consequently, I couldn't understand the feeling of danger that struck me late one afternoon. We had checked into the "family suite" at one of our usual economy motels. I was in my bedroom when this feeling came. It was so strong it really scared me. I looked around the room, smelled for gas, looked out the window at magnificent Mount Baker to make sure no plumes of smoke were coming from its top. Finally, stumped, I called out to Sun Bear.

We met in the kitchen. From the look on his face, I knew something was bothering him too.

"I have this sudden sense of danger," I told him.

"So do I," he replied.

Together we went over a list of possible physical dangers. We ruled those out. Then we considered possible earth changes in the area, but it didn't feel like that was what was happening either. We sat in silence for a while. Then, almost at the same time, we both said, "Something's wrong at home."

Economy motels don't have room phones. We went to the closest phone booth and called. Our premonition was very right. Shortly before we phoned, Louisa's son John and three of his radical friends—two Indian and one white—had come to the house. Finding Nimimosha, Running Deer, and War Dancer at home, they told them that they now knew what we were doing to Louisa.

"What are you talking about?" War Dancer asked.

"We know you all have been stealing money from Louisa," John said.

"What!" Nimimosha exclaimed, knowing that I had raised more money for Louisa than she had ever had raised before.

"She won't admit it, but we know it's the truth," John said with what Mosha described as a strange, ugly look on his face. "You've got the old woman hypnotized or something, but we can see right through all of you. You're up to no good. You're stealing her money just like you stole our land and our culture. That's all you whiteys know how to do: steal. We don't want your help no more. Especially, we don't want no more white women helping with our land fight, or anything else."

War Dancer, who had every bit as much Indian blood as John, and looked it, said, "You've got this one wrong brother. These folks are helping Louisa, not stealing anything."

"Who can believe you? You're with that Sun Bear and, even though he's Indian, he's stealing from his own people," John said angrily. "He's taking Louisa to the cleaners. That's the truth.

We're going to take care of him as soon as he puts his foot through the door. But now we're going to take care of you folks."

With that, one of John's friends took out a knife, grabbed Running Deer from behind and put the blade against his throat. Nimimosha reported that she felt faint when she saw that, but knew she had to protect the baby. She started to pray harder than she ever had, calling all the white light, all the good spirits to come and protect them.

"Do you feel loyal to Sun Bear now?", John sneeringly asked Running Deer. "Just admit he's stealing from Louisa and my buddy there will let you go."

Running Deer said nothing.

"Put that knife down!" Nimimosha commanded.

To her great shock, the man did. It was, she said, as though her words had broken a spell. While his buddy still had a hammerlock on Running Deer, John came over and threw some punches at him. War Dancer hardly hesitated before catching John's arm and pulling him away.

"Get out of here, man," War Dancer said.

"You can't tell me to get out," John replied. "This house and land belong to my family."

"I don't care. I'm getting sick of seeing your face, and if I get much angrier I'm going to go on automatic just like the Marines taught me to do in 'Nam," War Dancer said, stretching to show his full 6 foot 2 inch, 220 pound, muscular body. Out of the hammerlock, Running Deer began flexing his muscles and preparing to take a martial arts stance.

"Come on John, let's get out of here now," the white man said, "these guys are small potatoes. It's Sun Bear we want."

"Okay, okay," John said. "Just want to be sure these folks know we'll be back later, with reinforcements."

Running Deer reported that when the guy had him in the hold, the smell of alcohol was overpowering.

Nimimosha assured us they were all okay, and that they, Star Marker, and Wild Rose were taking turns guarding the house. They were ready to get out of there at a moment's notice.

"Good," Sun Bear told them. "Have you had council about what to do?"

"Yes," Mosha replied. "They mean business. We're going to have to leave."

"I want to talk with Louisa before we make any final decisions," Sun Bear told her, "but I think you're right. I'd start thinking about packing."

"We already have."

"We'll get there just as quick as we can," Sun Bear assured her. He talked to Running Deer for a moment and told him to watch Nimimosha and be sure she rested.

To his everlasting credit, Sun Bear did not say "I told you so" once to me as he related the story of what had occurred. He didn't have to. During that ride home I had plenty of opportunity to say it to myself. The words *terrible, guilt-ridden,* and *shamed* do not begin to describe how I felt about myself right then. I huddled in a corner of the back seat, shaking, while a battle that seemed of cosmic proportions took place within me.

I realized very clearly that it was my insistence on helping Louisa that had placed us all in danger. I had always felt I was doing the right thing by insisting we go there. I thought the land would be good for the community, and the community would be helpful to Louisa. I was right as far as I went in my thinking, but I didn't go far enough. And I had not believed Sun Bear's warning about donated land. I thought this time would be different, just because I wanted it to be so.

I knew Sun Bear had agreed to our being there most reluctantly, and only after I had purposely misinterpreted the dream about the grandmother to support my desires. He had warned me that going there would be a fork off the road of his vision, yet he had been willing to take it because I "needed the lessons on this fork." Moving to Louisa's land had been the logical choice, yet, apparently, it had been the wrong one. Painfully clearly I saw the trap my mind had created and how that had affected Sun Bear, the Tribe, and his vision.

In a flash, I realized that, in my own way, I had taken Sun Bear from his path as much as I had accused Spider Woman of doing. With that realization came tears: first bitter choking ones of shame, then gentle, cleansing sobs. While I was not yet ready to forgive myself for my actions, I realized I had, once again, done everything out of love as I understood it. That brought tears of self pity as I berated myself for my inadequate grasp of love. How could I be so intelligent in some areas and so stupid in others?

When I began to cry Spider Woman turned to comfort me, but

Sun Bear stopped her, and motioned her to silence. He knew that what I had to do then, I had to do alone.

After I had dried my tears, I asked Sun Bear to pull over for a moment. I knew we were in a hurry, but I also knew I had to apologize before I lost my nerve. We got out of the car and stood facing each other. Clearly, concisely I told Sun Bear what I had realized, and I apologized for interfering with his vision. I also apologized to Spider Woman for all the unjust accusations I had made both to myself and to Sun Bear about her taking Sun Bear off his path.

"I accept your apology, sister, and I am glad you have learned so many important lessons," he said. Then, with great warmth, he embraced me. Spider Woman followed suit.

When we got back in the car and continued speeding toward home, Spider Woman turned back toward me and said, "Wabun, when you talked to us back then, you didn't look like you do now. You looked like this wonderful old grandmother, with a face as wrinkled as the earth gets. And your eyes had so much love in them that it makes me cry thinking about it."

Hearing her say that made me add my tears to hers. It also made me remember clearly I had not seen or dreamed of the grandmother in a long time, not since I had lied to Sun Bear when I interpreted the dream in which she spoke to me about Louisa's land. No wonder I hadn't seen her! Why would she come to someone who had misused her words? Yet, from the description Spider Woman had given, I had looked like the grandmother just a few moments ago! I hoped that meant that she as well as Sun Bear had accepted my apology.

When the three of us got home, we were glad to learn John and his friends had not returned. War Dancer, drawing on his marine training, had taught the others what to watch for on guard duty. They, including Nimimosha, were rotating the job. As soon as War Dancer gave us his instructions, we were included in the rotations.

By dawn of the next day, Sun Bear and I were prepared to go see Louisa. Before we left, I explained to Sun Bear how I had handled all the expenses. All money for the land fight went into and out of a checking account that required both Louisa's and my signature. Louisa had wanted it that way so she wouldn't be tempted by her kids to use land money for personal items. The records made it clear that I had not only not stolen from Louisa but also had put a tidy sum of my writing money into her land fight.

When it was late enough that we were sure Louisa would be up, we went over to her place. As we suspected, John was there although, thankfully, his buddies seemed to be sleeping one off. John wouldn't let Louisa talk. Whenever she'd start, he would talk over her. He did the same when Sun Bear or I would try to say anything. It was impossible to have any kind of conversation with a broken record saying, "We know you stole from us. Nothing you say matters. We know the truth. You stole our money just like you stole our land and culture. We've had enough. We don't want any white woman working for us. You have to leave our land. Maybe you'll get off before we come and get you."

During his loud soliloquy, John wore a scowl that was much too familiar to me. His was the face of darkness, of ignorance: the face that scowls whenever it sees that the light is growing brighter. Once again that darkness was attacking the Tribe. This attack showed me clearly how bright a beacon the Tribe could someday be. I think it was at that moment, with John shouting his repetitive words, that I made my decision to stay with the Tribe.

Louisa sat there with tears streaming down her face. Looking at her, I felt moisture on my own cheeks. John wouldn't let me get near her. He kept playing his pitiable song.

"Let's go," Sun Bear said.

I knew there was no other choice. I waved at Louisa, and followed Sun Bear out.

We knew all the money the Tribe had put into buildings was gone, but we hoped to save as much of our equipment as possible. We arranged with the rancher who had become our buddy to store things in an old cabin on his place. We knew John and his friends would not dare to annoy this man. War Dancer and Running Deer built a camper to go on the back of our old yellow farm truck. Among that, our little pickup, and our latest recycled car, we packed as much as we could to take with us. We made sure all the inventory was easily accessible.

Our plan was to head north as soon as we got things stored safely. We would stop along the way to do shows and pow wows, but we'd keep traveling until we found land that felt right to all of us.

I worried a lot about the land we were leaving. Would anyone water the gardens? Would someone make prayers and offerings to the frogs, the hawks, the chipmunks, the stones, or the water in the irrigation ditch? And I was concerned about Louisa's land fight continuing. It seemed that everything was in good progress but with someone like John helping her, I was afraid everything could still fall apart. Aside from radicals fueled by racism, sexism, nationalism, or other forms of disguised rage, I've known some very good, sincere political people. I hoped some of them would come to work with Louisa and moderate John's angry stance.

I couldn't get any feeling of completion from my last meeting with Louisa. I asked Sun Bear if he thought it would be safe for me to go once more to the land Louisa sought. Maybe there I would again find peace and hope.

"I think it'll be okay," he said. "John and his buddies really have very little interest in being on the land. Be aware. If you see any of them, hide yourself until they leave."

When I arrived at the land, I carefully concealed the car. Since no one was around I walked down to the river, to the spot where Louisa and I had camped. I stood with my back against the grandmother fir, feeling her strength and peace. I watched the river flowing, and sang my song of thanks to the water people. I did the dances, and prayed that Louisa would be successful in her efforts. I felt better from my connection with the land, but I still felt unfinished with Louisa.

As I went back to where I had parked, I heard the noise of another vehicle. Heeding Sun Bear's instructions, I hid myself. I know that man is the most dangerous animal in the forests. I watched the vehicle get closer, and recognized Louisa's truck, but I couldn't see who was driving. When the truck passed my well-hidden car, it slowed down. I knew then it had to be Louisa. John would not have seen the car. My silent prayer had been answered.

Just to be sure, I waited until the car door opened. I was only mildly surprised when Louisa called out my name. I answered, and walked quickly toward her.

"I had a feeling you were here now, and I didn't want you to leave without our talking," she said.

We embraced, then she pulled back and said we needed to talk quickly. She could not be sure whether John was following her.

She said he was as bad as a puppy dog, especially if he thought she might be seeing any of us.

"Wabun," she said, "I am so sorry this has happened. Please tell Sun Bear and tell him everything I say. It breaks my heart to break my word to you. I would let you stay on the land no matter what John has said, but I can't control him or his friends. I can't be sure he wouldn't hurt one of you. I don't know what has gotten into him. He's always been angry, but he's never been this bitter and full of hate."

"This is terrible," she continued. "In the old days a son would banish himself for a time before he would treat his mother as John has treated me about this. A young man like him would never make an elder break her word."

"You all have been a gift to me from the Creator. From what you have done, I know the land will come back, and my vision will become a reality. I can only pray for John, either that the earth will touch him, or that he will banish himself from my land and life. I will pray very hard for you and Sun Bear and all of the Tribe. I will pray you get back some of the good you have given to me. I won't forget you, sister. I hope our paths may cross again in peace. Go now. It is dangerous to stay longer."

"I'll pray for you too, Louisa, and for your land."

I went to the car and drove back safely. I told Sun Bear what had happened.

"Louisa is a real good woman. I hope she succeeds, and I will pray, too, for John. He needs all our prayers, and a swift kick in the butt. I'll pray he gets that too," Sun Bear said, smiling at his latter thought.

When everything was packed or stored, we came together in a circle to pray for the lands and gardens. Then, while the rest kept guard, the four of us responsible for the boundary markers went out to pick them up. Sun Bear had explained to us it was important we withdraw our protection and energy from the land. That way we would not inadvertently interfere with whatever was to happen.

As I walked toward the east, I felt something following me. I looked back. About twenty feet behind me was a skunk, tail held high. I began singing my chant for calming animals, hoping it would quiet both me and sister skunk. I had become much more at home with nature here, but I was still skittish about skunk perfume. When I arrived at the actual east boundary of the land, I looked to my right. Waiting there was another skunk. I sang with even more gusto. As I walked the boundary, the two skunks followed me. They walked side by side, and kept the twenty foot distance. They watched as I removed the prayer marker and offered it, with thanks, to the energies of that direction. They accompanied me back to the point where I began walking south toward the house. They continued walking in an easterly direction.

I told people what had happened. Sun Bear said that skunks are the town criers of the animal kingdom. Apparently these two skunks were checking on what I was doing. Then they went their own way to pass the word to the other animals. Sun Bear said the animals and other beings on the land had felt the energy of our protection. Now that they knew that the energy had been withdrawn, they would change their behavior accordingly.

We finished our ceremonies, and watered the gardens for the last time. Calmly, but with no wasted motion, we got into our vehicles and took off. I didn't turn for one last look at the land. I knew it wasn't good to look back. Besides, I couldn't have seen anything. Tears of sadness were blinding my eyes.

14

BEGINNING TO BUILD

The first night after we left Louisa's land, I had a vivid dream of the Grandmother. We were heading toward the Pendleton Round-Up in Oregon, camping in view of the seven sister peaks of the Cascade range. The Grandmother came gliding toward me from the heavens, looking like a child who has just learned to use a sliding board. In this dream I could see her more clearly than I had before, even in the previous dream. No cheesecloth-like haze hung in the air. I saw she was dressed in white buckskins, which surprised me. She didn't look particularly Native. With her grand wrinkled face, she could have been of any nationality. Up close she looked the way I'd always imagined "a right jolly old elf" would whenever I'd heard or recited "T'was the Night Before Christmas." She looked enormously pleased, and I felt totally enchanted.

"It's good to see you again granddaughter. I hope you've learned it's not a good idea to make my words fit your desires. You know, you could have helped Louisa without moving to her land. Nonetheless, you did a good job for Louisa, and she is another one working to help me," she said. "I know it seems like the ending got botched up a bit. Don't worry. It will turn out fine. And you're even beginning to like Spider Woman, aren't you? Quite a bit of progress. How do you think you'd feel about Gayla if you saw her now?"

In my dream I told the Grandmother I did indeed like Spider Woman, and I was no longer feeling superior to her. I started to explain my revelation of the other day but she cut me off by saying she knew, and that I still did have a tendency to be too hard on

177

myself. I said I didn't think I'd like Gayla; that from my experience she didn't have the redeeming qualities Spider Woman did.

"Everyone has many sides, and most people have some redeeming qualities. But I thought you believed Spider Woman was Gayla. Have you changed your mind about that?" she asked.

I nodded yes and she continued, "You are accepting the other parts of you now, dear granddaughter, and your power is much stronger. Use it well. Soon you will find the mountain of vision. The circle begun there will spread far across the earth."

Giving me a big stage wink she continued, "If you keep going the way you are, sometime you might even find someone who reminds you of me walking around on two legs. I'm proud of you, my dear. Remember what the Iroquois grandmother told you. I'm counting on you as a spokeswoman. Keep taking care of Sun Bear and his vision. Or," she asked, raising her eyebrows, "is it solely *his* vision?"

With that question she smiled quizzically, turned, and glided back toward the sky.

I awoke the next morning feeling wonderful. Whoever the Grandmother was, she had certainly been in high humor in my dream. I smiled remembering it. Then her last question filled my mind, and I tried to formulate an answer. What was she trying to make me see? The Bear Tribe definitely was Sun Bear's vision, but now I shared parts of it. I wanted to see a community succeed as much as he did. But I had not been out Vision Questing, so how could that be my vision? Yet Richard Rainbow had told me some people got visions without questing. And certainly what happened with the dancing spirit was vision. But had the spirit told me to help form a community? But, but, but . . . there I was using my mind to confuse me again. I looked up at the seven peaks and, for a moment, I knew clearly the "buts" didn't matter. I was doing what I was supposed to.

As we continued driving to the Pendleton Round-Up, we stopped to look at land in some of the more rural parts of Oregon. There was beautiful land there but, if it had water, it cost more than we had. Sun Bear was insistent that this time we would get our own land and it would have its own water source. After the last land deal I arranged, I wasn't about to disagree.

With our farm truck and its funky, wooden, home-made camper, and with the pickup, the car with its box top, eight adults, two kids, and a couple of dogs, I felt as if we were finally doing a good imitation of something Sun Bear used to kid about when we were traveling the pow wow circuit—an old time medicine show. We were quite a sight pulling into the Round-Up.

Fortunately our medicine was running very strong. As soon as we began to unload, *someone* (the mythical creature that thrives in community settings) left a suitcase full of about $5,000 worth of our consigned turquoise jewelry sitting in the grass. I hadn't noticed it was missing until about an hour after we first began unpacking. To my true amazement, we went back and it was sitting in the grass just where the *someone* suspected they had left it. I didn't make any accusations, I didn't even lecture. I just made a prayer of thanks, and determined that I'd have to be extra careful of everything while I had so much help.

After the Pendleton Round-Up, we went to the west side of the Oregon Cascades and did a couple of shows, one in Eugene and one in Medford. We looked at land all along the way, but nothing we saw felt right to us. It was almost October and the nights were beginning to get chilly. We knew we couldn't keep camping forever. Another issue of *Many Smokes* was due out, and I didn't want to be too late getting it to subscribers and distributors. We needed a place to set up our graphic's materials and offset press.

We were having a counsel about our alternatives when I remembered Ruth had told me if we ever got stuck, she'd try to help us out. It felt as if this situation qualified as stuck. We decided to give her a call and see how she felt about taking in our traveling show. She felt fine. She even had a guest cabin of sorts she felt could house us and the magazine equipment.

Sun Bear was really feeling a push to find land, but agreed to our staying with her until the magazine was out. He said he'd scout out some land while we were doing *Many Smokes,* so that things could go faster later. We moved temporarily in at Ruth's place and got right to work. We were doing a literary issue of *Many Smokes,* which I really enjoyed. I'd happily work all day, and then stay up half the night talking with Ruth. Like many medicine people I've known, Ruth got more talkative when the sun went down. Maybe it's because many tribes used to tell stories only in the dark of winter, when all the work for the year was done.

What a month that was for me! It gave me the opportunity to learn from Ruth on an everyday basis. I have grown to value greatly such learning, realizing there are some things better communicated while cooking, shopping, working with plants, or doing dishes than sitting in a medicine meeting. What Ruth taught me then, as well as at other times in our relationship, was to be a human being. Human beings have to eat, sleep, and have pleasant surroundings as well as work with energies and healing, and commune with the spirit world. In fact, according to Ruth, keeping things in order on this plane of existence makes it much easier to reach other planes. She'd tell me the earth and other spheres were more closely intertwined than most folks realized. It's a good thing I had my magazine work to do or I would have been tempted to follow Ruth around all month, an invasion of privacy she would not have appreciated.

Once during the month Sun Bear, Spider Woman and I also traveled to do a show near Seattle. While there, we went to visit a friend who lived on the coast of Washington. Like me, George was of Welsh ancestry. But he had lived around the coastal Indians long enough that they had accepted him. In fact, he had been allowed to become part of one of their medicine lodges. While we were visiting him he asked me to lead us in a rainbow meditation one night. I was honored to do so.

When I was nearing the end, I felt a strange shift in my consciousness. Although I was able to continue saying the words to the meditation, most of me went somewhere else. I found myself standing by the Puget Sound, on a clear beach with forests around it. As sometimes happens in dreams and visions, I was watching, but I was also acting. The me acting was a young Indian man dressed only in a breechcloth. This young man me was chanting and dancing. The chant was more complex than most I'd heard, and the dance required strength and agility that the observing me certainly didn't have. It was a beautiful dance, very different from any I had seen, that reminded me of the movements of the osprey, one of my favorite birds. When it ended, I came back to the room where everyone else was sitting, and completed the meditation.

Sun Bear had noticed the long pause, and later asked me what had been happening. When I told him, he asked me to repeat the story to George. George asked how the dance looked and I showed him as much as I could manage. He was quiet for a minute and then told me I had just shown him a dance that would be very much at home in the medicine lodge. When I looked confused he said he would show me.

He arranged for us to accompany him the next night to a formal naming ceremony in the medicine lodge. At this ritual, a young man who had had a drug problem before he became involved with the lodge was going to receive a new name. It was quite an impressive event. The lodge was a very large wooden longhouse, the sides of which were lined with bleachers. Most of these were full of people, many of them in traditional Native dress. People were dancing around one of several drums in the big rectangle in the center. When we came in, they were doing the dancing I was used to seeing at pow wows.

Then the ceremony began and the young man received his adult name, along with a lot of blessings and support from the medicine people present, including Sun Bear, who was treated as an honored guest. After family members added their congratulations, his family did a large giveaway to celebrate. Once again I was amazed at the generosity of Native people. The family wasn't rich, but they had some gift to give every one of the approximately 150 people attending. I received some silk scarves with money tied in the corner, some fruit, and some kitchen towels. Sun Bear got scarves, fruit, some beadwork, and a new ribbon shirt.

After the giveaway, the dancing changed. People began to do individual dances they had been given either through their family or through vision. A good number of these dances honored the animals of the area. When I saw a dance for the red-tailed hawk, I saw what George had meant when he told me the dance I'd seen would fit in here.

Later I asked Sun Bear what it all meant. I had some ideas myself but wanted his opinion. He felt I had either seen the dance of someone who once lived here, or that I was seeing myself in an earlier existence, and remembering a dance I knew then.

"I'm not sure this one is mine," I told him.

"Well, it's not mine," he said. "You're not going to see me try to get this body in the positions you described."

"Shucks, I was looking forward to it."

I turned out to be right. The dance wasn't mine for this life. But I had not yet met the man to whom it would belong.

Eventually the literary issue of *Many Smokes* was completed and mailed, and it was time to move on. I didn't want to leave Ruth, but I knew I had to or she would do what she often threatened to with people avoiding their path: "Pry their fingers off the doorjam."

In his forays Sun Bear had not found a piece of land he felt was right but, from his dreams, he was certain it would be in the eastern Washington area. We headed there, arriving a few weeks before Thanksgiving. Now Thanksgiving isn't a big celebration for all Indian people. Some of them feel its a reminder of a bad decision on the part of their ancestors. But I still liked any excuse to bake and eat turkey, and other folks liked the latter activity, so we celebrated. Along with Christmas, Easter, and my birthday, Thanksgiving is a celebration date that is indelibly imprinted in my mind as one that divides up the year. Now these dates are joined by the solstices, the equinoxes, and the new and full moons.

We decided to stay in Spokane because it was central to the land around it. We went to an economy motel and rented a couple of family units, one of which actually had a bathtub. From there we looked for a place to rent for the winter. We had decided not to buy something hastily. Besides, we weren't sure we'd be able to afford land that already had buildings, and winter, we'd heard, could be pretty cold in this part of the country. A few days after we arrived, we saw for rent a resort at a place called Sacheen Lake, about thirty miles north of Spokane. It was perfect. The main lodge was heated both by electricity and wood, it had enough space, and the surroundings were magnificent. The lake was nestled in some foothills, and surrounded by many varieties of evergreens. The owner was happy to have someone to watch over the property, so the rental fee was low.

For the next month or so we familiarized ourselves with the land and people in the area. Being a mountain lover, I lobbied for property in northern Idaho, but the land available there was just too expensive for our budget. It seemed as if we'd be somewhere in the high-desert/foothill country of the Spokane area. But we couldn't find where. We looked at lots of pieces of land, but none felt quite right nor matched the land Sun Bear had seen in his dreams.

We had more success with the people we met, particularly

those who were involved with the Yantra Bookstore, then the alternative booksellers of Spokane. Sun Bear spoke to a good-sized group of people there about our work about a month after we arrived. Many of these folks later became friends and supporters. We also had pre-Christmas showings of some of our crafts at Yantra and at a general store near the Spokane Reservation. These gave us more opportunity to meet the local folks, and to pay the rent.

Sun Bear, Spider Woman, and I went into California to do another pre-Christmas show at a Western store where we had exhibited before. I was surprised how well I had finally settled into traveling with them. I had more or less accepted my role as maiden aunt, and I truly enjoyed Spider Woman's company a lot of the time. She was also a big help at shows. More important, I was really beginning to accept my place as Sun Bear's medicine helper. My self-revelations when we raced back to Louisa's land, my time with Ruth, and the dream of the Grandmother had all contributed to my understanding that I was helping Sun Bear do something I really wanted to do myself. He had envisioned a community; I wanted to figure out how to make one a reality. Sun Bear was pleased with my determination, and so were the other people in the counsel circle. I was more of a thinker, planner, and organizer than anyone else there, so they all gave me ample space to think, plan, and organize. That winter, working from Sun Bear's visions and ideas, I formulated the plans for many things that later became realities: the Bear Tribe Community, Bear Tribe Publishing, the Self Reliance Center, and self-reliance seminars.

With the winter slowing down the land search, the counsel circle spent more time theorizing with me about how to add on to the group already there. We read letters from people wanting to join us and tried to decide which folks to invite. We finally decided to go with my "balanced community" concept, and tried to choose people with a variety of skills, life experiences, and family situations. When we finally issued invitations, half the people had moved or had decided to do something else. We scheduled the other half to come over a period of time, beginning in the spring when we felt we'd be building on our own land. Ultimately, half of those we invited didn't show up, and the Tribe had not yet learned to refuse drop-ins, so our theorizing didn't yield much good that year. However, the experience did help me to hone my ideas about community.

I was also experimenting with fasting that winter—partly in the constant battle of the bulge, partly out of curiosity about its spiritual effects. I did one-, two-, three-, and four-day fasts. Then I tried fasting every other day. The longer fasts worked well. I found that I'd feel quite well, mentally and spiritually clear, after the initial hunger passed. These fasts helped to prepare me for understanding Vision Questing later. The every-other-day fasting was awful. I'd spend my fasting day thinking about what I'd cook and eat on my eating day. The other folks rather liked it. They got very elaborate meals every second day.

Nimimosha kept telling me it wasn't fair for me to lose weight while she was gaining so much. I thought she looked beautiful in her pregnancy. I took one photo of her silhouetted against a window that I think captures the bloom and grace of expectant mothers. I had my moments of envying Mosha, but she was so open with me about her experiences that they didn't last long. I think I put my hands on the outside of Mosha's stomach almost as much as she did. I felt one of the first kicks, and then the kicks increasing in strength. I felt the baby as she shifted her position, and as she moved around as we danced. I was enthralled with this developing being, and with the changes she brought to Mosha physically, mentally, emotionally, and spiritually.

It was a pregnant winter. Tsacha and Shasta also conceived almost as soon as we got to Spokane, and Mosha watched as Tsacha filled out, contending she was jealous at how quickly dogs formed their pups.

Earth Renewal ceremonies were small and quiet but powerful that year. Some of our new friends from Spokane came out to join us for the ceremonies. We missed having our sweatlodge and being able to roll in the snow after the heat of the lodge. When these ceremonies were completed, once again I flew East to visit family and friends for Christmas and New Years.

A week after I returned to Spokane, Running Deer saw an ad in a little paper for twenty acres of land with its own spring. He, Sun Bear, and Spider Woman went to see it that same day. They came back full of enthusiasm. The next day the rest of us went there. Not wanting to make a mistake, we all tried to find some

flaw in the land. We couldn't. It seemed perfect. It was about a
mile off a maintained county road, up an old lumber road that was
in fair shape. It was near the top of a small mountain, but had flat
areas. There was a foundation and root cellar left from an old
homestead. And there really was a spring that needed only minor
development. The water was sweet and fresh. The evergreens
were old and magnificent. There was a perfect building space for
a longhouse. Sun Bear said it looked like the land he had
envisioned.

Sitting in counsel we all agreed this was the right place. We
were even able to trade turquoise and silver jewelry for part of
the downpayment. It was some time after we purchased the land
that we found the petroglyphs on the other side of the mountain,
near Long Lake, These picture writings identified this mountain
as a place where the local Native people went for seeking vision.
The Spokane Indians called the mountain Axtú Leman Sumíx
which, translated loosely, means paint, power, or—as we came to
call it—Vision Mountain. When I found this out, I remembered
my most recent dream of the Grandmother, and her prediction
that we would soon find the mountain of vision.

As soon as we got the land, we began to build on it. We had
to move out of the resort in the spring, and we didn't think
camping with a newborn would be great fun. In the ice and snow,
people went to the land to bring in wood and begin to construct
a simple cabin over the root cellar that already stood. It was a
thirty-mile trek over country roads from the Sacheen Lake Resort
to Vision Mountain. Going there on poor roads in our yellow
truck was an act of bravery. As soon as the weather permitted,
some of the building crew began to camp there so they would
have more time for the building itself.

Nimimosha and I stayed at Sacheen Lake most of the time,
working on the magazine and correspondence and playing with
Goldenstar and Little Beaver. Both Mosha and Tsacha continued
to grow. In early February Tsacha labored all night to bring forth
five large puppies, three pure white and two black with a shepherd mask. Nimimosha began helping with the delivery, but it
went on most of the night. I suggested she get her sleep, and I
continued helping Tsacha. From the size of the pups, it was clear
that Shasta, who then weighed over 100 pounds, was the dad. He
came in a couple of times to see what was happening and nuzzle

Tsacha. It was a joyful night for me. The miracle of birth is another one of those phenomenons that elude words.

Almost two months later, Nimimosha went into labor, also at night. Because we were forty-five minutes from medical help, Mosha had decided to have the baby in the hospital, just to be safe. I accompanied her and Running Deer to the hospital at about 1 A.M. This was in the unenlightened days before birthing rooms, and before hospitals encouraged friends or family to be with the mother while she labored. They barely put up with the father's presence. However, by a stroke of good medicine, the labor room nurses thought I was Mosha's sister and a nurse myself. None of us said I was; the nurses just made the assumption and figured my presence would make their job easier. Consequently, they let me stay in the labor room. Mosha labored hard, and Running Deer and I were either both there or we took turns quietly being with her in those periods when it was clear she didn't really want to socialize. While I waited, I worked on the pouch for the baby's umbilical cord, and I prayed for a safe delivery. Toward the end it got easier for Mosha, and the baby came quickly. Her head crowned before they took Mosha to the delivery room, from which they barred anyone but the dad.

Within a few minutes after seeing the crown of her head, I first laid eyes on the child who would be named Yarrow. Before I knew what was happening, I was holding that little wonderwork. She seemed so fragile, so vulnerable, so innocent. She looked at me with her perfect baby-blue eyes, and my heart melted. I knew then that this little one would always be the firstborn daughter of my heart.

With her unmatchable generosity, Nimimosha said to her daughter, "Hey, little one, meet your other mother." And, as if on cue, Yarrow smiled at me. At that moment, one of the most precious bonds of my life was formed. The bond was sealed a few days later when Running Deer and Nimimosha announced they had decided to call the baby Yarrow Wabeno-wusk. That is the Ojibwa term for yarrow, the herb of the morning magicians. Part of the reason for the name was to honor the connection they felt between me and their child.

Having two available mothers a good part of the time makes infancy a lot easier for everyone. Outside of feeding, I did everything for Yarrow. It proved a good system. Yarrow rarely had to deal with a totally burnt out mother. And, even in community, it is the mother who spends most time with the child. I loved my time with Yarrow. It gave me the opportunity to practice a principle Ruth taught me was essential to Native culture: You never can give a child too much love. The more you give them, she told me, the more they will have to give back to their people.

Just before Yarrow's birth I had travelled with Sun Bear to Boise, Idaho to speak to a group formed by Phyllis Huffman Atwater, who has since gone on to write a book entitled *Coming Back to Life: The After-Effects of the Near-Death Experience.* At that time Phyllis was publishing a newsletter called *Inner Forum,* and she and I had been corresponding and exchanging articles for a number of years. This trip was noteworthy for a number of reasons. First was that it was here I first heard about a man who would eventually learn with me what love and commitment can really mean. He was away for the weekend, but I heard a lot about him and his work from a number of the people there. Second, Phyllis had done astrology charts for both Sun Bear and I, and arranged to have them read by Johnny Lister, a well-known astrologer. This was the first time I had been exposed to real astrology, and I was fascinated with how accurately my chart described some aspects of my being. Third and last, the trip was noteworthy because Sun Bear pulled a fast one on me.

Without warning in the middle of his talk he said, "Now Wabun is going to tell you more about what we are doing." I was on, and I wasn't prepared to be. I had done quite a bit of public speaking in school, but that was a long time ago. I got up and began to speak, and I sounded like Minnie Mouse because my throat was so closed. I knew the only way out of it was through it, so I kept talking. Eventually, my squeak filled out and I sounded like a human being, albeit a soprano rather than my usual deep alto.

In later years when I've taught other people how to teach lectures and workshops about the earth, I've always tried to remember my first talk. It helps me keep my perspective, and it reminds me that people can overcome many speaking problems if they really care about what they are saying. Care I did. This was my opportunity to begin doing what the Iroquois grandma had told me to: teach my own people some of what I had learned.

I had more opportunities that spring and summer. Sun Bear and I talked to school classes in Spokane about Native culture. We spoke to a group of seventy-five at the Yantra Bookstore about our idea for a Self-Reliance School. We made a cross-country trip talking to foundation people about this idea. Later we arranged a class at the local Unity church about self-reliance. By that time, I was a little more comfortable with speaking publicly. My chances to speak would always come at unexpected times in the middle of Sun Bear's talks. Knowing that chances might come, I had tried to get my thoughts together, and do a little practicing. But I never knew what topic Sun Bear would ask me to speak about. I could never figure out if he was doing this purposely to teach me extemporaneous speaking, or whether he would just introduce me when he wanted a rest. When I asked him, he claimed to not know what extemporaneous meant, so he said he couldn't be doing that. Since he could sometimes out-vocabulary me, I took his answer to mean he wasn't going to tell me, and I'd better be prepared on a variety of topics.

On our trip to talk with foundation people, we also went to a couple of East Coast pow wows. A lot of Eastern Native people were just beginning to come back to their old ways at this time and it was exciting to witness. Sun Bear said it was sort of like the Native Renaissance he had experienced in the Los Angeles area. At the Wampanoag Pow Wow in Massachusetts we met Slow Turtle, their medicine person. He and his family took us in and became people whose friendship we've really valued over the years. Sun Bear had met another well-known Wampanoag named Manitonquat (Medicine Story), a storyteller and writer, a few years earlier, and was glad to see him again at this event. I was happy to meet him, to listen to his stories and community ideas, and to get him to agree to write for *Many Smokes*.

On this trip we also met several people who would come later to the community. I began to see how all our work fit together. Through the traveling and shows we met people who became interested in the vision and community. Also through the shows, we were able to make the money that allowed the community to continue, and to expand our subscribers to and advertisers in *Many Smokes*. Through *Many Smokes* people learned about our work and schedule, and invited us to visit, or came to shows to meet us. It was a good circle.

The community had a lot of people passing through that summer. Sun Bear contended that it must have been harder to live in community than to have made it through Green Beret training, since we had a higher drop-out rate. Out of 200 people, perhaps two would stay for any length of time. The high pass-through rate made us core people feel as though we were living in a fishbowl. Sometimes this was hard to take. For example, one week somebody would come through and tell us we were terrible because we ate meat, then the next week someone would come and say we should be like the Indians and eat only meat. Every person who passed through seemed to be an expert on community. Why, I wondered, were they living alone and traveling by themselves?

War Dancer began staying out more on the pow wow circuit. Star Marker and Wild Rose made a long trip to visit relatives. When the number of people overwhelmed me, I retreated often to a special spot on the mountain. Running Deer retreated to one in the opposite direction. Either he or I usually took Yarrow. That left our gregarious group—Sun Bear, Spider Woman, and Nimimosha—to socialize with the visitors.

While people were there, we put them to work on our gardens and on building our longhouse. The little cabin was only meant to be a temporary structure, and it was small even for that. Half the core group, and all the visitors had been camping out during the summer. Our kitchen was outdoors in a kitchen shed, and the outhouse was down the path. We went to Long Lake to swim and get clean, although some of us had the one-gallon bath and hair wash down pat by now. For that you use a quart of woodstove-heated water in a bowl to soap up, another quart in another bowl to rinse off. Then you combine these and use it to shampoo your hair. The other half-gallon is used to rinse your hair. For real luxury, we'd go to the YWCA in town and pay for a swim, suana, and shower there.

The longhouse we built that summer has unique construction—inevitable in any building planned and carried out by committee. The counsel had decided the most important thing was that everyone have equal-sized bedrooms. That way there would be no jealousy about who got the bigger rooms. So we had planned four downstairs bedrooms, and four upstairs ones, figuring that would give us room for twelve or more people, depending upon how many were in couples. Unfortunately, two of the four upstairs bedrooms were windowless. That meant that, despite the equal size, the people in these rooms would have reason for jealousy. This upstairs construction ultimately led us literally to raise the longhouse roof in one of the many remodelings the house has undergone.

Again that summer, Sun Bear, Spider Woman, and I went to the Omak Stampede, Chief Seattle Days, and the Pendleton Round-Up. While we were gone, people continued to come and go, the longhouse rose ever taller, and Yarrow seemed to grow overnight.

In the fall we gave a thank-you dinner for thirty people from Spokane who had helped us build the longhouse in one way or another. Some had donated materials; others had helped with the labor. With the shell of the longhouse almost complete, it looked as if we'd have a roof over our heads that winter, even if the interior would be a bit rough.

Living in the community now were the eight adults and two children who had made the move with us, Yarrow, and two new people. That made the twelve-plus-founder I'd been waiting for, and I was sure the community was now ready to grow in quantum leaps. Karen, one of the new folks, had been a legal secretary. I had tried to recruit her when I met her at an Eastern show, both liking her and knowing how helpful her skills would be to the magazine, the correspondence, and to some new projects we planned. I was glad she had finally come. Soon after her arrival, she and War Dancer got seriously involved. Logan, the other new resident, was a professional carpenter, someone whose skills and sense of humor we really valued.

Soon all that remained to do with the longhouse shell was the roofing. Luckily, some folks from Canada came down to help with that. It turned out they were involved with the final stages of planning the First World Symposium on Humanities, sponsored by Yogi Bhajan's 3HO organization, which was to be held in Vancouver, Canada. Jerome Twin Rainbows, Lester, and Suellen had heard about Sun Bear and our new community and decided to take a weekend to come down and see for themselves what we were doing. On the Halloween of the year that Jimmy Carter was elected president, with their help, we finished the longhouse shell and moved us and the building equipment inside. The first snow flurries came the next day.

15

ACCEPTANCE

J erome, Suellen, and Lester must have liked what they saw
during their visit. Within a few days after their return to
Canada, Sun Bear received an invitation to speak at the First
World Symposium on the Humanities. To the best of my knowledge, the First World Symposium was the initial large interna-
tional, multicultural event that brought together the prime
movers of what would later be called "The New Age." At this
point, however, we were still being referred to as alternative,
countercultural, human potential, communal, hippie, yippie, and
psychedelic types. This was 1976, the middle of the decade when
some of us were hoping the sixties would stage a comeback, and
others were trying to figure out what, if anything, could head off the
strut our culture seemed to be taking toward another era of
crass materialism.

In the interim between the invitation and the Symposium, Sun
Bear, Spider Woman, and I went to a show in the Seattle area.
On the Saturday of that weekend, Spider Woman and I went out
for dinner together, while Sun Bear visited with our friend
George. Spider Woman and I ended up talking and laughing
deep into the night. Even as we were talking, I was reflecting
about the remarkable changes in the way I felt about this other
woman. From rival, she had become sister, and a sister I truly
valued. I enjoyed watching her lovely face as she talked, particularly now when she'd let it express her sadness or anger. I'd
noticed she allowed herself more expression in my company.
When she was around Sun Bear or other men she still tended
toward what I call the "Miss America Smile." That is, the amazing

smile that beautiful women can keep on their face no matter what else they are saying or doing. You could ask them a question such as, "How would you feel if I spent the night with your husband?" and, still smiling, they would answer, "I'll rip every hair out of your head, one by one."

When I went to bed, I continued my reverie. I was amazed at how the relationship between Spider Woman and myself had evolved. It had grown from fear, jealousy, anger, and hatred to appreciation, liking, and sisterly love. We were very different people, but now had enough respect for each other that we could laugh about our differences. I had explained the "Miss America Smile" to her once, and she had laughed so much she cried. Then she had me laughing hysterically while she did a parody of herself smiling while talking about the girl who tried to steal her prom date.

At one point early this year I had tried to talk to her about my initial feeling that she was a pawn for some negative forces when she first arrived. She became so upset when I broached the subject that I decided to drop it. It truly hurt her that I believed she could ever wish ill upon me, Sun Bear, or anyone in the Tribe. I knew that no matter how much we talked, she would have her ideas about what had happened when she arrived, and I would have mine. I didn't feel I had to pursue the subject. After the night with the dancing spirit, I had never suspected that Gayla had something to do with Spider Woman.

Despite my positive personal feelings for Spider Woman, I still didn't find her to be my idea of the model community member. She flirted with new men who came by to visit the Tribe whenever she could, and ten minutes of her flirting made many of them ready to leave their wives or long-term mates, at least for a fling. This created emotional chaos whenever it happened, but I now believed Spider Woman when she said she didn't mean to cause trouble. She didn't. Most of the time she didn't even like the man, and had no intention of flinging. Flirting was her way of communicating, like philosophizing was mine. I was beginning to learn you can't fault people for what they are. You can point out automatic habits, you can support people in changing them, but you can't change anyone but yourself, and even that is quite a task. Later I would theorize about this flirtatious energy Spider

Woman oozed; now I just experienced it, sometimes with humor, and sometimes with ire.

What I hadn't realized until the past summer was that Spider Woman happily would be almost as concerned, loving, and caring about me as she was about Sun Bear. The lady really had a loving heart. It was just that most women were so afraid of her they never got close enough to perceive it. And having been the object of her concern, I could better understand why it was so attractive to men. Spider Woman had a real talent for making me feel good about myself. Doing that for someone is a real gift. I was observing Spider Woman to see if I could learn to give that gift myself.

Thinking about Spider Woman eventually made my thoughts turn to Sun Bear. I realized how fully I had settled into being his spiritual partner, medicine helper, and community organizer. After Spider Woman and I had returned from the show that brought us together, he had slowly but surely regained his balance, and his interest in his vision. Since I had accepted Spider Woman, his enchantment with her had moderated steadily. It was there, but it wasn't overwhelming everything else. It occurred to me that by accepting Spider Woman, I had freed all three of us from the web she had spun, whether intentionally or inadvertently.

Sun Bear was now almost back to being the visionary I had first met; almost, but not quite. His love for Spider Woman had changed him too, made him seem more human, more vulnerable. I envied her the ability to touch him in this way, and I still wished somewhere within me that I could do the same. But I was a lot happier now than I had been when I was living in fantasyland. Accepting my relationship with Sun Bear as it was, rather than trying to change it, made the rest of my life a lot more pleasant. I was overjoyed to be over the "true love paranoia" that gave me suspicious eyes whenever I saw him talking to another woman. Now I could talk to the women myself, and make the sisterly connections that had always before been so important to me.

I wondered a lot about this "true love" business. Part of the myth I'd been fed with my Gerbers was that true love made you love the world, at least in the few minutes you had free from Prince Charming. No one had told me you'd want to bat Prince Charming around every time his eyes landed on another female, and that he'd be experiencing the same desire if his best friend took your hand. How could you love the world if a casual glance could send you into rage? How could possessiveness make you a better person? It certainly hadn't done much for my personality or self image.

I no longer blamed myself quite so stringently. When I met Sun Bear and Star, I had been starving for love. The New York honeymoon of unconditional love fed me so much that I became greedy for more. I thought the honeymoon would go on forever. But honeymoons rarely do. The reality of daily living generally intrudes. Then you have to work at love for it to grow.

I was beginning to think the only kind of love I wanted in the future was the kind that would help me look upon others with kindness and compassion, not with suspicion and fear. But I wasn't sure such love could exist over any period of time, and particularly in romantic relationships. If it did, people seemed to do a good job of hiding it.

There were times when I felt lonely watching Sun Bear and Spider Woman or Nimimosha and Running Deer, but for now I'd rather be lonely than be that small-minded, spiteful person I had found within myself when Spider Woman first came. I sometimes wondered why I could not have been as gracious to Spider Woman as Morning Star had been to me. The business with Gayla aside, I theorized that Star had always seen the close relationship with Sun Bear as transitory, where I had been convinced I could make it permanent.

My contemplations had made me hungry, so I went to the kitchen of George's house. With good Welsh hospitality, similar to that of Native people, George had told us to help ourselves to anything in the kitchen. I was heating water for tea, and checking the refrigerator for possibilities, when I heard footsteps. I looked up and Sun Bear was there. I made him tea, and found us some sandwich makings. We sat at the table eating.

"You were thinking pretty loud tonight Wabun," Sun Bear said.

"You mean I still haven't learned how to shield my thoughts from you?" I asked.

"You're getting better at it," he acknowledged. Then, still showing he had that maddening ability to read my mind he said, "Great Spirit showed me part of your path when we first met, the part where your path joined with mine. That's how I knew you were to be my medicine helper. It's unusual for the Creator to let someone see part of another person's vision but, in your case, it probably was necessary. If you remember, you weren't exactly open to the idea of vision when we first met. Trying to get you even to believe you had a path was quite a job. You're turning into one of the best medicine helpers I could want, but you sure were a pain-in-the-ass student a lot of the time."

"Thanks, I think," I responded.

Laughing, he continued, "You are very welcome sister."

He reached out, took my hand and said, "Go ahead, ask me."

"Okay. Do you really love Spider Woman as much as you seem to?"

"Well, you shielded your thoughts on that one. I thought you were going to ask me how things would go in the future. Wabun, you don't really want me to answer that. If I say 'no' you won't really believe me. If I say 'yes', you'll be hurt. Let's just say that Spider Woman came along at a time when things were going hard with my vision, and she offered me some very wonderful relief. She is a beautiful sister, inside as well as out."

I nodded in agreement.

"Remember," he continued, "I once told you that many of Spider Woman's lessons were for you. Do you see that now?"

"I sure do."

"Good, and good night, or we'll both be beat tomorrow. Stop thinking so loud, and get some sleep."

When we got home, I was glad for the sweet interlude that show had provided. A call had come in just before we arrived saying that Spider Woman's mother was very ill. It had been some time since Spider Woman had been back to Illinois to see her, so she decided she had better go now. Although I was sorry she wouldn't be going to the Symposium with us, I knew she was doing what she needed to do. Sun Bear took her to the airport early the next morning.

A few days later Sun Bear spoke at the Yantra Bookstore along with Gunther, a young man from Germany who was an herbalist and healer. Gunther was from northern Germany and knew about the Native people of his own land. He had spent an undetermined number of years studying with some Native medicine people in the wilds of British Columbia. Now he lived in a beautiful part of

Montana. Someone from the Yantra group had met him there and arranged for Sun Bear and him to speak together, both privately and to a group.

This wonderkid, who was only a couple of years older than I, irritated me at first sight. He was too good to be true I thought, and he sounded like a walking, talking German version of a Carlos Castenada book. He seemed to like me in direct proportion to my amount of irritation. He began to verbally court me. I thought, "Oh, no, not again," being fairly certain I recognized his form of courtship as that used by a teacher who has recognized a potential star pupil. He had great respect for Sun Bear so I knew he wasn't trying to get me to leave the Tribe and help with his burgeoning community. I didn't know what he was trying to do, but, whatever it was, it nettled me. I was glad when that talk was over, and he and his students left for home. As he hugged me goodbye he assured me we would see each other again soon.

A few days after the talk, Sun Bear and I traveled to Vancouver and the First World Symposium on the Humanities. This event was being held right in downtown Vancouver, at the Hyatt Hotel. There were over 1,000 people there, possibly close to 2,000. Being around that many similarly minded people was intoxicating in itself. Having it at the Hyatt made me feel as though the counterculture would indeed become "the movement" of the seventies, even if, with our long hair, our ethnic clothes, and our beads we must have looked like the Woodstock Festival moved uptown.

The speaker's list was long and impressive. I managed to hear David Spangler speak about the Findhorn Community, Buckminster Fuller talk about the future, Patricia Sun do her sacred sounds, and Rolling Thunder speak about his medicine and his camp in Nevada. I met Steven Gaskin, Ken Keyes, and Swami Kriyananda, all founders of alternative communities that seemed to be working well, and moving away from the guru-centered model. That was exciting. I went with Sun Bear to the Indian Center in Vancouver where he had been asked to speak about his work. We had a couple of meals with Rolling Thunder and his people, and participated in a sunrise ceremony he conducted one morning.

All this was exhilarating business. I had the feeling we were part of history in the making. But, underlying the excitement were some spiritual and political disagreements between people and groups participating. This undercurrent was creating a definite drain on the energy of the event.

Sun Bear and I discussed this between ourselves, and with Jerome, Lester, and Suellen. It seemed to us as if the Symposium were reflecting one of the major problems of society in general: lack of grounding in the Earth Mother. Being in the ballroom of the Hyatt Hotel, surrounded by people and technology, it was hard for participants to remember they were connected to the great circle of life. We felt this issue of grounding and devisiveness had to be addressed or the First World Symposium might be the last. Jerome discovered there was a speaking slot open that afternoon so he went off to try to arrange for us to have it.

We waited around for a while then, when Jerome still hadn't returned, we decided to go to the coffee shop and have a cup of coffee. As soon as the cups came, Jerome found us and said to come right now. We had the speaking slot and only a few minutes to get to the room. We hastened upstairs to one of the ballrooms. Since this talk had only been scheduled, we didn't expect much attendance.

We went into a room full of people, somewhere between 500 and 600. Sun Bear was introduced. Instead of getting up on the stage and distancing himself from his listeners, he sat on the edge of the stage, motioning me beside him. He invited people to sit in a circle on the floor so they could remember the great circle of life. Early in his talk he addressed the undercurrents that were threatening to divide the group. He told people it didn't matter what our race was, or nationality, or religious preference, because all truth comes from the same source, and we are all nourished by the same Earth Mother. "No matter what your beliefs," he continued, "it's important to remember we all gather sand from the same seashore."

The crowd roared their agreement. After he had spoken for a while, he looked at me, took my hand and said, "Now I'd like you all to hear from Wabun, my medicine helper, a woman who, like most of you, grew up in the dominant society. She was a writer in New York when I met her. Like many of you, she locked herself in every night. I think she had three locks on her apartment. They have to lock up animals in the zoo, but they can get people in cities to do it themselves."

Sun Bear handed me the microphone and I sat holding it while the laughter died down. I tried to smile without it being a "Miss America Smile." I wasn't too worried about that. I'd always found it hard to show that much teeth. But I was petrified that I'd open my mouth and sound like a mouse again. I prayed for strength, courage, timbre, and volume.

My prayers were answered. I began to talk to people about my own experiences in learning how to reconnect with the earth. I told them about the sacred circle, and how good it felt to realize I was a part of it. I spoke about my special place on the mountain and how I yearned to see it as much as I longed to see the faces of loved ones. I talked about our relations in the other kingdoms—the elements, the plants, the animals, the spirit and energy forces—and how important it was to honor them. I explained that I had been just like many people: that if someone had drawn an accurate picture writing of me in New York it would have had a very big head, a little stick body, and a dot for a heart. I told them I now prayed daily that I can walk with more feeling and more balance on the earth.

I assured them that the changes I had made felt very good: that one sickness of the cities is that all you see all the time is people, and so you begin to believe that people are the only things that matter in the universe. When you reconnect with the earth, you realize that while people are important in the circle of life, so is everything else.

When I finished, people gave me a big round of applause, and even a couple of roars of agreement. I was pleased, humbled, and a bit embarrassed. I could tell this getting out in front of people would take a lot of getting used to. I gave the microphone back to Sun Bear and he spoke for a bit more. After our talk, people told us our presentation was "a historic moment," and "the turning point" of the Symposium.

The rest of the Symposium passed in a haze of newness and excitement for me. After that presentation, a lot of people wanted to talk with us personally and some of them issued invitations for us to speak in different parts of the continent. As the Symposium continued, it became increasingly obvious that a new phase of work was opening for us, and for the Bear Tribe.

When the Symposium ended, we went to Susanville once again to do a pre-Christmas jewelry show at our friend's Western store there. After we finished the second day of the showing, Sun Bear called home. When he came back to the room he had a strange look on his face.

"What's up?" I asked.

"It seems like Spider Woman called and said she has decided not to come back," he replied.

"Oh, no," I said, shocked. "Why?"

"She didn't say. I tried to call her mother's house to talk with her in person, but no one was home."

While I was sad, I expected Sun Bear to be devastated.

"I'm sorry," I said, more sincerely than I would have believed possible. "How are you feeling?"

"I'm sad," he replied, "but not surprised. The lessons have been learned all around."

I didn't know what to say, so I took his hand. I really tried to think of some consoling words, and then the irony of the situation overcame me and I began to laugh.

"I'm not laughing at you," I assured Sun Bear. "It's just that the etiquette books never told me how to handle the situation of trying to console the man you love because his girlfriend has left him."

"You left the familiar ground of etiquette books a long time ago sister."

"Yeah, Emily Post didn't tell me how to hold my knife for cow butchering or which fork to use for road-kill pheasant, sans glass," I answered, giving Sun Bear a tentative smile.

"I'm okay, Wabun," he said. "But I'm going to take a long walk now. I need time to think."

I was glad to be alone. I needed to think myself. Spider Woman's departure raised a host of interesting questions. I was going to enumerate them to myself when, through the window, I saw the moon begin to rise over the mountains to the east. I went outside to see Grandmother Moon more clearly. Under her light I decided to think about my questions another time. Right now, no one was around, and it felt like a perfect time to dance.

Afterword

Over a dozen years have elapsed since that night I danced under the moon. Each one of them has been as full of lessons, challenges, magic, and movement as the six years described in this book.

Gunther did become a teacher, one who opened me to my own deep knowledge of the feminine. Spider Woman returned a few more times—always in a different guise—until I truly learned the lessons she had to teach me. The Bear Tribe Community began to grow and develop and reach out to the world in ways I wouldn't have dreamed were possible. I met Grandmother Twylah Nitsch and some other clan mothers who reinforced the lessons Ruth continued to give me. Sun Bear and I settled into a relationship of friendship, love, and trust, laced with a lot of mutual respect.

We began to travel across the country, then around the world teaching people how to have a better relationship with the earth and all of her children. When the media discovered the New Age, Sun Bear became one of the more prominent people in it.

I worked a lot with feminine energy—both my own and other people's—over these years. I developed a unique theory of world history, and some strong views about what each person on the planet now needs to do to help the earth at this critical time. I've taught about these theories and views to at least a couple of thousand people a year since the late seventies. In between traveling to talk, teach, and sell, I helped build the Bear Tribe Community and became a strong, independent woman in the process of doing so.

Just when I thought I had my life all put together in a viable but solitary way, that old coyote of the south came along to trick me, and I fell in love with the man who is now my husband. Shortly after we met, the grandmother came to me again—this time in human form. But all of that is another long story, one I'll save for another day.

Over the years of my odyssey, I have gained a great deal of respect for the culture and philosophy of Native people, both in this country and elsewhere. I particularly admire their method of teaching through stories. Stories stick where lectures don't. For example, I don't remember much of the subject content I learned in the first grade, but I've never forgotten the little engine that could.

I have used a storytelling mode in relating the beginning of my own spiritual odyssey. Believe me, it's been a real challenge to tell my story without lecturing. I've become used to teaching in situations in which I am able to state the points I want to make, make them, then review them once again.

Throughout writing *Woman of the Dawn* I promised myself that once I told my story, and let you know that it continues, I could have just a few pages to review the points I wanted to make. There is a precedent for this in some Native storytelling traditions. After the storyteller had finished her tale, she would be allowed to ask the people listening (adults as well as children), "What did you learn from this story?" Then she would get to add any points they had missed.

So, borrowing from that tradition, and hoping that you, dear reader, will bear with me (pun intended), I now ask "What have you learned from my story?"

If you are really willing to humor me, write your answers, or, even better, discuss them with a friend. When you've concluded, go to the next page, and see how your list compares with mine.

THE LESSONS

1. Every person on this earth has her own vision, her own path, and her own reason for being here.

2. Part of our responsibility as human beings is to find that vision, then seek ways to fulfill it.

3. All life is sacred, and all life is connected.

4. We are responsible for our own lives, and for the way we connect with all other life.

5. Humans are not necessarily the universal big cheeses we sometimes think we are.

6. We all want to get love.

7. We all need to learn how to give love.

8. When you embrace your shadow, it disappears.

The Moral:
YOU MAKE A DIFFERENCE!

We are currently in the midst of what Native prophecies refer to as "The Earth Cleansing." This is a time in which the earth will cleanse herself of the poisons placed upon her by man.

To me, the earth cleansing is a real situation of reaping what we have sown. While scientists and officials debate whether there really is a connection between toxic waste and acid rain; between destruction of the rain forests and the greenhouse effect; between nuclear testing and earthquake activity, the dominant society continues to destroy the planet. Native prophecies, some of them thousands of years old, foretell this time.

Most prophecies say the planet will survive, but some of them warn that humankind might not. The dinosaurs seemed pretty powerful too when they "ruled" the planet.

I've been taught that *each individual alive now can make a difference in whether our species survives.*

That means *you do* make a difference. I urge you to start making it now.

"Who, me?" you might ask.

Yes, you; each one of you. If you've gotten this far you obviously care deeply about life and about the earth. But what can you do?

Native people believed the best teaching came from example. What I've tried to show in my life and in this book are:

1. *Don't be afraid of your feelings, and don't be ashamed to admit you have them.* The shadow of the rational society is the feeling aspect of human nature. Much of our education is designed to make us guilty about emotions and sensations; in short, about much of the energy with which we are all born. The more people who learn to embrace their feelings, the less power the rational society will have to reject them.

2. *Speak your truth firmly and clearly.* This is a particularly important lesson for women. Many of us hide our wisdom because we've been conditioned to believe we must defer to men. Please look around and see what such deferral has wrought in our lives and on the planet.

3. *Find your path and purpose and follow it.* I firmly believe in the Vision Quest experience as a way to find your path. I've seen the magic that comes over people who have been blessed with the opportunity to spend time alone with the Great Mother. Realizing that, at this point, Vision Quests are not available to all people, I support you in any way you can use to find your path. For some people talking with friends helps; others do better praying to the Creator. While you're looking for your path, remember it's there, it's special, and you are the only person who can walk it.

4. *Respect the visions of others.* If we *really* did this, we would transform the earth.

5. *Get involved.* Sun Bear often tells people, "If you don't like the world you live in, help to create the world you like."

Participate. Get involved. Don't wait for someone else to do it. If you do, it might not get done.

Pick a subject you care about, then get involved with it. Whether the subject is politics, religion, children's rights, women's rights, the environment, education, storytelling, art, music, poetry, relationships, counselling, healing, ceremonies, nutrition, prochoice support, the homeless, animals, endangered species, spiritualism, science research, psychology, human development, storytelling, antinuclear activities, birth control, law, AIDS research and support, strip mining, Native rights, traditional peoples, bioregionalism, permaculture, or anything else you can think of, *your help is needed now.*

Often we're quick to complain about what's wrong with the world. We need to learn to be as quick to find ways to try to make it right.

Just in case you can't think of anything you care about, I have three visions I'd love to see become reality.

First, I'd like the Vision Quest to become part of the curriculum of every school in the country. For more information about this ancient rite of passage so relevant to today I refer you to *The Book of the Vision Quest* and *The Roaring of the Sacred River,* both by my dear friends Steven Foster and Meredith Little.

Second, I'd like to see seniors graduating from high school or college have the chance to live in a community setting for three or six months after graduation. If that could happen we might produce a generation capable of meeting John Kennedy's challenge to "ask not what your country can do for you; ask what you can do for your country."

There are many things I have to say about community. However, to keep this section short, as promised, I'll simply state that wisely-structured community life can be a pressure-cooker that helps evaporate a lot of the hurt, shame, guilt, anger, and sadness that otherwise weigh down many humans.

Third, I'd like to help establish grandparent's lodges throughout the country in which two of our most ignored populations, children and seniors, could help each other. In many Native societies the grandparents raised the children. The parents, who were more physically able to do so, took care of providing food and shelter for both their elders and their children. The grandparents had the wisdom of their years, the patience of their wisdom, and the gentleness of their love to give to the children. This system worked for hundreds, even thousands, of years for some tribes. It could help a lot of people today.

For further information about these ideas, or to learn more about my current speaking, writing, and ceremonial work, write to me at:

Wind Communications
16141 Redmond Way, Suite 308
Redmond, WA 98052

If you want to hear about some other good ideas in which to become involved, contact Sun Bear at:

The Bear Tribe
P.O. Box 9167
Spokane, WA 99209-9167

If you write either place, please enclose a stamped, self-addressed envelope, and be patient. We get a lot of mail.

• • •

Thank you for joining me for the beginning of my odyssey. As you travel your own path, may you learn better with each day to walk in balance upon this very beautiful Earth Mother.